GW00566840

SOUPS

3. Put the meat, bones and water into a saucepan, bring to the boil, skim, simmer for about 3 hours, skimming occasionally to remove fat. Replace water as it boils away, so that there will be 1 quart of stock when finished. Strain and leave to cool.

4. Heat the fat in a saucepan, put in the vegetables cut in small pieces and cook for about 5-10 minutes until brown.

5. Mix in the flour, and cook for about 5 minutes until brown.

6. Stir in the strained stock gradually, bring to the boil, skim. Add bouquet garni, and simmer for 1½ hours, skimming occasionally.

7. Strain the soup, return to the saucepan and bring to the boil. Add sherry and lemon juice. Correct for seasoning and consistency, and serve.

HOLLANDAISE SOUP

1½ pts. white stock.	½ pt. milk.
½ oz. butter.	2 egg yolks.
½ oz. flour.	½ gill cream.

Salt and pepper.

Garnish :—1 tablesp. diced cucumber ⎱ ⅛ inch dice.
1 tablesp. diced carrot ⎰
1 tablesp. peas.

1. Boil the stock, add a good pinch of salt. Put in the carrot and cook for about 20 minutes, then add the green peas and cucumber and cook until all are tender.

2. Strain off the stock and keep for the soup. Keep the vegetables hot.

3. Make a white roux with the butter and flour, cool slightly and add the stock slowly.

4. Boil soup for 5 minutes, stirring all the time. Add half of the milk.

5. Beat yolks of eggs with the remainder of the milk and cream, add the soup slowly to them. Season.

6. Return to the saucepan with the cooked vegetables. Reheat carefully, but do not boil.

RICE CREAM SOUP

2 ozs. onion.	1 oz. butter or margarine.
2 ozs. white turnip.	1 oz. flour.
2 sticks of celery.	½ pt. milk.
1 quart of white stock.	Salt and pepper.
1½ ozs. rice.	½ gill cream (if liked).
Bouquet garni.	½ teasp. finely-chopped parsley.

1. Prepare the vegetables, and cut them into small pieces.

2. Put the stock, vegetables, washed rice and bouquet garni into a saucepan. Bring to the boil and simmer for about 1½ hours.

3. Remove bouquet garni and rub soup through a fine sieve.

4. Rinse the saucepan, put in the butter and heat until melted, add the flour and mix well together, cook for 3 minutes, draw aside and cool a little.

5. Add the milk and sieved soup gradually, stirring well. Stir until it boils for 5 minutes. Correct seasoning, pour on to the heated cream. Sprinkle parsley on top.

PARSNIP SOUP

½ lb. parsnips.	1 oz. butter or margarine
4 ozs. potatoes.	1 oz. flour.
4 ozs. onions.	½ pt. milk.
1 quart white stock.	1 tablesp. sieved cheese.
Bouquet garni.	Salt and pepper.

1. Prepare vegetables and cut into small pieces.

2. Put them into a saucepan with the stock and bouquet garni. Bring to the boil and cook until the vegetables are tender, about 1½ hours.

3. Remove bouquet garni and rub soup through a sieve.

4. Rinse the saucepan and put in the butter. When melted, add the flour and mix well together. Cook for 3 minutes, and cool slightly.

5. Add the milk and sieved soup slowly, and stir until it boils for 5 minutes. Correct seasoning and serve. Sprinkle cheese on top.

CREAM OF CELERY

½ lb. celery.	2 ozs. butter or margarine.
4 ozs. onions.	2 ozs. flour.
1 qt. white stock.	½ pt. milk.
Bouquet garni.	1 tablesp. cream (if liked).
Salt and pepper.	¼ teasp. chopped parsley.

1. Prepare vegetables and slice thinly.

2. Put them into a saucepan with the stock and bouquet garni, bring to boil, and simmer for about 1½ hours.

3. Lift out the bouquet garni and rub soup through a fine sieve.

4. Melt the butter in the rinsed saucepan, stir in the flour, and blend together. Cook for 3 minutes and cool slightly.

5. Add the milk and sieved soup slowly and boil for 5 minutes. Season.

6. Pour on to the heated cream in the hot soup tureen, and stir while doing so. Sprinkle finely-chopped parsley on top.

SOUPS

VEGETABLE MARROW SOUP

1 lb. vegetable marrow (prepared).	Salt and pepper.
2 ozs. onion.	2 ozs. butter or margarine.
2 sticks celery.	2 ozs. flour.
1 quart of white stock.	½ pt. milk.
Bouquet garni.	¼ teasp. finely-chopped parsley.

1. Prepare the vegetables and cut into small pieces.
2. Put the vegetables, stock, bouquet garni and salt into a large saucepan Bring to the boil, simmer until the vegetables are soft.
3. Remove bouquet garni, rub soup through a fine sieve.
4. Rinse the saucepan, put in the butter, when melted stir in the flour, cook for 3 minutes, cool a little and add the sieved soup and milk. Stir until it boils for 5 minutes. Correct seasoning.
5. Serve in a hot soup tureen and sprinkle the parsley on top.

CUCUMBER SOUP

1 large cucumber.	2 ozs. flour.
2 ozs. onion.	½ pt. milk.
1 quart of white stock.	Salt and pepper.
2 ozs. butter or margarine.	Green colouring.

1. Peel the cucumber and cut into pieces, peel and slice the onion.
2. Put the cucumber, onion, stock and salt into a saucepan. Cook until tender. Rub through a fine sieve.
3. Make a roux with the butter and flour, cool slightly, and add the milk and sieved soup. Boil for 5 minutes, stirring all the time. Correct colour and seasoning. Serve in a hot soup tureen.

ARTICHOKE SOUP

¾ lb. Jerusalem artichokes.	Salt and pepper.
2 ozs. onion.	2 ozs. butter or margarine.
1 stick of celery.	2 ozs. flour.
Bouquet garni.	½ gill cream (if liked).
1 quart of white stock	½ teasp. finely-chopped parsley.
½ pt. milk.	

1. Prepare the artichokes and other vegetables and cut into slices.
2. Put them into a saucepan with the stock, bouquet garni and salt. Bring to the boil, simmer for about 1½ hours.
3. Remove the bouquet garni and rub soup through a fine sieve.
4. Rinse the saucepan and make a roux with the butter and flour, cool a little, and add the milk and sieved soup gradually. Boil for 5 minutes, stirring all the time. Correct seasoning.
5. Pour on to the heated cream in a hot soup tureen and sprinkle the parsley on top.

CREAM OF TOMATO

¼ lb. tomatoes or	2 ozs. flour.
2 ozs. tin tomato purée.	2 ozs. butter or margarine.
2 ozs. carrot.	½ pt. milk.
4 ozs. onion	½ teaspoonful sugar.
2 sticks of celery.	Salt and pepper.
1 quart of stock.	Pink colouring.
Bouquet garni.	¼ gill cream.

1. Slice the tomatoes. Prepare all the vegetables and cut into small pieces.

2. Put the tomatoes or tomato purée and vegetables into a saucepan with the stock, bouquet garni and seasoning. Bring to the boil and simmer for about 1½ hours.

3. Remove the bouquet garni and rub the soup through a sieve.

4. Rinse the saucepan and make a roux with the butter and flour, cool slightly and add the milk, sieved soup and sugar.

5. Stir until it boils for 5 minutes. Correct consistency, seasoning and colouring.

6. Put the heated cream into a hot soup tureen, pour in the soup and stir while doing so.

WHITE ONION SOUP

¾ lb. onions.	1 quart white stock.
2 sticks celery.	Bouquet garni.
2 ozs. butter or margarine.	Salt and pepper.
2 ozs. flour.	½ pt. milk.

1. Peel and blanch the onions. Wash the celery. Cut the vegetables into small pieces.

2. Melt the butter in a saucepan, add the vegetables. Cover with a round of greaseproof paper and a lid and cook for 10 minutes without browning.

3. Remove the paper, stir in the flour and cook for a few minutes.

4. Add the stock, a little salt and the bouquet garni. Bring to the boil, skim, simmer for about 1¼ hours. Rub through a fine sieve.

5. Rinse the saucepan and return the soup to it. Add the milk and bring to the boil, correct for consistency and seasoning.

6. Pour into a hot soup tureen, sprinkle parsley on top and serve.

SOUPS

SPRING PURÉE

2 ozs. white turnip.	1 quart of white stock.
4 spring onions.	A sprig of mint.
4 ozs. potato.	A bunch of parsley.
1 head of lettuce.	2 ozs. butter or margarine.
A few leaves of spinach.	2 ozs. flour.
1 gill of peas.	$\frac{1}{2}$ pt. milk.

Salt and pepper.

1. Prepare vegetables. Cut the onion, turnip and potato into small pieces.
2. Put them into a large saucepan with the peas, stock and mint. Bring to the boil and simmer until the vegetables are soft, about 1$\frac{1}{4}$ hours. Put in the bunch of parsley, shredded lettuce and spinach for the last 15 minutes. Rub the soup through a sieve.
3. Melt the butter in the rinsed saucepan. Stir in the flour and cook for 3 minutes, cool slightly. Add the sieved soup and milk and boil for 5 minutes. Correct seasoning, and serve.

BEETROOT SOUP

$\frac{3}{4}$ lb. beetroot.	Bouquet garni.
2 ozs. onion.	2 ozs. butter or margarine.
2 sticks of celery.	2 ozs. flour.
1 quart of stock.	$\frac{1}{2}$ pt. milk.

Salt and pepper.

1. Prepare beetroot, celery and onion. Simmer the beetroot in boiling water until about half-cooked—1-1$\frac{1}{2}$ hours. Remove skin from beetroot. Cut all the vegetables into pieces.
2. Put into a saucepan with the stock and bouquet garni, and simmer for about 1$\frac{1}{2}$ hours.
3. Remove bouquet garni, and rub soup through a fine sieve.
4. Make a roux with the butter and flour, cool a little and add the milk and sieved soup gradually. Boil for 5 minutes, stirring all the time. Correct seasoning, and serve.

SPINACH SOUP

1 lb. spinach.	1 quart of white stock.
2 ozs. butter or margarine.	$\frac{1}{2}$ pt. milk.
2 ozs. flour.	A little green colouring.

Salt and pepper.

1. Pick off the leaves of the spinach and put to cook in the boiling stock for 3 minutes. Remove the spinach and rub it through a sieve or put it through a mincer. Return it to the stock.
2. Melt the butter in a saucepan, stir in the flour and cook for 3 minutes. Cool a little and add the milk and stock gradually. Boil for 5 minutes, stirring all the time.
3. Season, add a little green colouring, if necessary, and serve.

ALMOND SOUP

2 sticks of white celery.	2 ozs. butter or margarine.
2 ozs. onion.	2 ozs. flour.
4 ozs. ground almonds.	½ pt. milk.
1 quart of white stock.	½ gill cream.
Bouquet garni.	½ teasp. finely-chopped parsley.

1. Prepare vegetables, slice thinly, and put into a saucepan with the almonds, stock, and bouquet garni. Bring to the boil, simmer for about 1 hour.

2. Remove bouquet garni, and rub the soup through a fine sieve.

3. Rinse the saucepan and put in the butter; when melted, add the flour and mix until smooth. Cook for 3 minutes and cool slightly.

4. Add the milk and sieved soup slowly, and stir until it has boiled for 5 minutes. Correct seasoning. Pour on to the cream and stir while doing so. Sprinkle a little parsley on top.

ASPARAGUS SOUP

½ lb. tin of asparagus.	2 ozs. flour.
1 stick of celery.	½ pt. milk.
2 ozs. onion.	Salt and pepper.
1 quart of white stock.	Pinch of sugar.
2 ozs. butter or margarine.	Green colouring.
Bouquet garni.	½ gill cream.

1. Cut the tips from the asparagus for garnish, cut the stalks into small pieces. Prepare the celery and onion and cut into small pieces.

2. Put the onion, celery, stock and bouquet garni into a saucepan and bring to the boil. Add the asparagus and cook for about 1 hour.

3. Remove the bouquet garni and rub the soup through a sieve.

4. Make a roux with the butter and flour, cool a little and add the milk and sieved soup slowly, stirring all the time. Boil for 5 minutes. Correct colouring and seasoning. Pour on to the heated cream and asparagus tips, and serve.

CRÈME DUBARRY

1 small cauliflower.	2 ozs. butter or margarine.
3 ozs. chopped onion.	2 ozs. flour.
1 oz. chopped leek.	½ pt. milk.
1 quart white stock.	Salt and pepper.
Bouquet garni.	

1. Melt the butter. Put in the onion and leek, cover with a round of greaseproof paper and a lid, cook slowly for about 5 minutes.

2. Remove all the green leaves from the cauliflower, cut into small flowerettes. Add to the onion and leek, stir all together, cover and cook for 5 minutes. Remove the paper.

3. Add the flour and cook slowly for 5 minutes, stirring all the time. Do not allow to colour.

4. Add the stock and bouquet garni, bring to the boil, skim, season and cook for about 1 hour. Remove the bouquet garni.

5. Rub through a sieve, add the milk, bring to the boil, correct seasoning, and serve.

MUSHROOM SOUP

2 sticks of celery.	2 ozs. flour.
2 ozs. onion.	½ pt. milk.
¼ lb. mushrooms.	1 teasp. mushroom ketchup.
2 ozs. butter or margarine.	1 teasp. lemon juice.
1 quart of white stock.	Salt and pepper.
½ gill cream (if liked).	

1. Prepare the celery and onion, and cut them into small pieces. Wash the mushrooms, nd cut up finely.

2. Put the mushrooms, celery, onion, a little salt and the stock into a saucepan. Bring to the boil, simmer until the vegetables are soft—about 1½ hours.

3. Rub through a fine sieve. Melt the butter in the rinsed saucepan, stir in the flour and cook for 3 minutes. Cool a little and add the milk and sieved soup gradually.

4. Add the mushroom ketchup and lemon juice and boil for 5 minutes, stirring all the time. Correct for consistency and seasoning.

5. Pour on to the heated cream in the hot soup tureen, stirring while doing so.

CHESTNUT CREAM SOUP

½ lb. Spanish chestnuts.	1 oz. flour.
2 ozs. onion.	½ pt. milk.
1 stick celery.	Pepper and salt.
1 quart of white stock.	Pinch of sugar.
Bouquet garni.	¼ gill of cream.
1 oz. butter or margarine.	Pink colouring.

1. Slit the chestnuts on the flat side and bake them in a hot oven—15-20 minutes until the shells split, or boil for about 10 minutes. Remove the shell and inner skin and break nut into pieces.

2. Prepare the onion and celery and cut into small pieces.

3. Put the chestnuts, vegetables, bouquet garni and stock into a saucepan and boil until the chestnuts are soft—about 1 hour.

4. Lift out the bouquet garni and rub soup through a fine sieve.

5. Make a roux, cool slightly and add the milk and sieved soup. Boil for 5 minutes, stirring all the time. Correct seasoning, and add sugar and a drop of pink colouring to make a pale shrimp colour.

6. Pour on to the heated cream in a hot soup tureen, and stir while doing so.

HARE SOUP

1 hare.	3 ozs. fat.
2 tablesp. seasoned flour.	4 quarts brown stock.
2 ozs. white turnip.	Bouquet garni.
4 ozs. onion	6 ozs. flour.
4 ozs. carrot.	1 glass of port wine.
2 sticks of celery.	1 tablesp. red-currant jelly.

Salt and pepper.
Garnish :—Pieces of hare meat.
To serve :—Forcemeat Balls (page 222).

1. Skin and paunch the hare (page 74). Cut it into small pieces and toss in the seasoned flour.

2. Prepare the vegetables, and cut them into small pieces.

3. Heat the fat, and when smoking hot, fry the pieces of hare and vegetables until lightly browned. Add the flour, and cook until golden brown.

4. Add the stock and bouquet garni, bring to the boil. Skim. Simmer for 2½ hours, or until the flesh of the hare comes easily from the bones.

5. Turn into a sieve, remove a few pieces of meat, cut into ¼-inch cubes and use for garnish.

6. Rub the remainder of the meat and vegetables through the sieve and return to the rinsed saucepan.

7. Add the blood of the hare, the wine, red currant jelly and seasoning. Re-heat, but do not boil.

8. Put the garnish into a hot soup tureen and pour the soup over. Serve forcemeat balls on a dish paper on a small dish.

LOBSTER BISQUE

1 small hen lobster with spawn.	2 ozs. flour.
¼ lb. of mixed vegetables.	½ pt. milk.
1 quart of fish stock.	Salt and pepper.
Bouquet garni.	½ glass of sherry **or** white wine.
1 oz. butter or margarine.	½ gill of cream.

1. Remove the spawn from the lobster, leave aside and use for colouring the soup.

2. Cook the lobster and remove meat as on page 37, keeping back the firm flesh for a lobster dish. The soft lobster meat is used in the bisque. Break up the shells and wash them.

3. Prepare the vegetables, and cut them into small pieces.

4. Put the cold stock into a saucepan. Add the lobster meat, the shells, the vegetables and the bouquet garni. Simmer for 1½ hours.

5. Turn into a fine sieve, remove shell and bouquet garni and rub the remainder through.

6. Rinse the saucepan and make a roux with the butter and flour, cool slightly and add the soup.

7. Wash and dry the spawn, pound in a mortar and rub through a fine sieve.

8. Add the spawn to the soup. Boil for 5 minutes, stirring all the time.

9. Add the milk, seasoning, and wine. Re-heat.

10. Pour on to the cream in a hot soup tureen, stirring while doing so.

NOTE.—If there is no spawn in lobster, colour a faint pink with pink colouring.

FISH

FISH À L'ORLY

1 lb. white fish (filleted).

Marinade :

2 tablesp. olive oil.
1 tablesp. white wine or
wine vinegar.

1 teasp. minced onion.
1 teasp. chopped parsley.

Salt and pepper.
To coat :—Rich Coating Batter (page 223).
To fry :—Bath of fat.
To garnish :— 1lb. of potato purée. 2 tomatoes. Parsley.
To serve :—Hot Tartare Sauce or Dutch Sauce.

1. Make the marinade by mixing all the ingredients together on a plate.
2. Skin the fish, wash and dry it and cut into neat pieces. Soak in the marinade for 20 minutes.
3. Drain out of the marinade and dip fish in the batter.
4. Fry in smoking hot fat. Drain on kitchen paper.
5. Put the potato purée into a forcing bag fitted with a large rose pipe and make a double row of potato roses down the centre of the dish. Arrange the pieces of fish on top and garnish with parsley and heated tomato.

GRILLED SOLE

1 sole.   Olive oil or melted butter.
Salt and pepper.
1 oz. Black Butter (page 128).
To garnish :—Cut lemon and parsley.

1. Prepare fish, remove the black skin, and scale the white skin. Wash and dry the fish.
2. Brush over with oil or melted butter and sprinkle with salt and pepper.
3. Have the griller red hot, grease the bars of the gridiron.
4. Grill the white skin side first for 4 or 5 minutes, turn and grill the other side until cooked. Time about 15 minutes.
5. Lift on to a hot entrée dish. Pour the black butter over the fish, and garnish with lemon and parsley.

FILLETS OF SOLE VIN BLANC

1 black sole—use the bones for the fish stock.
Fish Velouté Sauce :

½ pt. fish stock.　　　　　1 oz. flour.
　　1 oz. butter or margarine.

___

1 teasp. finely chopped onion.　A little white wine.
¼ pt. fish stock.　　　　　Salt and pepper.

To garnish :—Parsley.

1. Skin and fillet the sole. Wash the fillets, dry well, fold in two and leave aside while making the fish stock.
2. Make the fish stock, measure off ½ pt. for the sauce and keep the remainder for poaching the fish.
3. To make the Fish Velouté Sauce—Melt the butter, add the flour, cook until sandy but not coloured. Add the fish stock and cook slowly with the lid on for about 10 minutes.
4. Grease a shallow stewpan, put in the onion and then the fish, pour the fish stock over, add white wine, salt and pepper. Place a round of greased paper on top and poach the fish for about 12-15 minutes until cooked.
5. Lift the fish on to a warm greased plate, cover with the greased paper and keep hot. Reduce the liquor in which the fish was poached until slightly thick. Strain into the sauce. Correct consistency and seasoning.
6. Put a little of the sauce on a heated entrée dish, arrange the fish neatly, mask with the sauce, and garnish with parsley.

FILLETS OF SOLE VERONIQUE

Make as for Fillets of Sole Vin Blanc, adding 2 ozs. skinned and stoned green grapes to the sauce a few minutes before serving.

FILLETS OF SOLE BONNE FEMME

1 black sole—use the bones for the fish stock.
Fish Velouté Sauce :

¼ pt. fish stock.　　　　　½ oz. flour.
　　½ oz. butter.

___

2 ozs. mushrooms.　　　　　A little white wine.
1 dessertsp. finely chopped onion.　Salt and pepper.
¼ pt. fish stock.　　　　　1½ ozs. butter.

To garnish :—Parsley.

1. Skin and fillet the sole, wash the fillets, dry well, fold in two and leave aside while making the stock.
2. Make the fish stock.

3. To make the Fish Velouté Sauce—Melt the butter, add the flour, cook until sandy but not coloured. Add the fish stock and cook slowly with the lid on for about 10 minutes.

4. Wash the mushrooms, remove the stalks, peel and slice thinly. Keep stalks and skins to use in soups or sauces.

5. Grease a shallow stewpan, put in the onion, mushrooms and a little chopped parsley. Place the fish on top. Add the fish stock, white wine and seasoning. Place a round of greased paper on top and poach for about 12-15 minutes until the fish is cooked.

6. Lift the fish on to a warm greased plate, cover with the greased paper and keep hot. Reduce the cooking liquor until slightly thick. Remove from the heat and add the 1½ ozs. butter in small pieces, rotating the stewpan to mix in the butter, do not stir to avoid breaking the garnish.

7. Add the Velouté Sauce a little at a time. Correct seasoning. Put a little sauce on a heated entrée dish, arrange the fish neatly, mask with the sauce, put under the grill to brown slightly. Garnish with a little parsley.

FILLETS OF FISH MEUNIÈRE

4 fillets of plaice or sole.	2 ozs. butter.
Seasoned flour.	Juice ½ lemon.

Chopped parsley.

1. Remove the black skin. Scale the white skin. Wash the fish and dry well.

2. Pass through seasoned flour.

3. Heat a little butter on a heavy pan, put in the fish and fry until brown. Turn and brown the other side. Shake the pan gently while cooking. Time about 7 minutes.

4. Lift the fish on to a heated dish. Put the remaining butter on the pan and heat until brown.

5. Sprinkle the fish liberally with chopped parsley. Squeeze the lemon over, mask with the browned butter, and serve.

FILLETS OF FISH DUGLÈRÉ

4 pieces of fish.	¾ pt. fish stock or water.
1 large tomato.	2 teasps. lemon juice.
1 teasp. chopped onion.	1 oz. butter or margarine
1 teasp. chopped parsley.	1 oz. flour.

Salt and pepper.

1. Skin the fish, wash and dry it.

2. Skin the tomato, cut in two, remove the seeds and chop the flesh roughly.

3. Grease a shallow stewpan, put in the onion, tomato and parsley. Place the fish on top, add the stock, lemon juice and seasoning. Place a round of greased paper on top and poach for about 12-15 minutes until the fish is cooked.

4. Put the butter and flour on a plate and work together with a knife until creamy.

5. Lift the fish on to a warm greased plate, cover with the greased paper and keep hot. Reduce the cooking liquor to about half, while boiling add the creamed butter and flour in small pieces whisking to prevent lumping—the sauce should be just thick enough to mask the back of a spoon. Correct seasoning.

6. Put a little sauce on the heated dish, arrange the fish neatly, mask with the sauce and garnish with a little parsley.

STUFFED ROLLS OF PLAICE

4 fillets of plaice.   1 tablesp. milk or fish stock.

Stuffing :
2 ozs. breadcrumbs.   1 oz. butter or margarine (melted).
1 teasp. chopped parsley.   Salt and pepper.
$\frac{1}{2}$ oz. chopped onion.

$\frac{1}{2}$ lb. potato purée.
To garnish :—1 tomato, parsley.
To serve :—Tomato sauce.

1. Remove the skin from the fish and wash the fillets.

2. Make the stuffing and spread a little of it on each fillet. Roll up and tie with a piece of thread.

3. Place on a deep plate with 1 tablespoonful milk or stock. Cover with a second plate and steam over a saucepan of boiling water for about 20 minutes.

4. Put the potato purée into a forcing bag, fitted with a large rose pipe, and make a double row of potato roses down the centre of the dish.

5. Remove the thread from the rolls of fish and place them on top of the potatoes.

6. Garnish with heated tomato and parsley. Pour a little sauce around and serve remainder in a hot sauceboat.

SCALLOPED FISH

1 lb. cooked white fish. $\frac{3}{4}$ pt. white coating sauce.
1 oz. sieved cheese.   Salt and pepper.
$\frac{3}{4}$ lb. potato purée.

1. Grease 4 or 5 scallop shells and pipe potato roses round the edges.

2. Remove all skin and bone from the fish and flake.

3. Fill the shell with fish, coat with white sauce to which cheese and seasoning have been added.

4. Sprinkle a little cheese on top and bake for about 20 minutes in a moderate oven. Garnish with parsley and serve.

ALL IN THE COOKING

FISH QUENELLES

6 ozs. white fish.	1 oz. breadcrumbs.
1 oz. butter or margarine.	Pinch of mace.
1 oz. flour.	1 egg.
¼ pt. milk.	Salt and pepper.
1 lb. potato purée.	

To garnish :—Paprika pepper and chopped parsley.
To serve :—½ pt. Anchovy Sauce, or Cheese Sauce (coating consistency).

1. Make a thick white sauce with the butter, flour and milk. Skin, bone and shred the fish. Mix with the sauce, breadcrumbs, mace, salt and pepper, and bind with the beaten egg.
2. Shape like an egg, using a dessertspoon and a knife dipped in boiling water to smooth the top.
3. Grease a stewpan or deep frying pan. Lift the quenelle from the spoon by slipping a second dessertspoon half into the bowl of the first and putting the quenelle gently into the pan. Do not have them touching.
4. Pour enough boiling fish stock or water down the side of the pan to half cover the quenelles.
5. Place a piece of greased paper over. Cover and poach gently for about 15 minutes.
6. Lift out and drain well. Pipe a double row of potato roses down the centre of a heated dish, arrange the quenelles on top. Mask quenelles with sauce and garnish with parsley and a very little paprika pepper.

CASSOLETTES OF FISH

Cassolettes :

1¼ lbs. mashed potato.	Beaten egg.
Salt and pepper.	¼ oz. butter (melted).

Filling :

½ lb. cooked fish.	½ pt. Béchamel coating sauce.
1 teasp. lemon juice.	Cayenne pepper and salt.

To garnish :—Parsley.

1. Skin, bone, and flake the fish. Heat in the sauce, add the seasoning and lemon juice.
2. Make cassolettes (page 82). Put the filling into the centre.
3. Serve on a plain dish paper on a hot dish. Garnish with parsley.

HOT FISH CREAM

½ lb. raw or cooked fish.	Pinch of mace.
2 ozs. butter or margarine.	Rind and juice of ½ lemon.
2 ozs. flour.	1 oz. breadcrumbs.
½ pt. milk.	1 tablesp. cream.
2 eggs.	Salt and pepper.

To garnish :—Cut lemon and green peas.
To serve :—Anchovy Sauce or Suprême Sauce.

1. Remove all skin and bone from the fish, and flake.

FISH

2. Make a thick white sauce with the butter, flour and milk. Cool a little, add the eggs one at a time and beat well. Add the mace, grated lemon rind, lemon juice, breadcrumbs, cream, fish, salt and pepper. Mix well.

3. Turn into a well-greased border mould, cover with greased paper. Steam until firm to the touch. Time—about 1 hour.

4. Turn out on to a hot dish and fill the centre with freshly-cooked peas. Garnish with cut lemon.

HALIBUT WITH PICCALILLI SAUCE

2 cuts of halibut.	Salt.
1 oz. butter.	1 tablesp. piccalilli.
1 teasp. chopped onion.	½ pt. fish stock or ¼ pt. fish stock
½ oz. of flour.	and ¼ pt. milk.

1. Wash the fish and dry well.

2. Melt the butter in a saucepan, put in the onion and fry. Put in the flour, salt and piccalilli, cook for a few minutes, cool slightly, add the stock slowly, and boil for 5 minutes. Cool.

3. Put in the fish and cook gently for about half an hour. Serve on a hot dish.

BAKED HALIBUT

1½ lbs. halibut.	1 oz. finely chopped onion.
1½ oz. butter.	Squeeze of lemon juice.
Salt and pepper.	

1. Wash the halibut and dry well.

2. Put the onion into a greased fireproof dish, place the fish on top. Squeeze a little lemon juice over and place the butter in small pieces on top.

3. Cover and bake in a moderate oven for about ½ hour.

4. Remove the skin, garnish with parsley, and serve.

BOILED TURBOT

1½ lbs. turbot.	Boiling water.
Salt.	Lemon juice or vinegar.

To garnish :—Lemon and parsley.
To serve :—Hollandaise Sauce (page 125).

1. Wash the turbot. Rub over with a piece of cut lemon, and if the black skin is very thick, score to prevent cracking.

2. Put into boiling salted water to which a few drops of lemon juice or vinegar are added. Simmer gently for about 15 minutes.

3. Drain well, serve on a folded table-napkin on a hot dish. Garnish with cut lemon and parsley.

VOL AU VENT OF FISH

8 ozs. puff pastry (page 155).

Filling :

½ pt. white coating sauce.   1 teasp. lemon juice.
½ lb. cooked fish.   Pinch of mace.
Salt and pepper.

To garnish :—Lemon and parsley.

1. Make and bake four Vol au Vent cases with puff pastry as on page 112, and keep hot.
2. Remove skin and bone from the fish and break into pieces. Add flavourings, seasonings and fish to the sauce, and heat well.
3. Fill each pastry case with the mixture and put on the pastry lid. Serve on a dish paper on a hot dish and garnish.

FRIED TROUT

2 trout.

Butter.   Seasoned flour.

To serve :—Hollandaise or Dutch Sauce.

1. Remove the heads, tails and fins from the trout. Scale, clean, wash well and dry.
2. Pass through seasoned flour. Fry in butter until cooked—about 10-20 minutes according to size.
3. Serve on a hot dish. Garnish with parsley.

GRILLED TROUT

2 trout.
To serve :—Maître d'Hôtel Butter or Black Butter.

1. Remove the heads, tails and fins from the trout. Scale, clean, wash well and dry.
2. Make three diagonal cuts on each side of the thick part of the back. Brush with oil or clarified butter.
3. Heat the griller and grease the bars. Place the fish on them and grill each side for about 1 minute. Reduce the heat and grill until the fish is cooked, turning frequently. Time—about 15-30 minutes according to size.
4. Serve on a hot dish and place a pat of Maître d'Hôtel Butter on top or mask with Black Butter.

BAKED TROUT

2 trout.   1 teasp. capers.
1 oz. butter.   1 tablesp. lemon juice.
Salt and pepper.

To garnish :—Thin slices of lemon.
To serve :—Hollandaise Sauce.

3. Add the chutney, apple and sliced or squashed tomatoes, cook for a few minutes.

4. Stir in the stock gradually, bring to the boil, skim, add the salt and cook for about 1 hour, skimming frequently.

5. Strain, return to the rinsed saucepan, bring to the boil, correct for consistency and flavour and serve in a hot soup tureen.

6. The rice is handed separately in a small dish garnished with parsley.

OXTAIL SOUP

1 oxtail.	2 ozs. white turnip.
3 ozs. fat.	1 leek.
4 ozs. flour.	2 sticks celery.
2 quarts stock or water.	4 ozs. tomatoes.
4 ozs. onion.	Bouquet garni.
4 ozs. carrot.	Salt and pepper.

1. Wipe the oxtail well with a damp meat cloth. Cut it into pieces, splitting the larger joints into two.

2. Heat the fat in a large saucepan, put in the oxtail and fry until brown.

3. Add the vegetables cut in small pieces and cook for about 5-10 minutes until brown.

4. Mix in the flour and cook for about 5 minutes until brown, add the sliced tomatoes and cook for a further 2-3 minutes.

5. Stir in the stock gradually, bring to the boil, skim. Season and add bouquet garni. Cook for 2½-3 hours, skimming occasionally.

6. Strain the soup. Lift out some of the pieces of tail, cut off the meat and cut it up finely for garnish.

7. Return the soup to the saucepan, correct for seasoning and consistency. Add the pieces of meat. Bring to the boil and serve in a hot soup tureen.

MOCK TURTLE SOUP

Half a calf's head.	2 ozs. white turnip.
Salt.	2 ozs. fat.
2 quarts of water.	Bouquet garni.
4 ozs. onion.	2 ozs. flour.
2 sticks of celery.	½ glass of sherry.
4 ozs. carrot.	1 teasp. lemon juice.

Pinch of cayenne pepper.

1. Steep the head in cold water and salt overnight. Wash well, put into a saucepan, cover with cold water, bring to the boil and pour off the water.

2. Remove all meat from the bones and cut into small pieces. Break the bones.

SOUPS

à l'Italienne.—Small pieces of vermicelli, spaghetti, macaroni, or any Italian paste preparation, cooked in boiling salted water.

Macédoine.—Several kinds of vegetables cut in fancy shapes and cooked in boiling salted water.

à la Russe.—Shreds of carrot, celery and leek cooked in boiling salted water.

Julienne.—Fine match-like strips of carrot and white turnip cooked until tender in boiling salted water.

MINESTRONE

1 quart stock.	½ oz. fat.
½ lb. mixed vegetables.	1 oz. streaky bacon.
1 tomato.	1 oz. spaghetti.
¼ clove garlic (crushed)	Bouquet garni.

Salt and pepper.

To garnish :—1 teasp. chopped parsley.
To serve :—1 oz. Parmesan cheese.

1. Heat the fat in a saucepan, add the bacon cut into strips and fry until beginning to brown.
2. Prepare the vegetables, i.e., carrot, onion, white turnip, leek, celery, potato, French beans, cabbage, and cut into small pieces.
3. Put into the hot fat, cover with a circle of greaseproof paper and the saucepan lid. Leave over a low heat for about 15 minutes.
4. Remove the skin from the tomato and cut the flesh into small pieces. Break the spaghetti into one-inch pieces and wash.
5. Add the tomato, spaghetti, hot stock, bouquet garni, salt and pepper to the other vegetables. Bring to the boil and simmer for about ¾ hour.
6. Prepare the French beans, cut into small pieces. Shred the cabbage. Cook both in the soup for the last 10-15 minutes.
7. Add the parsley. Serve Parmesan cheese separately.

MULLIGATAWNY SOUP

4 ozs. chopped onion.	2 ozs. fat.
2 ozs. chopped cooking apple.	2 ozs. flour.
2 tomatoes.	1 dessertsp. curry powder.
1 teasp. chutney.	1 quart of brown stock.

Salt.

To serve :—1 oz. boiled rice.

1. Heat the fat in a large saucepan, add the onion and fry until golden brown.
2. Add the flour and cook for a few minutes. Add the curry powder and cook for a further 3 or 4 minutes.

15

3. Bring to the boil, skim and wipe away any scum from the inside of the saucepan. Simmer for about 3 hours, skimming constantly and replacing water as it boils away. Do not cover the saucepan.

4. Strain through muslin. Return to a clean saucepan and bring to the boil. Correct seasoning, add sherry and serve very hot.

CLEAR SOUP

Clear soup consists of clarified double stock. Lean beef and whites and shells of eggs are added to clear the stock. The stock is clarified during the coagulation process of the protein of the egg and beef. The clear soup takes its name from the particular garnish served in it, e.g., Consommé Julienne, Consommé Royale.

3 pints of double stock.	Salt.
¼ lb. lean beef.	6 peppercorns.
White and shell of 1 egg.	½ gill sherry.

1. Remove the fat from the stock and strain through muslin.

2. Remove all the fat from the meat. Chop or mince it.

3. Put the meat into a heavy saucepan with the white and shell of egg and salt. Mix well with a wooden spoon to draw out the blood from the meat.

4. Add the cold stock a little at a time, mixing thoroughly.

5. Bring to the boil very slowly, stirring occasionally. Simmer for 1 hour, with the lid off the saucepan. Do not skim.

6. Draw aside, cover and leave to stand for 20 minutes.

7. Strain through double muslin which has been wrung out of cold water. Ladle or pour very gently, keeping back the scum.

8. Return the clear soup to a clean saucepan, bring to the boil, add sherry and seasoning if necessary.

9. Put the garnish into the heated soup tureen. Pour the clear soup over and serve very hot.

CONSOMMÉ GARNISHES

Royale.—Savoury custard made from one yolk of egg, seasoning and one tablespoonful of milk, beaten together, put into a greased dariole mould. It is then covered with a piece of greased paper and steamed until set. The custard is then turned out and placed in cold water for a short time, after which it is sliced thinly and cut into small diamond or other shaped pieces.

Brunoise.—Mixed vegetables cut in ⅛-inch dice and cooked.

Jardinière.—Carrot and white turnip cut into pea-shaped pieces (using a vegetable cutter) and cooked in boiling salted water.

Célestine.—Fine shreds of savoury pancake, made from ½ gill milk, 1 oz. flour, ½ egg, ½ teaspoonful chopped parsley, ½ teaspoonful chopped tarragon, salt and pepper. Prepare batter and make into very thin pancakes. Roll tightly and slice thinly.

SOUPS

DOUBLE STOCK

2 quarts of water.	4 ozs. tomatoes.
1 lb. leg beef.	1 leek.
2 lbs. beef bones.	2 sticks celery.
2 ozs. bacon rinds.	6 peppercorns.
8 ozs. carrots.	Salt.
8 ozs. onions.	Bouquet garni.

1. Break up the bones, remove the fat. Put the bones on a roasting tin and place in the oven to brown for about $1\frac{1}{2}$ hours.

2. Cut the meat into very small pieces or mince it.

3. Put the meat, bones, salt, peppercorns, bouquet garni and cold water into a large pot. Bring slowly to the boil. Skim. Simmer slowly 2-3 hours. Skim frequently. Replace the water as it boils away.

4. Cut the bacon rinds into small pieces, fry in a hot pan until brown and the fat is extracted. Prepare the vegetables and cut them into small pieces, fry them with the bacon rinds until brown. Drain all well. Add with the tomatoes to the stock and simmer for a further 2-3 hours.

5. Strain immediately into an earthenware vessel. Skim off all fat.

6. Keep uncovered and bring to the boil daily in hot weather or keep in a refrigerator.

BOUILLON

1 lb. shin of beef.	2 sticks of celery.
2 lbs. bones.	3 quarts of water.
4 ozs. carrots.	Bouquet garni.
4 ozs. onion.	$\frac{1}{2}$ glass sherry (if liked).
1 leek.	Salt and pepper.

1. Remove fat from meat and bones. Cut the meat into small pieces and put into a saucepan with the water, bones, salt and bouquet garni. Bring to the boil and skim.

2. Prepare the vegetables, cut into pieces and add to the other ingredients in the saucepan.

13

MIXED FRUIT COCKTAIL

1 small tin of pineapple.	¼ lb. grapes.
2 oranges.	1 tablesp. lemon juice.
6 cherries.	A little sugar.

1. Cut the pineapple into small pieces.
2. Cut the orange in two crosswise and remove the pulp with a teaspoon.
3. Stone the cherries and cut into pieces.
4. Stone the grapes and cut them.
5. Mix all the ingredients together and add some of the pineapple syrup.
6. Leave in a cold place until required. Serve in small glasses.

ORANGE JUICE

Squeeze oranges and strain juice. Sweeten a little if liked. Serve in small glasses.

LOBSTER COCKTAIL

3–4 ozs. lobster meat.	Squeeze of lemon juice.
2 tablesps. mayonnaise.	A few leaves of lettuce.
2 tablesps. cream.	Salt and pepper.
1–2 teasps. tomato purée.	1 dessertsp. brandy or sherry.

1. Prepare the lobster meat as on page 37. Cut into small pieces.
2. Mix the mayonnaise with the tomato purée and half-whipped cream. Add lemon juice, brandy and seasoning to taste.
3. Cut the lettuce into small shreds and keep it covered in a cold place until ready to serve the cocktail.
4. Place a dessertspoonful of lettuce into each of four stemmed glasses and place on top about 1 oz. lobster meat. Mask with the sauce, using about 1 tablespoonful in each glass.
5. Garnish with a little finely-chopped parsley or powdered coral (page 37).

PRAWN COCKTAIL

Make as for Lobster Cocktail, substituting 1 doz. prawn tails (page 35) for the lobster meat.

SCAMPI

Cooked prawn tails (page 35).   Rich Coating Batter (page 223).
To Fry :–Bath of Fat.
To Serve :–Cut lemon, Tartare or Rémoulade Sauce.

Put the prawns in the batter, lift out and fry in smoking hot fat. Drain and serve.

HORS D'OEUVRE

RICE SALAD VALENCIENNE

Add to 3 ozs. cooked rice, 2 tablespoonfuls of diced cooked ham and the same amount of diced flesh of tomatoes and cooked peas. Dress with French Dressing and serve.

FRESH GRAPEFRUIT

Cut the fruit in halves crosswise. Remove the core. Loosen the fruit from the skin with a grapefruit knife and separate the sections. Remove pips. Sweeten and flavour with sherry, if liked. Put a maraschino cherry in the centre.

CHILLED MELON

Wash, dry and cut in wedge-shaped pieces. Remove seeds and serve on a fruit plate. Hand castor sugar and ground ginger separately.

MELON COCKTAIL

Cut prepared melon into $\frac{1}{2}''$ cubes. Serve in grapefruit glasses. Sprinkle with castor sugar.

GRAPEFRUIT COCKTAIL

Cut a deep slice from the top of the grapefruit, exposing the fruit. Peel the grapefruit in a spiral fashion leaving no pith on fruit, using a saw-like action. Cut each segment of fruit out and put in a bowl. Squeeze the core to collect juice. Sweeten if liked. Put into grapefruit glasses and put a maraschino cherry on top.

FLORIDA COCKTAIL

Make as for Grapefruit Cocktail, using grapefruits and oranges. Omit cherries.

NASSAU COCKTAIL

Make as for Grapefruit Cocktail, using grapefruits, oranges and pineapple. Cut the pineapple into small pieces. Omit the cherries.

TOMATO COCKTAIL

2 tomatoes.	1 tablesp. lemon juice.
$\frac{1}{2}$ teasp. finely-chopped onion.	1 tablesp. white vinegar.
1 tablesp. finely-chopped celery.	$\frac{1}{2}$ oz. castor sugar.

Put the tomatoes in boiling water for 1 minute and then in cold water. Remove skins and eyes and mash to a pulp. Mix with the other ingredients and leave in a cold place for about half an hour. Sieve and serve in small glasses.

OLIVES

Serve the olives in the dish without dressing. They may also be bought stuffed with pimento.

RED CABBAGE SALAD

Shred the red cabbage. Wash well and drain. Toss in French Dressing. Arrange neatly in dish.

COLE SLAW

Shred the white cabbage. Wash well and drain. Toss in French Dressing. Shredded celery, sultanas, or shredded pineapple may be added if liked. Arrange neatly in dish. Garnish with chopped parsley.

RUSSIAN SALAD

Mix diced cooked carrot, diced cooked white turnip and cooked peas together. Dress with Mayonnaise. Arrange neatly in dish. Garnish with parsley.

EGG MAYONNAISE

Remove shells from hard-boiled eggs. Cut each in two or cut in slices. Mask with Mayonnaise. Arrange neatly in dish. Decorate with a pinch of cayenne pepper.

EGG SALAD

Cut the hard-boiled eggs in two on the length. Remove the yolk, mash it with a fork. Mix it with some Mayonnaise and pipe it back into white of egg, using a bag and rose pipe. Garnish with small sprigs of parsley. Arrange neatly in a dish.

RADISHES

Wash the radishes well, top and tail, slice thinly. Toss in French Dressing. Arrange neatly in dish. Garnish with parsley.

CELERY SALAD

Wash the celery well. Shred and dress with Mayonnaise. Arrange neatly in dish. Garnish with parsley.

GREEN PEAS

Shell the peas, cook, cool and toss in French Dressing. Arrange in a dish.

RICE SALAD CRÉOLE

Boil 3 ozs. rice, drain well and dry. When cold add 2 tablespoonfuls cooked diced mushrooms and 2 tablespoonfuls flesh of tomatoes. Mix well and dress with French Dressing. Season, arrange neatly in dish and garnish with chopped parsley.

HORS D'OEUVRE

PATÉ DE FOIE

Cut in slices and serve with hot toast and butter or serve on croûtes of bread.

CHICKEN AND HAM SALAD

Cut left-overs of chicken and ham into dice, mix with Mayonnaise and arrange neatly on a dish on a few small leaves of crisp lettuce. Garnish with parsley.

BEETROOT SALAD

Cook the beetroot, when cold remove skin, cut in match-like strips. Toss in French Dressing. Arrange neatly in dish and garnish with chopped parsley.

CARROT SALAD

Prepare the carrot, cook and cool. Cut in $\frac{1}{2}''$ dice, toss in Mayonnaise, arrange neatly in dish. Garnish with chopped parsley.

POTATO SALAD

Wash potatoes, cook with skins on and cool. Peel, cut in $\frac{1}{2}''$ dice, toss in Mayonnaise. Arrange neatly in dish and garnish with parsley. A little very finely diced onion may be added if liked.

APPLE SALAD

Peel the apples, cut in match-like strips, toss in lemon juice. Arrange neatly in dish.

POTATO, APPLE and CELERY SALAD

Mix Potato Salad, Apple Salad and some shredded celery together. Arrange neatly in a dish. Garnish with finely chopped parsley.

CAULIFLOWER SALAD

Prepare the cauliflower, cook, cool, break into flowerettes and mix with Mayonnaise. Arrange neatly in dish. Garnish with chopped parsley.

TOMATO SALAD

Put tomatoes in boiling water for 1 minute and then in cold water. Remove skins and eyes. Cut in thin slices, put into a bowl with French Dressing, a little extra salt, a pinch of sugar, and mix. Arrange neatly in dish and garnish with chopped parsley.

CUCUMBER SALAD

Wash the cucumber, cut in very thin slices, put in a bowl and dress with French Dressing. Arrange neatly in dish. Garnish with chopped parsley.

5. Then remove the beard with the edge of the knife and loosen the oyster from the lower shell and turn it over to make sure it is fresh.

6. Remove any small pieces of shell which may have got in when opening. The liquid is served in the shell.

7. Arrange the deep shells with the oysters in them on a soup plate with broken ice underneath the shells. Garnish with cut lemon, watercress or parsley.

CAVIARE

Open the jar or tin and place it in a bed of crushed ice on a soup-plate. Use a bone spoon to serve. Arrange small segments of cut lemon around the jar, allowing one segment per person.

SARDINES

Arrange the sardines neatly on the dish, pour the oil from the tin over them. Garnish with chopped parsley.

ANCHOVIES

Curl the anchovy fillets round the point of a knife, place a caper on top. Arrange neatly in the dish.

SMOKED SALMON

Cut in thin slices, arrange on plates, sprinkle French Dressing or lemon juice over. Garnish with small segments of lemon and parsley. Serve thin brown bread and butter and have a peppermill and cayenne pepper on the table.

KIPPERED HERRINGS

Boil the kipper for 5 minutes, remove the flesh from skin and bone. Flake, toss in French Dressing or Mayonnaise. Arrange neatly in dish.

SMOKED HADDOCK

Boil the smoked haddock for about 10 minutes, remove flesh from skin and bone. Flake, toss in French Dressing, or Mayonnaise. Arrange neatly in dish.

SALAMI

Cut in thin slices.

LIVER SAUSAGE

Cut in thin slices.

GERMAN SAUSAGE

Cut in thin slices.

ALL IN THE COOKING

HORS d'OEUVRE

Hors d'oeuvre is the name given to the first course of a full luncheon or dinner menu. It consists of small, tasty, appetising morsels of food, which help to stimulate the appetite ; they should be daintily and attractively served. Some hors d'oeuvre are served in their natural state, e.g., oysters, grapefruit, melon, while others are dressed with a well flavoured dressing and served in small dishes which are part of an hors d'oeuvre set, or on individual plates. Savoury mixtures on small croûtes or canapés may also be served as hors d'oeuvre. The housewife should have no difficulty in preparing hors d'oeuvre from the following suggestions, if she uses her imagination and ingenuity.

The hors d'oeuvre may be put at each place before the guests enter the dining room, or, as in the case of hors d'oeuvre variés, canapés, or croûtes, they may be handed around.

OYSTERS AU NATUREL

6 oysters per person.

To garnish :—Cut lemon, watercress or parsley.
Accompaniments :—Thin slices of brown bread and butter.
Vinegar and seasoning.

1. Oysters should always be alive when purchased. They should smell fresh and the shell should be tightly closed. Buy them from a reliable source when they are required.
2. Scrub the oysters well and rinse them in clean cold water.
3. Place the oyster with the deep shell downwards on a board and hold it firmly with a cloth in the left hand, having the hinge towards the right.
4. Using an oyster knife, prise it gently but firmly into the hinge, then cut the oyster free from the top shell. before removing the top shell.

7

PREFACE TO THE SECOND EDITION

We have pleasure in presenting to the public this second edition of ALL IN THE COOKING.

As in the first edition, our aim has been to offer to the Irish housewife and to the student of cookery an authentic and easy reference book, ideally suited to their needs.

Many new recipes have been tested and included, with a view to arousing greater interest in the art of cooking.

To all who, by their suggestions and criticisms, have helped us in the preparation of this second edition we offer our most sincere thanks.

JOSEPHINE B. MARNELL
NORA M. BREATHNACH
ANN A. MARTIN
MOR MURNAGHAN

CONTENTS

The City of Dublin Vocational
Education Committee have approved
the use of this book, entitled *All in
the Cooking*, as an official Text-book
for all their Schools.

This facsimile edition first published 2022 by
The O'Brien Press Ltd.
12 Terenure Road East, Rathgar, Dublin 6, D06 HD27, Ireland.
Tel: +353 1 4923333; Fax: +353 1 4922777
E-mail: books@obrien.ie; Website: obrien.ie
and
The Educational Company of Ireland
Ballymount Road, Walkinstown, Dublin 12, Ireland.
Tel: +353 1 4500611; Fax: +353 1 4500993
E-mail: info@edco.ie; Website: www.edco.ie
First published 1963 by Longman, Browne & Nolan.

ISBN: 978-1-78849-325-3

Copyright © the authors 1963
The moral rights of the author have been asserted.
Cover design by Emma Byrne.

All rights reserved. No part of this publication may be reproduced or utilised in
any form or by any means, electronic or mechanical, including photocopying,
recording or in any information storage and retrieval system, without
permission in writing from the publisher.

1 3 5 7 9 10 8 6 4 2
22 24 26 27 25 23

Printed and bound in Poland by Bialostockie Zaklady Graficzne S.A.
The paper in this book is produced using pulp from managed forests

Published in

ALL IN THE COOKING
BOOK II

COLAISTE MHUIRE BOOK
of
ADVANCED COOKERY

Compiled by
JOSEPHINE B. MARNELL,

NORA M. BREATHNACH,

ANN A. MARTIN,

Diplomées of Irish Training School of Domestic Science ;

MOR MURNAGHAN,

Diplomée of St. Catherine's Training School of
Domestic Science

(*Staff Teachers, Coláiste Mhuire, Cathal Brugha St., Dublin*)

THE O'BRIEN PRESS
DUBLIN

THE EDUCATIONAL COMPANY OF IRELAND, LIMITED
89 Talbot Street, Dublin

PRAISE FOR

ALL IN THE COOKING
BOOK I

'The book has attained near legendary status over the years. Chefs and students of Home Economics remember it well, but nobody could get their hands on a copy! Until now ... An absolute gem to add to any cookbook collection.'
WWW.IRISHFOODGUIDE.IE

'There are many gems and timeless classics in this book as well as some 'interesting' recipes from bygone days ...There was much to make me smile. I remember how posh I thought potato roses were – a little mashed potato nest with peas in the centre ...The various recipes and explanations contained in it are the result of varied and scientific experience, and have been compiled with minute care and detail.'
DARINA ALLEN, IRISH EXAMINER

'Old school, no frills, no messing – but hugely useful for generation after generation.'
EVENING ECHO

'*All in the Cooking* really is a gem, a cookbook that deserves pride of place in every Irish kitchen. Full of practical information that's still relevant today, this wonderful book will definitely be on a lot of Christmas lists this year and hopefully will lead to more generations of Nanas and Grandchildren baking and cooking together and making memories to treasure forever just like I did.'
KARYN RYAN, IRISH BAKING ADVENTURES

'Many a granny will happily reminisce over the disciplined, informative, thoroughly indexed and photo-free pages that are so typical of the era, and recall the successes (and maybe a few failures) of working from one of the many dog-eared copies that were in daily use in Ireland at the time.'
GEORGINA CAMPBELL, WWW.IRELAND-GUIDE.COM

ALL IN THE COOKING BOOK I
is available to buy from www.obrien.ie
and in all good bookshops

1. Remove the heads, tails and fins from the trout. Scale, clean, wash well and dry. Lay them head to tail on a greased fire-proof dish.

2. Put the chopped capers, lemon juice, salt and pepper, and pieces of butter on top.

3. Cover with greased paper and bake in a moderate oven for about 20 minutes.

4. Garnish with thin slices of lemon.

BOILED SALMON

2 lbs. centre cut of salmon. Boiling water to cover salmon.
Salt (1 teasp. to 1 quart of water).

To garnish :—Lemon, cucumber and parsley.
To serve :—Hollandaise or Hot Tartare Sauce.

1. Clean and wash the fish.

2. Add the salt to the boiling water. Place the salmon on a plate, tie in a piece of muslin and lower into the boiling water.

3. Simmer until cooked, allowing 10 minutes to each pound of salmon and 10 minutes over at the end.

4. Lift out the salmon, remove muslin and drain.

5. Serve salmon on a folded table-napkin on a hot dish. Garnish with alternate slices of notched cucumber and lemon and a few sprigs of parsley.

SALMON FLAN

4 ozs. short pastry.

Filling :

½ lb. of cooked salmon. Pinch of ground mace.
¼ pt. coating sauce. 2 teasps. lemon juice.
Salt and pepper. 1 egg.

¼ lb. potato purée.

To garnish :—Parsley.

1. Roll out the pastry about 1 inch larger than the flan ring. Lift the pastry into the greased ring and press into shape.

2. Make a roll on the edge by pressing back the pastry and trim off the surplus pastry by running the rolling-pin over the top. Bring up the edge to rest on the top of the ring.

3. Finish the edge as desired, lift the flan ring on to a greased tin. Place a round of greased paper in the centre and fill with beans or crusts of bread.

4. Bake in a moderate oven for about 20 minutes. Remove the beans or crusts and return to the oven for about 5 minutes to dry out.

5. Remove skin and bone from the fish. Add the beaten egg, flavourings, seasoning and fish to the sauce.

6. Put the mixture into the flan case and bake in a moderate oven until lightly browned.

7. Decorate with roses of heated potato purée and garnish with parsley. Serve on a hot dish.

SALMON MAYONNAISE

1½ lbs. tail end of salmon.

Mayonnaise Aspic :
¼ gill mayonnaise (page 126).   ¼ gill aspic jelly. (page 221)

To garnish :—1 head lettuce, 3 tomatoes, 1 gherkin, chopped aspic jelly.

1. Steam the salmon, remove the skin and leave until cold.

2. Loosen the salmon from the bone, lift off the top piece, remove the bone and place pieces together again. Lift on to a clean dish.

3. Have the aspic jelly cold and beginning to thicken, mix with the mayonnaise and use to coat the fish.

4. Before serving, decorate with thin strips of tomato and gherkin. Arrange a few lettuce leaves, quarters of tomato, and chopped aspic jelly around the fish.

NOTE.—If not required for cold buffet coat with mayonnaise without the aspic jelly.

SALMON PATTIES

8 ozs. puff pastry.
Filling :—½ pt. white coating sauce.
8 ozs. of cooked salmon.
2 teasps. lemon juice or vinegar.
Pinch mace, salt, pepper.

1. Make and bake patties as for Vol au Vent cases, (page 112) cutting them 3½ inches in diameter.

2. Remove skin and bone from the fish and flake with a fork.

3. Add the flavourings, seasonings and fish to the sauce and heat well.

4. Fill the hot patty cases with the mixture and put on the pastry lid.

5. Serve on a dish paper on a hot dish and garnish with parsley.

GRILLED SALMON

Cutlets of salmon.
To serve :—Cut lemon, parsley, Hollandaise Sauce.

1. Clean the salmon, wash it and dry well. Brush over with melted butter or oil.

2. Heat and grease the bars of the griller.

3. Put on the fish, grill one side for about 1 minute, turn and grill the other side for the same time, reduce the heat and cook on each side for about 5 minutes until the fish is cooked.

4. Serve on a hot dish, garnish with cut lemon and parsley.

SALMON SOUFFLÉ

Make as for Lobster Soufflé, using cooked salmon.

PRAWNS

Break off the tail piece. Take hold of the centre fan of the tail, loosen gently and then draw out to remove the vein. Wash the prawn tails, put into boiling salted water and cook 2–3 minutes. Crack the centre of the shell gently to loosen it. Pull out the flesh from the shell.

Prawn tails may be bought cooked and prepared.

CRAB

Choice

1. Buy alive.

2. Choose one of medium size and heavy in proportion to its size.

3. A crab with a rough shell and large claws is best.

4. Incrustations upon the shell are indications of age.

TO BOIL CRAB

Put the crab into a saucepan of boiling salted water (1 oz. salt to 1 gal. water). Boil for 15-20 minutes according to size.

TO REMOVE THE MEAT FROM CRAB

1. Twist off the large claws, crack with a weight and lift out the meat.

2. Remove the small claws, wash four and keep for garnish, crack the others and lift out the meat.

3. Insert the handle of a spoon at head end and prise out the body of the crab. Scoop out the meat from the shell with the handle of a small spoon. Break away the shell from each side at the natural division. Remove the remainder of the meat.

4. Remove the grey gills, the stomach (which is a small bag lying just below the head) and the intestine. These three parts must be discarded, the remainder of the meat and soft part are edible.

5. Pick out all the meat from the shell, using a skewer. The claws provide white meat and the body grey meat—for some dishes these are not mixed together.

6. If the shell is required—scrub well, rinse, dry and polish with a little salad oil.

HOT DRESSED CRAB

1 crab.	A few drops of lemon juice or vinegar.
1 oz. breadcrumbs.	1 dessertsp. sherry.
½ oz. butter (melted).	Pinch of mace.
¼ teasp. chopped onion.	Salt and pepper.

To garnish :—Browned crumbs, chopped parsley, cut lemon.

1. Cook the crab and remove the meat as on page 35. Flake the crab meat and mix with the other ingredients. Heat thoroughly and pile into the heated prepared shell.

2. Dust over with the browned crumbs and garnish with lemon and parsley. Serve on a dish paper on a hot dish and arrange small claws around.

COLD DRESSED CRAB

1 crab.	Cayenne pepper and salt.
2 tablesps. mayonnaise or cream.	A few lettuce leaves.
1 dessertsp. lemon juice.	1 tomato.

1. Cook the crab and remove the meat as on page 35. Scrub the shell well, dry and polish it with a little salad oil.

2. Flake the claw meat and keep aside. Mix the body meat with mayonnaise, lemon juice and seasoning.

3. Fill the claw meat into the sides of the shell, leaving a triangular space in the centre with the apex towards head end. Put the body meat into the space and smooth both with a knife, keeping a slight hollow between the two meats.

4. Place a line of finely-chopped parsley along this hollow. Serve the crab on a small dish and arrange lettuce leaves and pieces of tomato around.

LOBSTER

Choice

1. Lobsters should be bought alive, if possible. They are then black in colour. After boiling, the colour changes to a cardinal red.

2. If bought already cooked, the tail should be pressed close to the body and it should spring back quickly when opened out straight.

3. The hen lobster contains the spawn which is used to add colour to soups and sauces.

4. The meat from the cock lobster is considered superior in flavour to that of the hen lobster. It is also firmer in texture.

LOBSTER SPAWN

The spawn is a mass of tiny greenish balls found underneath the tail.

36

FISH

To Use.
1. Remove the spawn before cooking the lobster.
2. Wash, drain well and pound in a mortar.
3. Mix with 1 oz. butter and rub through a sieve.
4. Heat in the soup or sauce to give colour and flavour.

CORAL
This is a strip of bright red matter which extends from the lower part of the body along the top of the tail.

To Use.
1. Wash, and dry in a cool oven.
2. Rub through a fine sieve.
3. Use to garnish lobster salad, etc.

LOBSTER BUTTER
Pound shells, soft meat and lobster spawn in a mortar, then mix with creamed butter. Rub through a sieve, and use for colouring lobster soup or sauces.

TO BOIL LOBSTER
Put the lobster head foremost into a large saucepan of boiling salted water (1 oz. salt to 1 gal. water). Boil for 20-30 minutes depending on the size of the lobster. Do not overcook—this will make the meat hard and thready. Lift out lobster and leave until cold.

TO REMOVE MEAT FROM COOKED LOBSTER
1. Twist off the large and small claws. Crack them with a weight and lift out the meat. Some of the small claws are usually kept for garnish.

2. Split the body and tail piece lengthwise, cutting first from centre joint to tail, then turning the lobster and cutting from centre joint to head. Use a large chopping knife to split the lobster.

3. Remove the intestine—the dark strip which runs the length of the tail. If there is any coral—this is bright red and runs down the centre of the lobster—remove it carefully and keep for garnish.

4. Lift out the lobster meat from the shell, remove the grey gills and the stomach—this is a little bag lying near the head. All the rest of the meat is edible. Remove the soft part with a spoon and use a skewer to pick out the remainder of the meat.

LOBSTER SALAD

1 lobster.	Lettuce.
¼ cucumber.	1 slice of onion.
1 bunch radishes.	Juice of ½ lemon.
1 hard-boiled egg.	Pinch of cayenne pepper.
1 teasp. chopped capers.	Salt.

To serve :—Mayonnaise.

1. Prepare the lobster as on page 36. Do not split the head portion, prise out the body from the shell with the handle of a fork or spoon, inserting it under the eyes.

2. Reserve the head, coral, long feelers and the tips of the claw meat for decoration. Remove the eyes from the head, wash, dry and polish the shell with salad oil.

3. Prepare the coral, if there is any in lobster (page 37). Cut the lobster meat into small pieces and sprinkle it with lemon juice, salt and pepper.

4. Prepare the other ingredients as for Salads. Arrange in layers with the lobster meat in a salad bowl.

5. Stand the head upright in the centre and decorate the salad with the pieces of lobster meat, coral, cucumber, radishes and egg.

LOBSTER SOUFFLÉ

3 ozs. of cooked lobster.	½ pt. milk.
2 ozs. butter or margarine.	3 eggs.
2 ozs. flour.	1 teasp. lemon juice.
Salt and pepper.	

To garnish :—Pieces of lobster meat and parsley.
To serve :—Fish Velouté, Supréme or Hollandaise Sauce.

1. Grease a mould well with clarified butter or margarine.

2. Chop the lobster meat, keeping back the tips of the claw meat for garnish.

3. Make a white sauce with the butter, flour and milk. Cool a little, add the yolks of eggs one at a time and beat well. Mix in the flavourings and lobster meat.

4. Beat the whites of eggs stiffly and mix 1 tablespoonful into the sauce, fold in the remainder. Half fill the prepared mould and place a piece of greased paper on top.

5. Place the mould in a deep tin three-quarters full of hot water, put the tin on top of the stove and cook over a gentle heat until the soufflé has reached to the top of the mould—about 20 minutes.

6. Then place the deep tin in a moderate oven and cook until the soufflé is set—about 20-25 minutes more.

7. Lift the soufflé mould out of the water, remove the paper, turn the soufflé on to a heated dish, lifting the mould carefully from the soufflé. Garnish with heated claw meat and parsley. Serve a little sauce around the soufflé.

LOBSTER MAYONNAISE

1 lobster prepared as on page 36.
¼ cucumber.
1 bunch radishes.
1 hard-boiled egg.
1 teasp. chopped capers.

1-2 heads lettuce.
1 slice of onion.
Juice of ½ lemon.
Pinch of cayenne pepper.
Salt.

To serve :—Mayonnaise.

1. Line the salad bowl with the lettuce.
2. Arrange the lobster meat and other ingredients in layers in the centre of the bowl, sprinkling some thin mayonnaise between the layers.
3. Coat the top with thick mayonnaise or half aspic jelly and mayonnaise.
4. Sprinkle the top with the prepared coral.
5. Put the heart of the lettuce in the centre and stand the long feelers around.

LOBSTER CUTLETS

½ lb. lobster meat or ¼ lb. tin of lobster.
1 oz. butter or margarine.
1 oz. flour.
Salt and pepper.

¼ pt. milk.
1 teasp. lemon juice or vinegar.
½ egg.

To coat :—Egg and breadcrumbs.
To garnish :—Parsley, a stick of macaroni.

1. Make a thick white sauce with the butter, flour and milk.
2. Flake the fish. Mix with the sauce and other ingredients. Spread on a wet enamel plate and leave until cold.
3. Cut into eight pieces. Lift each triangular piece on to a floured board. Shape like a cutlet.
4. Coat with beaten egg and breadcrumbs. Put an inch piece of macaroni in the narrow end of each to imitate the bone of a cutlet.
5. Fry in smoking hot fat until a golden brown colour. Drain on kitchen paper.
6. Serve overlapping on a dishpaper on a hot dish. Garnish with parsley.

CREAMED LOBSTER WITH EGGS

½ lb. lobster meat or ½ lb. tin of lobster.
½ pint white coating sauce.
1 tablesp. cream.
Pinch of mace.
1 lb. potato purée.

Salt and cayenne pepper.
Lobster spawn (page 36),
   or
Pink colouring.
4 eggs.

To garnish :—Tips of lobster claws and parsley.

1. Cut the lobster meat into small pieces.
2. Heat the potato purée thoroughly, put into a forcing bag with a large rose pipe. Make a border of potato on a hot entrée dish and keep hot.
3. Add the mace, seasoning and colouring to the sauce, mix in the lobster meat and cream, heat well.
4. Poach the eggs, drain well and place in the centre of the dish.
5. Pour the creamed lobster over the poached eggs and garnish with parsley.

LOBSTER AU GRATIN

1 lobster.
1 oz. butter or margarine.
1 oz. flour.

½ pt. milk.
Salt and pepper.
1 oz. sieved Parmesan or 2 ozs. of other cheese.

1. Prepare the lobster as on page 36, and cut the meat in small pieces.
2. Make a white sauce with the butter, flour and milk. Season, add the lobster meat and re-heat thoroughly. Add the cheese— do not allow to boil again. Correct seasoning and colour pale pink.
3. Arrange the four pieces of shell on a grillpan, fill each with lobster mixture. Sprinkle a little sieved cheese on top and brown under the griller. Garnish with parsley.

LOBSTER PATTIES

Make as for Salmon Patties, using either tinned or cooked lobster meat. Omit the lemon juice.

CURRIED PRAWNS

2 doz. prawn tails (page 35).

Curry Sauce :
1 oz. fat.
1 oz. chopped onion.
1 oz. flour.
1 teasp. curry powder.

½ apple.
¾ pt. stock.
1 dessertsp. chutney.
1 soft tomato *or* ½ teasp. tomato purée.
Salt.

To serve :— 6 ozs. boiled rice (page 225).

1. Melt the fat, add the onion and cook very slowly with the lid on the saucepan for about 5 minutes.

2. Add the flour and curry powder and cook until sandy, add chopped apple, chutney and tomato, cook for a further few minutes.

3. Work on the stock, bring to the boil, skim, add salt and simmer for about 20 minutes, skimming occasionally.

4. Strain into a clean saucepan. Correct the sauce for consistency and flavour. Put in the prawn tails and cook gently for about 15 minutes.

5. Make a border of rice around the entrée dish and serve curried prawns in the centre. Garnish the rice with chopped parsley.

MEATS, POULTRY AND GAME

HAMBURGERS

1 lb. minced lean steak.	1 teasp chopped onion.
1 teasp. chopped gherkins.	1 tablesp. tomato sauce.
1 teasp. chopped capers.	Pepper and salt.
1 teasp. chopped parsley.	1 oz. clarified fat.
To serve :—½ lb. potato purée.	Espagnole Sauce.
To garnish :—Parsley.	

1. Mix the meat with the other incredients and mix well together. Shape into round cakes, about 3 inches in diameter.

2. Fry on a pan in a little hot fat until cooked and browned. Time—10-12 minutes.

3. Make a double row of potato roses on a hot entrée dish, and arrange the meat on top. Garnish with parsley.

GRENADINES OF VEAL

1 lb. lean veal (cut thinly).	2 tomatoes.
1 lb. potato purée.	Pepper and salt.

1 tablespoonful of seasoned flour.
To coat :—Beaten egg and breadcrumbs.
To fry :—Bath of fat.
To serve :—Espagnole or Réforme Sauce.

1. Wipe the meat and cut into oval pieces. Pass through seasoned flour and coat with beaten egg and breadcrumbs.

2. Fry in hot fat for 10–12 minutes. Drain and keep hot.

3. Sli e the tomatoes, season and heat them.

4. Pipe rounds of hot potato purée on to a heated entrée dish. Place a grenadine on each round of potato and place a slice of tomato on top. Garnish with parsley. Pour a little sauce around.

ESCALOPE OF VEAL

4 pieces fillet of veal (about ½-inch thick).
Seasoned flour.   1 oz. clarified fat.

To coat :—Beaten egg and breadcrumbs.
To garnish :—4 slices of lemon.
                 4 anchovy fillets. Capers.

1. Batten the veal. Pass through seasoned flour. Coat with egg and fine breadcrumbs.

2. Fry on both sides in very little hot fat until brown and cooked, about 10 minutes.

3. Garnish each piece of veal with a slice of lemon, place a ring of anchovy on the lemon and place a caper on top.

BLANQUETTE OF VEAL

1 lb. veal.	1 carrot.
1 onion.	1 oz. butter or margarine.
2 cloves.	1 oz. flour.
Bouquet garni.	Salt and pepper.

¼ lb. button onions. ¼ oz. butter.

2 ozs. button mushrooms. Lemon juice.

To garnish :—Croûtes of fried bread.
Chopped parsley.

1. Cut the veal into pieces, put into a heavy saucepan, add sufficient cold water to cover the meat—about 1 quart. Bring to the boil and skim.

2. Add the bouquet garni, carrot, salt, and the onion stuck with the cloves. Cover and cook slowly until the meat is tender—about 1 hour. Skim.

3. Lift out the meat and keep hot, strain the stock into a jug.

4. Peel the mushrooms and cook in a little of the veal stock with a squeeze of lemon juice, salt and pepper. Time—about 15 minutes.

5. Cook the button onions in very little boiling veal stock until tender, add a nut of butter, remove the lid and allow the liquid to evaporate and the butter to glaze the onions. Time—about 30 minutes.

6. Melt the butter in the saucepan, add the flour and cook until dry and sandy. Draw aside and work on about ¾ pint of the veal stock. Stir until it boils. Correct consistency and seasoning.

7. Add the veal to the sauce and cook for a further ¼ hour. Add mushrooms and onions, reheat.

8. Serve in a hot entrée dish. Garnish with croûtes of bread and parsley.

BLANQUETTE OF LAMB
Make as for BLANQUETTE OF VEAL (page 43).

BLANQUETTE OF MUTTON
Make as for BLANQUETTE OF VEAL (page 43).

VEAL QUENELLES

¼ lb. raw lean veal.	1 egg.
½ oz. margarine **or** butter.	1 teasp. lemon juice.
½ oz. flour.	Salt and pepper.
¼ gill milk.	1 lb. potato purée.

To coat :—½ pint Velouté Sauce.
To garnish :—Chopped parsley, paprika pepper **or**
yolk of hard-boiled egg.

1. Wipe the meat and mince finely twice.
2. Make a white sauce with the margarine, flour and milk. Add the meat, beaten egg, lemon juice, salt and pepper, and mix well.
3. Shape into egg shapes on a dessertspoon, smooth the top with a knife dipped in boiling water.
4. Grease a stewpan or deep frying pan. Lift the quenelle from the spoon by slipping a second dessertspoon half into the bowl of the first, and putting the quenelle gently into the pan. Do not have them touching. Pour enough boiling stock or water down the side of the pan to half-cover the quenelles. Put a piece of greased paper on top and poach gently for about 30 minutes.
5. Lift out and drain well. Pipe a double row of potato roses down the centre of a heated dish, arrange the quenelles on top. Mask each quenelle with Velouté Sauce and garnish with parsley and a very little paprika pepper or sieved yolk of egg.

RÉFORME CUTLETS

1½ lbs. fair end of mutton.	1 lb. potato purée.

¾ pint Réforme Sauce.
To coat :—Beaten egg and breadcrumbs.
To fry :—Bath of fat.
To garnish :—Strips of gherkin and cooked carrot.

1. Wipe the meat, trim and divide into cutlets as for Mutton Cutlets.
2. Pass the cutlets through seasoned flour, brush them over with beaten egg, toss in breadcrumbs and fry in hot fat until cooked and browned. Time—about 10 minutes.
3. Make a bank of potato roses down the centre of a hot entrée dish, and arrange the cutlets at each side.
4. Pour a little of the sauce around and garnish with vegetable strips at the four corners.

KIDNEYS À L'ESPAGNOLE

4 mutton kidneys.	2 tomatoes.
Pepper.	8 rounds of fried bread.
1 oz. butter.	½ pint Espagnole Sauce (page 121).
To garnish :—Parsley.	

1. Skin, core and divide each kidney in two.

2. Have butter sizzling hot on pan, season the kidneys and fry for about 10 minutes, turning them occasionally, and keeping them basted with the butter.

3. Slice the tomatoes and heat, place them on the rounds of fried bread. Place the kidneys on top.

4. Arrange on an entrée dish, and pour a little of the sauce around. Garnish with parsley.

DEVILLED KIDNEYS

3 mutton kidneys.   1 oz. Devil Butter (page 128).

2 tomatoes.

To serve :—½ lb. potato purée.

To garnish :—Finely-chopped parsley.

1. Skin, core and divide each kidney in two.

2. Fry in Devil Butter, basting all the time until the kidneys are cooked—about 10 minutes. Slice the tomatoes and heat them.

3. Pipe rounds of hot potato purée on to a heated entrée dish and place a slice of tomato on each.

4. Put each half kidney on top of each slice of tomato and sprinkle with parsley. Pour the Devil Butter over.

CASSEROLE OF KIDNEY

1 beef kidney.	2 tomatoes or a little tomato purée.
1 oz. flour.	1 oz. white turnip.
1 oz fat.	2 ozs. mushrooms.
1 pint brown stock.	Bouquet garni.
2 ozs. onion.	Salt and pepper.
4 ozs. carrot.	½ glass of red wine (if liked).

To garnish :—Parsley.

1. Skin the kidney and remove the core. Cut the kidney into small pieces and wash.

2. Melt the fat in a heavy saucepan and when smoking hot add the kidney and fry until brown.

3. Cut the carrot and turnip into small pieces, chop the onion. Fry the vegetables until brown.

4. Stir in the flour and cook for a few minutes, cool slightly and add the stock, stirring all the time.

5. Bring to the boil, skim, add tomato and bouquet garni, put on the lid and cook slowly for about 1 hour. Stir occasionally during cooking. If liked it may be cooked in a moderate oven, and in this case no stirring is required.

6. Lift the kidney into a clean saucepan or casserole. Strain the sauce, add the wine, correct consistency, colour and seasoning and pour over the kidney.

7. Peel the mushrooms and cut in halves, add to the kidney and put all back to cook for a further ½ hour.

8. Garnish with parsley and serve very hot.

CASSOLETTES OF KIDNEY

½ beef kidney or 2 mutton kidneys.	1 tomato or a little tomato purée.
½ oz. flour.	½ oz. white turnip.
½ oz. fat.	1 oz. mushrooms.
1½ gills brown stock.	Bouquet garni.
1 oz. onion.	Salt and pepper.
2 ozs. carrot.	½ glass red wine (if liked).

4 or 5 potato cassolettes (page 82).
To garnish :—Parsley.

1. Stew the kidney as in previous recipe for Casserole of Kidney.
2. Fill into the hot cassolettes. Serve on a hot entrée dish and garnish with parsley.

PORK FILLETS WITH TOMATO

1 lb. porksteak.	4 tomatoes.
1 oz. butter or margarine.	Pepper and salt.

Apple Sauce :—½ lb. apples.	A little water.
A little brown sugar.	½ oz. butter or margarine.
Pinch of nutmeg.	

To serve :—Thickened Brown Gravy.
To garnish :—Parsley.

1. Wipe the pork and cut into ¾-inch slices. Fry in the hot fat until cooked—about 20 minutes.
2. Make the Apple Sauce.
3. Skin the tomatoes. Cut in halves and fry for a few minutes.
4. Serve the pork fillets on a bed of Apple Sauce on a hot entrée dish. Place a piece of tomato on each piece of pork. Garnish with parsley.

BAKED HAM WITH PINEAPPLE

2½ lbs. lean ham (cut about 1½ inches thick).	
1 small tin pineapple.	Made mustard.
¼ lb. brown sugar.	6 cloves.

1. Coat the ham thinly with the made mustard. Stick in the cloves.
2. Put the ham into a shallow fireproof dish. Pour the pineapple syrup over and put the brown sugar on top.
3. Bake in a moderate oven for about 1½ hours.
4. Put the pineapple on top. Baste with the syrup and bake for a further 15 minutes.
5. Garnish with chopped parsley and serve.

MEAT, POULTRY AND GAME

BRAISING

This is a method of cooking suitable for pieces of meat which are not of sufficiently good quality to roast. It is a combination of two methods of cooking, i.e., frying and stewing—the meat being first fried and then stewed on a bed of root vegetables in a well-flavoured thin brown sauce. Joints suitable for braising are : rump, housekeeper's cut, and thick flank of beef ; shoulder, centre-cut, breast and leg of mutton ; tail-end, fillet, centre-cut and flank of veal ; gammon and shoulder from the bacon pig. The meat should be lean and in one piece.

METHOD OF BRAISING

1. Wipe the meat and lard it to make it tender and to give it flavour. This is done by inserting strips of fat bacon into the meat with a larding needle or larding pin.

2. Make a marinade by mixing two parts oil and one part wine or wine vinegar together and adding sliced onions and carrots, sprig of thyme, bayleaf and a few parsley stalks tied together. The oil gives flavour and the wine helps to make the meat tender as well as giving flavour.

3. Put the meat into the marinade, rub it all over the meat and leave overnight if possible.

4. Next day remove the meat from the marinade, drain well, season and put it into a heavy saucepan with a little hot fat. Fry on all sides until brown.

5. Remove the meat and pour off the fat, add the vegetables from the marinade, putting them together in the centre of the saucepan, place the meat on top of them. Pour in sufficient Thin Brown Sauce (page 120) to come half-way up the meat. It is important to use a saucepan which will just hold the meat, otherwise too much liquid is required.

6. Add a little of the marinade, one or two tomatoes or 1 teaspoonful tomato purée or chutney. Bring to the boil, skim well, cover with a very tightly-fitting lid and cook gently for about 1½-2 hours.

7. Lift the meat into a clean saucepan. Skim the sauce very well, correct for seasoning, colour and consistency and strain over the meat. If using vegetable garnish add it, cover again and cook for another ¾ hour. See that the garnish is cooked.

BRAISED VEAL

2 lbs. lean cut of veal.	1 oz. fat.
Lardons of fat bacon.	Salt and pepper.
1 pint Thin Brown Sauce (page 120).	

Marinade :

2 tablesps. olive oil.	1 carrot.
1 tablesp. wine or wine vinegar.	Sprig of thyme.
1 onion.	Bayleaf.
A few parsley stalks.	

Garnish :—Strips of carrot and white turnip.

1. Wipe the meat and braise as on page 47.
2. Carve the veal, arrange the slices down the centre of the dish, the garnish at sides. Mask with a little sauce and serve remainder in a sauceboat.

BRAISED BEEF

2 lbs. lean cut of beef.	1 oz. fat.
Lardons of fat bacon.	Salt and pepper.
1 pint Thin Brown Sauce (page 120).	

Marinade :

2 tablesps. olive oil.	1 carrot.
1 tablesp. wine or wine vinegar.	Sprig of thyme.
1 onion.	Bayleaf.
A few parsley stalks.	

Garnish :—Cubes of carrot and white turnip.
Button onions.

1. Wipe the meat and braise as on page 47.
2. Carve the beef, arrange the slices down the centre of the dish, the garnish at sides. Mask with a little sauce and serve remainder in sauceboat.

BRAISED MUTTON

2 lbs. lean cut of mutton.	1 oz. fat.
Lardons of fat bacon.	Salt and pepper.
1 pint Thin Brown Sauce (page 120).	

Marinade :

2 tablesps. olive oil.	1 carrot.
1 tablesp. wine or wine vinegar.	Sprig of thyme.
1 onion.	Bayleaf.
A few parsley stalks.	

Garnish :—Mushrooms.

1. Wipe the meat and braise as on page 47.
2. Carve the mutton, arrange the slices down the centre of the dish, the garnish at sides. Mask the meat with a little sauce and serve remainder in a sauceboat.

Sweetbreads

Sweetbreads are light and easily-digested glands. They are got from the calf, lamb or ox—the first-mentioned being the ones generally used. Ox sweetbreads are usually coarse and are rarely used. A " pair " consists of the heart and throat sweetbreads. They are considered a great delicacy, but are expensive. The heart sweetbread is the more appreciated of the two, it is white and firm and is suitable for serving whole. The throat sweetbread, which is the thymus gland of the animal, is longer and darker in colour. It is often rather membraneous and is more suitable in dishes where it can be cut up in small pieces.

To Prepare Sweetbreads:

1. Wash them well and steep in cold water and salt for about an hour. Change the water a couple of times while they are steeping.

2. Blanch in water to which a few drops of lemon juice have been added.

3. Lift out, put into cold water and remove any fat, discoloured parts and skin without spoiling the shape. Press (if required) until cold between two plates having a light weight on top.

BRAISED SWEETBREADS

3 pairs sweetbreads.	1 oz. fat.
Lardons of fat bacon.	Salt and pepper.
1 pint Thin Brown Sauce (page 120).	

Marinade :

2 tablesps. olive oil.	1 carrot.
1 tablesp. wine or wine vinegar.	Sprig of thyme.
1 onion.	Bayleaf.
A few parsley stalks.	

To garnish :—Cooked peas.

1. Wash, soak, blanch and prepare the sweetbreads as directed above, and press them.

2. Braise as on page 47.

3. Arrange the sweetbreads in a hot entrée dish, mask with a little sauce and put the garnish around. Serve remainder of sauce in a sauceboat.

SWEETBREADS EN CASSE

1 pair calf's sweetbreads.	3 tablesps. cooked diced carrot.
1 pint stock.	3 tablesps. diced cucumber.
Bouquet garni.	3 tablesps. cooked green peas.
½ onion.	½ pint Hollandaise Sauce.

To garnish :—Chopped parsley.

1. Wash, soak, blanch and prepare the sweetbreads as directed above, but do not press them.

2. Put the stock, sliced onion and bouquet garni into a saucepan, bring to the boil, put in the sweetbreads and simmer gently until cooked—time, about 1½ hours.

3. Drain sweetbreads well, cut into dice and mix with the vegetables and sauce.

4. Pile into individual fireproof dishes. Place in a very moderate oven to heat. Sprinkle chopped parsley on top and serve.

CREAMED SWEETBREADS

3 pairs sweetbreads.	1 carrot.
1 onion.	1 oz. butter or margarine.
2 cloves.	1 oz. flour.
Bouquet garni.	Salt and pepper.

1–2 tablespoonfuls of cream.

To garnish :—Croûtes of fried bread.
Grilled rolls of bacon.   Parsley.

1. Wash, soak, blanch and prepare the sweetbreads as on page 49.

2. Put them into a saucepan with the onion stuck with the cloves, bouquet garni, carrot and about 1½ pints water. Bring to the boil and skim. Cover and cook slowly for about 1 hour.

3. Melt the butter in a saucepan, add the flour and cook until dry and sandy. Allow to cool.

4. Lift out the sweetbreads and keep hot, strain the liquid into a jug and measure off 1 pint. Add to the roux, bring to the boil, stirring all the time. Correct seasoning and consistency. Add the sliced sweetbreads and cook gently for about ½ hour. Add the cream.

5. Serve in a hot entrée dish. Garnish with croûtes of fried bread, bacon rolls and parsley.

FRIED SWEETBREADS

3 pairs of sweetbreads.
To coat :—Beaten egg and breadcrumbs.
To fry :—Bath of fat.
To serve :—6 croûtes of fried bread.
½ pint Tomato or Velouté Sauce.
To garnish :—Fried parsley (page 223), cut lemon.

1. Wash, soak, blanch and prepare the sweetbreads as on page 49, but do not press them. Put to cook in boiling salted water to which a few drops of lemon juice are added, simmer until tender—about 1¼ hours.

2. Place the saucepan under the cold tap, and let the water run slowly until the sweetbreads are cold. Drain well and press between two plates with a light weight on top.

3. Roll in seasoned flour, coat with egg and breadcrumbs. Fry in hot fat until golden brown and drain well.

4. Serve each sweetbread on a croûte in a hot entrée dish. Pour a little sauce around. Garnish with cut lemon and parsley.

CHICKEN MARYLAND

1 Chicken.   Butter.

To coat :—Seasoned flour, egg and breadcrumbs.

Accompaniments : Horseradish Sauce, Grilled Rashers, Sweet Corn Pancakes, Fried Bananas (or Banana and Pineapple Fritters, if liked).

1. Disjoint the chicken as on page 221.

2. Coat the chicken with seasoned flour and then with beaten egg and breadcrumbs.

3. Heat some butter or other cooking fat in a heavy pan. Fry the dark meat (drum-sticks and thighs) first, after 5 minutes put in the white meat (breast) and fry for about 20 minutes, until cooked. Turn when half-cooked.

4. Arrange on a hot dish with the grilled rashers, Sweet Corn Pancakes and fried banana. Serve with Horseradish Sauce.

Fried Banana

Peel the bananas, cut in two and split each piece. Pass through seasoned flour, and fry.

Banana and Pineapple Fritters

Prepare the bananas as above. Drain the pineapple, and cut each ring in half. Dip the bananas and pineapple in batter and fry in hot bath of fat. Drain and serve.

Batter : 4 ozs. flour.   1 egg.
Pinch of salt.   ¼ pt. milk.

Sieve the flour and salt into a bowl. Make a bay in the centre of the flour, drop in the egg, add half of the milk gradually, stirring with a wooden spoon. Allow the flour to fall in gradually from the sides. Beat for 5 minutes. Add remainder of the milk and allow to stand for at least 1 hour before use.

Sweet Corn Pancakes

Take about half of the above batter and mix with 1 table-spoonful of sweet corn. Fry on a hot greased pan as for Dropped Scones, or cook in muffin rings.

KROMESKIES

½ oz. butter or margarine.   1 teasp. Tomato Sauce.
½ oz. flour.   1 teasp. Mushroom Ketchup.
½ gill milk.   Pinch of nutmeg.
3 ozs. minced cooked veal.   Salt and pepper.
1 oz. minced cooked ham.   6 ozs. streaky rashers.
Rich Coating batter (page 223).

To fry :—Bath of fat.

To garnish :—Parsley.

1. Make a white sauce with the butter, flour and milk.

2. Add the meat, tomato and mushroom sauces, nutmeg and seasoning. Mix well and bring to boil. Cool and form into cork-shaped pieces.

3. Remove the rind and any bone from the rashers, cut in two, and flatten out on a board. Put a piece of meat mixture on each piece of rasher and roll up.

4. Coat with the batter, lift out on a skewer and drop into the smoking hot fat. Fry until cooked and brown, drain well.

5. Serve on a dish paper on a hot entrée dish. Garnish with parsley.

NOTE.—Any poultry, meat or game may be used instead of veal.

BRAINS À L'ITALIENNE

3 sets of calf's brains.	Salt.
Cold water.	1 tablesp. vinegar.

To coat :—Beaten egg and breadcrumbs.
To fry :—Bath of fat.
To serve :—3 croûtes of fried bread. ½ pint Tomato Sauce.
To garnish :—Cooked spaghetti.

1. Wash brains in cold salted water, remove skin and soak them in fresh cold water for half an hour. Change the water once or twice. Blanch them.

2. Put them into a saucepan, cover with cold water, add salt and vinegar. Bring to the boil, skim, and cook gently for 10–12 minutes. Put the saucepan under the cold tap, and let the cold water run until the brains are cold.

3. Dry the brains, toss in seasoned flour, coat with beaten egg and breadcrumbs. Fry in hot fat and drain well.

4. Serve on croûtes of fried bread on a hot entrée dish. Pour a little of the sauce around and garnish with spaghetti.

PICKLING OF MEAT

General Directions.

Pork and Beef are the two meats generally pickled. The meat chosen must be fresh and of very good quality, and it is usually boned. Before pickling, trim the meat carefully and remove any discoloured parts, kernels or traces of blood. Wipe it, rub it with common salt and leave for at least twelve hours.

Parts of Meat usually Pickled

Brisket, Round, and Tail Piece of Beef.
Head, Shoulder, Leg, Streaky, Shank, and Feet of Pork.

There are two methods of pickling—the wet and the dry method. Dry pickling is more suitable for home use.

Rock salt or common salt may be used for pickling, but a mixture of the two in equal quantities is better. Saltpetre gives colour to the meat, but must only be added in very small proportion, as it tends to harden it. Brown sugar mellows and helps to soften the texture.

SPICED BEEF

1 lb. salt.	¼ oz. ground cloves.
1 oz. saltpetre.	¼ oz. ground mace.
½ oz. black pepper.	½ teasp. chopped thyme.
½ teasp. cayenne pepper.	6 bay leaves.
¼ lb. brown sugar.	3 chopped shallots.
½ oz. allspice.	¼ lb. treacle.

The above will spice from 7–10 lbs. beef.

1. Prepare the meat as above.

2. Mix the salt, saltpetre, sugar, shallots, spices, seasoning and flavourings together. Rub this mixture into the meat on all sides.

3. Leave for two days, then pour the treacle over. Rub in the mixture every day for about a fortnight.

4. Tie into shape, cook as for salt meat. Press and dust with meat spice.

DRY PICKLE FOR MEAT

½ lb. rock salt.	½ oz. black pepper.
½ lb. common salt.	1 teasp. allspice.
½ lb. brown sugar.	¼ teasp. ground ginger.
½ oz. saltpetre.	¼ teasp. ground cloves.

1. Pound all the ingredients together and mix well.

2. Prepare the meat (page 52), and put it into the pickling basin or dish. Sprinkle the pickle over and rub well into the meat.

3. Repeat the rubbing every day for about 10 days and turn the meat each day. Remove from the pickle and wash. Boil as for salt meat.

RAISED VEAL AND HAM PIE

Filling :

½ lb. lean veal.	Grated rind and juice of ¼ lemon
¼ lb. ham.	2 slices of onion (finely-chopped).
1 hard-boiled egg.	Pepper and salt.
1 tomato.	2 ozs. breadcrumbs.

Stock.

Raised Pie Crust.

½ lb. flour.	¾ gill water.
4 ozs. shortening.	¼ teasp. salt.

To glaze :—Beaten egg.
To garnish :—Parsley.

1. Wipe the meat, trim off any fat and bone, and cut it into neat pieces about ½ inch square. Put into a bowl with the onion and rind and juice of the lemon. Add seasoning.

2. Make the pastry (page 156). Cut off a quarter for the lid and put it back into the bowl to keep warm.

3. Put the remainder into the greased mould and press it into the bottom and sides of the mould, keeping it even in thickness.

4. Brush the inside of the pastry with white of egg.

5. Put breadcrumbs in the bottom of the mould and fill up with the prepared meat filling. Half-fill with stock.

6. Brush the edge with beaten egg. Roll out the piece kept for the lid and cover the pie with it. Press the edges together, trim and decorate them. Brush the top with beaten egg.

7. Make a hole in the centre, and with the trimmings make three or four leaves. Arrange them neatly around the hole, damp underneath the tips to keep them in position, and brush them with beaten egg.

8. Bake in a moderately hot oven for about 2 hours. When brown place a piece of greaseproof paper on top.

9. Remove the paper and tin about half an hour before pie is fully cooked, and brush the sides with beaten egg. If necessary, additional boiling stock may be added to the pie through the hole in the top.

10. Serve the pie on a plain dish paper on a hot dish.

NOTE (a).—Raised pies may also be raised and cooked without a special mould, as follows :—

1. Prepare the pastry and cut off a quarter of it for the lid. Put this piece back into the bowl and keep it warm.

2. Knead the remainder into a smooth flat round. With the back of the hand press down the middle of the pastry to ⅜-inch in thickness and to about 4 inches in diameter.

3. Raise up the thick edge of the pastry, using both hands to form a case about ⅜-inch in thickness. Brush the inside of the pastry with white of egg.

4. Put in the filling. Flatten out the remaining piece. Damp the top edges of the pastry and proceed as above.

NOTE (b).—Raised pies are sometimes served cold. In this case, stock, which will form a jelly when cold, must be used. If stock is not strong enough, soak a sheet of gelatine in tepid water until soft, squeeze it out of the water and dissolve it in the hot stock.

RAISED PORK AND VEAL PIE

Filling :

4 ozs. minced pork.	2 ozs. breadcrumbs.
4 ozs. minced veal.	½ teasp. finely-chopped sage.
2 ozs. chopped ham.	Pepper and salt.
1 hard-boiled egg.	Stock.

½ lb. Raised Pie Crust.

To glaze :—Beaten egg.
To garnish :—Parsley.

Make as for Raised Veal ana Ham Pie (page 53.)

GRILLED STEAK AND BANANAS

1 lb. sirloin steak.	Pepper.
Olive oil or melted butter.	2 bananas.

Lemon juice.

To serve :—Maître d'Hôtel Butter.

1. Wipe meat, sprinkle with pepper and brush over with olive oil or melted butter. Grill 12–15 minutes.

2. Skin the bananas, cut in two and split each piece. Sprinkle with lemon juice. Fry in butter.

3. Serve steak on a hot dish, place a few pats of Maître d'Hôtel Butter on top and garnish with fried bananas.

VEAL AND HAM PIE

5 ozs. Puff or Rough Puff Pastry.

½ lb. veal.	Grated lemon rind.
½ lb. cooked ham.	½ gill stock.

Forcemeat :

2 ozs. breadcrumbs.	Rind and juice of ¼ lemon.
1 tablesp. chopped suet.	Pepper.
1 teasp. chopped parsley.	Salt.
¼ teasp. mixed herbs.	A little stock to bind.

To glaze :—Beaten egg.
To garnish :—Parsley.

1. Roll out pastry a little larger than top of pie dish, and leave in a cold place.

2. Wipe the veal and remove bone and fat from it. Cut the ham and veal into neat pieces.

3. Mix the ingredients for the forcemeat and put a layer of it in the bottom of the pie-dish, then a layer of veal sprinkled with grated lemon rind, and next a layer of ham. Continue until pie-dish is full, having a layer of forcemeat on top.

4. Pour in a little stock. Cover the pie with the pastry. Make a hole in the centre of the pastry and decorate with leaves of pastry. Brush over with beaten egg.

5. Bake in a hot oven for about ten minutes. Reduce the heat and cook for about 1½ hours. If necessary, additional boiling stock may be added to the pie through the hole in the top.

6. Serve pie on a dish paper on a hot dish and garnish with parsley.

BAKED HAM

½ ham (fillet or (shank).

To serve :—½ pint Réforme Sauce (page 123).

1. Weigh and wash the ham. If very salty or highly-smoked, soak for 24 hours, changing the water 3 or 4 times. Scrape, removing any rusty or discoloured parts.

2. Wrap the ham up in aluminium foil, making sure that it is completely covered by it.

3. Place on a roasting tin and bake in a moderate oven, allowing 25 minutes to each pound and 25 minutes over at the end.

4. When cooked, remove the foil and skin. Put the ham back to crisp in the oven for a few minutes, or crisp in front of a bright fire. Serve on a hot dish.

GRILLED CUTLETS

4 cutlets   Pepper
½ oz butter or other fat.

To serve :—Grilled mushrooms or tomatoes.
Watercress.

Prepare cutlets, sprinkle with pepper and brush over with melted butter. Grill 8–10 minutes. Arrange on a hot dish. Garnish with mushrooms or tomatoes and bunches of watercress.

STEWED OX-TAIL

1 oxtail.	Bunch of fresh herbs.
2 ozs. seasoned flour.	2 ozs. dripping.
1 carrot.	1½ pints brown stock.
1 white turnip.	2 soft tomatoes or
1 onion.	1 teasp. tomato purée.

1 glass sherry (if liked)

To garnish : Julienne Strips (page 222).
or, Cooked cauliflower divided into flowerettes,
or, ½ lb. cooked green peas

1. Wash the tail and divide at the joints. Trim off the fat. Blanch and rinse in cold water. Drain and dry in a meat cloth, and toss in the seasoned flour.

2. Prepare the carrot, onion and turnip. Cut carrot and turnip into neat pieces and slice the onion. Wash the herbs.

3. Melt the dripping and fry the pieces of oxtail in it until browned. Lift them out and add the remainder of the flour. Stir until browned. Cool a little. Add the stock gradually, stirring all the time. Boil for 5 minutes. Add the meat, vegetables, herbs and tomatoes.

4. Cover with a tightly-fitting lid and stew gently until the meat is tender—about 2 hours. Lift the pieces of oxtail into a clean saucepan, correct the sauce, skim well and strain over the meat. Put back to cook for a further half-hour. Add sherry.

5. Lift the meat on to a hot entrée dish, pour a little sauce over and garnish.

BEEF OLIVES

1 lb. round steak (cut very thin).	1 oz. fat.
1 pint Thin Brown Sauce (page 120).	Pepper and salt.

Forcemeat :

2 ozs. breadcrumbs.	1 teasp. finely-chopped onion.
1 tablesp. finely-chopped suet.	Pinch mixed herbs.
1 teasp. finely-chopped parsley.	Pepper and salt.
A little stock to bind.	

Marinade :

2 tablesps. olive oil.	1 carrot.
1 tablesp. wine or wine vinegar.	1 onion.
Sprig of thyme.	Bayleaf.
A few parsley stalks.	

To garnish :—Julienne strips.

1. Wipe the meat with a damp meat cloth, and trim. Cut into oblong pieces about 3 ins. by 2 ins. Beat with the back of a wooden spoon. Put into the marinade. Leave for about 1 hour.

2. Make forcemeat by mixing all the dry ingredients together, and bind with stock.

3. Spread a little forcemeat on each piece of meat and roll up. Tie with a piece of coarse white thread.

4. Braise as on page 47 and serve in a hot entrée dish.

MUTTON FLAN

5 ozs. Short Pastry.

Filling :

1 oz. clarified fat.	Pepper and salt.
1 oz. flour.	1 oz. chopped onion.
½ pint brown stock.	¾ lb. cooked mutton.
1 teasp. tomato purée.	

To garnish :—2 tomatoes.   1 lb. potato purée.
Chopped parsley.

1. Make a flan case as on page 33, put a piece of greased paper in the centre with some beans or crusts of bread on it to

prevent the pastry from rising. Bake in a moderate oven for about 20 minutes. Remove the beans and paper and return the flan case to the oven to dry out for about 5 minutes.

2. Heat the fat, add the onion and flour. Cook until the flour browns, stirring well. Draw aside and stir in the stock. Cook for 5 minutes. Skim. Add tomato purée and season.

3. Prepare the meat, cut it into ¼-inch cubes and add to the sauce. Mix well, bring to the boil and reheat thoroughly.

4. Put the flan case on a hot dish, put in the filling and pipe roses of hot potato purée on top. Garnish with the tomatoes which have been cut in quarters and heated in the oven. Sprinkle chopped parsley on top.

GOULASH

1 lb. round steak.	1 oz. flour.
1 oz. paprika.	1 pint stock.
1 oz. fat.	1 teasp. tomato purée or 2 tomatoes.
4 ozs. onion (chopped).	Salt

To garnish :—Parsley.

1. Cut the meat into 1-inch squares and toss in the paprika.

2. Heat the fat in a heavy saucepan and fry the meat quickly on all sides. Add the onion and fry until golden brown.

3. Add the flour and cook over a moderate heat until brown, stirring to prevent burning. Cool a little and add the stock, stirring all the time. Bring to the boil and skim. Add tomato and salt, put the lid on the saucepan and stew gently for about 2 hours. Skim the stew occasionally while cooking.

4. Lift the meat into a hot entrée dish. Correct the sauce and strain over the meat. Garnish with parsley.

BEEF GALANTINE

1 lb. round steak.	Pinch of mixed herbs.
½ lb. sausage meat.	Pepper and salt.
6 ozs. breadcrumbs.	1 egg.
1 dessertsp. Worcester Sauce.	A little stock.
1 dessertsp. Tomato Ketchup.	¼ lb. streaky rashers or cooked ham.
½ teasp. finely-chopped onion.	1 hard-boiled egg.
¼ teasp. finely-chopped parsley.	1 tomato.

To garnish :—Meat Glaze (page 223). Parsley.
Savoury butter (page 223). Lettuce leaves.
Tomatoes.

1. Dip a pudding cloth into boiling water, wring out as much water as possible and brush over with hot fat.

2. Remove any fat and bone from the meat, wipe and mince it. Put into a mixing bowl, add the sausage meat, breadcrumbs, sauces, onion, parsley, herbs, pepper and salt. Mix well together, bind with beaten egg and a little stock.

3. Turn on to a lightly-floured board and flatten out into an oblong piece about 1 inch in thickness and about 9 inches in width.

4. Rind and bone the rashers, flatten out on a board and place them over the meat.

5. Slice the hard-boiled egg and tomato and arrange them in rows on the rashers.

6. Roll up and tie in the prepared cloth. Sew up the opening.

7. Put down in boiling salted water, and simmer gently for 1¼ hours.

8. Lift out and place on a board. Place another board on top with a 2 lb. weight on it, and leave until cold. Remove the cloth, wipe over the meat with a cloth dipped in boiling water.

9. Brush over with liquid meat glaze, trim the ends and decorate with Savoury Butter and parsley.

10. Lift on to a dish, and garnish with lettuce leaves and tomatoes cut in quarters.

JELLIED TONGUE

1 ox tongue.	¾ pint pot liquor (in which tongue
¾ oz. leaf gelatine.	was cooked).

Meat Glaze (page 223).

To garnish : —Lettuce or parsley.　　　　Tomatoes.

1. Boil the tongue allowing about 3 hours. Test the tip with a skewer. Take it out of the liquor in which it was cooked and allow the cold water to run on it for a few minutes, the skin should then peel off easily.

2. Remove all the bones at the root of the tongue and trim away some fat. Roll up and place it in a cake tin 6 inches to 7 inches in diameter.

3. Soak leaf gelatine in a bowl of tepid water, leave until soft, squeeze out of the water.

4. Strain off ¾ pint of the pot liquor and remove all trace of fat from it. Add the gelatine and dissolve it in this liquor. Pour over the tongue and leave until cold and set.

5. Slip a pointed knife around the edge and dip the tin in boiling water for a second. Turn out, and brush over with liquid meat glaze.

6. Serve on a dish and garnish with lettuce or parsley and tomatoes.

GLAZED TONGUE

1 ox tongue.	Meat Glaze (page 223).

To garnish :

1 oz. Savoury Butter (page 223).	Chopped Aspic Jelly (page 221).
2 tomatoes.	Parsley.

1. Boil the tongue, take it out of the liquor in which it was cooked and allow the cold water to run on it for a few minutes— the skin should then peel off easily.

2. Shape it on a board by fastening it down with two fine skewers at the root end. Slip the neck of a narrow bottle under the thick part of the tongue to give it an arched appearance. Fasten down the tip of the tongue with a fine skewer.

3. When cold, remove the skewers and bottle, and trim away some of the fat from the root end. Brush the tongue over with liquid meat glaze. Decorate with Savoury Butter and parsley.

4. Fasten a paper frill around the root and keep it in position with two fancy skewers, or two small pieces of pointed wood.

5. Serve on a dish paper on a dish, and garnish with cut tomatoes, Aspic Jelly and parsley.

ROAST TURKEY

1 turkey.	Few slices of fat bacon.

1 lb. Veal Forcemeat (page 225) *or* 1 lb. Sweet Stuffing (page 225) *or* 1 lb. Chestnut Stuffing (page 222).

To serve : Ham or Sausages.   Thin Brown Gravy.
Bread Sauce *or* Cranberry Sauce.

Prepare, draw, truss and roast as for Roast Chicken.

Have the oven moderately hot for the first $\frac{3}{4}$ hour and reduce to very moderate for the remainder of the time.

Protect the breast with a piece of aluminium foil.

Approximate times for cooking turkey—

About 9–11 lbs. (purchased weight) allow about 2 hours.
  ,,   11–14   ,,   (,,   ,,   )   ,,   ,, $2\frac{1}{2}$,,
  ,,   14–17$\frac{1}{2}$,,   (,,   ,,   )   ,,   ,,   3   ,,
  ,,   18–22   ,,   (,,   ,,   )   ,,   ,, $3\frac{1}{2}$,,

If cooked the meat of the thigh should be soft when tested with a skewer or pressure from fingers.

ROAST GOOSE

1 goose.	A little hot fat.

Potato Stuffing :

1$\frac{1}{2}$ lbs. mashed potatoes.	3 ozs. butter or margarine.
3 ozs. chopped onion.	3 teasps. chopped parsley.
Pinch of mixed herbs.	Pepper and salt.

To serve :—Thickened Brown Gravy.   Apple Sauce.

1. Pluck, singe and draw the goose as for chicken, taking care to remove all the soft fat from the inside. Cut off the first bone of the wing. Leave on the feet, scald and skin them and cut off the toe-nails.

2. To make the stuffing : fry the onion in butter until soft, then mix in the other ingredients.

3. Stuff the goose, truss it and cook as for Roast Duck, allowing 2–2$\frac{3}{4}$ hours to cook, according to size.

ROAST GUINEA-FOWL

1 guinea fowl.	A slice of fat bacon.

Veal Forcemeat: (page 225)

4 ozs. breadcrumbs.	2 ozs. butter or margarine.
1 teasp. chopped parsley.	1 oz. chopped onion.
Pepper and salt.	

To serve :—Thin Brown Gravy.   Rolls of bacon.
       Bread Sauce *or* Cranberry Sauce.

1. Pluck, singe, draw, stuff and truss the guinea-fowl **as for** Roast Chicken.

2. Place a slice of fat bacon over the breast. Roast, allowing about 1¼ hours, and serve as for Roast Chicken.

NOTE.—Guinea-fowl may also be treated as game.

ROAST DUCK

1 duck.	A little hot **fat.**

Sage and Onion Stuffing :

6 ozs. breadcrumbs.	Pepper and salt.
3 small onions (parboiled).	1½ ozs. butter or margarine.
6-8 sage leaves (chopped).	A little stock.

To garnish :—Watercress.

To serve :—½ pint Thickened Brown Gravy.   Green peas.
       Apple Sauce.   Potato Ribbons.

1. Pluck, singe and draw the duck as for chicken and cut off the first bone of the wing. Leave on the feet, scald and skin them, and cut off the toe-nails. Wipe the inside of the bird with a damp cloth.

2. Mix the breadcrumbs, chopped onions and sage together and season. Add melted butter and bind with a little stock.

3. Put into the body at the tail end, and put the tail through the hole left by cutting away the vent.

4. Dislocate the legs at the knee joints and turn them back and under on to the back. Fan the feet across the back and draw the flap of skin from the neck end over the back.

5. Put a trussing needle threaded with some fine twine through the joint of the right wing, joint of right leg, through the body, out through the joint of the left leg and through the joint of the left wing.

6. Take a stitch through the flap of the skin, and tie the twine at the side.

7. Put the trussing needle through the top of the right wing, through the body and out through the left wing at the other side. Tie at the side.

8. Cover the breast with greased paper, and roast, allowing 1½–2 hours.

9. About ten minutes before being fully cooked, remove the paper, dredge the breast with flour, and return to the oven to brown.

10. Lift the duck on to a plate, remove the twine, serve **on a** hot dish and garnish with watercress.

SAUTÉ OF CHICKEN WITH MUSHROOMS

1 chicken.	1 glass white wine.
½ lb. mushrooms.	¾ pt. Chicken Velouté (page 124).
2 ozs. butter.	½ gill cream.
1 teasp. lemon juice.	Salt and pepper.

1. Disjoint the chicken as on page 221.
2. Make stock with the chicken carcase and use to make the Velouté Sauce.
3. Prepare the mushrooms and cook in a little butter in a small saucepan.
4. Heat some butter in a heavy pan. Put in the dark meat first (drum-sticks and thighs); after about 5 minutes put in the white meat (breasts and wings) and cook without colouring for about 15 minutes. Turn when half-cooked.
5. Add the lemon juice, white wine, and Chicken Velouté, cook for about 5 minutes. Put into a casserole and cook in a very moderate oven for about 20 minutes. Add the heated cream and mushrooms. Correct seasoning and serve.

CHICKEN OR TURKEY MAYONNAISE

1 boiled chicken or cooked turkey meat.	Pepper and salt.
4 sticks of celery.	½ pint cream.
2 ozs. chopped walnuts.	½ pint mayonnaise.

To garnish—Lettuce leaves.   Tomatoes. Parsley.

1. Cut the chicken or turkey meat into ½-inch cubes and put into a bowl with chopped celery, walnuts and seasonings. Mix well together and bind with ¼ pint of whipped cream and ¼ pint of mayonnaise.
2. Turn on to a large dish, form into a pile and shape into an oval with palette knife.
3. Coat with mayonnaise, decorate with seasoned whipped cream and garnish with tomatoes, parsley and lettuce.

COLD CHICKEN CREAM

Aspic Jelly (page 221).   Chilli rings.   Parsley.

½ pt. Béchamel Sauce (page 120).	8 ozs. minced cooked chicken.
¼ oz. gelatine.	2 ozs. minced cooked ham.
1 teasp. lemon juice.	¼ pint aspic jelly.
Pepper and salt.	¼ pint cream.

To garnish :—Lettuce.   Tomato.   Chopped Aspic Jelly.

1. Line the mould with Aspic Jelly and decorate with parsley and chilli rings (page 224).

2. Soak leaf gelatine in a bowl of tepid water, leave until soft, squeeze out of the water when required. If using powdered gelatine mix with 2 tablespoonfuls of water, leave for a short time and use.

3. Make Béchamel Sauce, add the gelatine and stir until dissolved. Cool and mix in the lemon juice, pepper, salt, chicken, ham and tepid aspic jelly. Leave until beginning to set.

4. Fold in the half-whipped cream and pour into the prepared mould. Leave until set.

5. Loosen the edge with a pointed knife, then dip the mould in hot water. Turn the cream out on to a dish and garnish with lettuce leaves, tomato, and chopped Aspic Jelly.

HOT CHICKEN CREAM

1 oz. butter or margarine.	1 teasp. lemon juice.
1 oz. flour.	Pinch of ground mace.
1½ gills milk.	2 eggs.
Pepper and salt.	6 ozs. minced cooked chicken.

½ gill cream

To serve :—Dutch or Tartare Sauce or Sauce Mornay.
¼ lb. cooked green peas.

1. Make a white sauce with the butter, flour and milk. Add pepper, salt, lemon juice, and mace.

2. Drop in the eggs one by one and beat well. Add the chicken and cream and mix thoroughly.

3. Put the mixture into a greased border mould, cover with greased paper and steam slowly 30-40 minutes.

4. Turn on to a hot dish, fill the centre with freshly-cooked green peas and pour a little of the sauce around.

CHICKEN SOUFFLÉ

2 ozs. butter or margarine.	Grated lemon rind.
2 ozs. flour.	Pinch grated nutmeg.
½ pint milk.	6 ozs. cooked minced chicken.
3 eggs.	2 ozs. cooked minced ham.

Pepper and salt.

1. Grease a mould with clarified butter or margarine.

2. Make a white sauce with the butter, flour and milk. Cool a little, add the yolks of eggs one at a time and beat well. Mix in the flavourings, chicken and ham.

3. Beat the whites of eggs stiffly and mix 1 tablespoonful into the sauce, fold in the remainder. Half-fill the prepared mould and place on a baking tin.

4. Place over a slow heat (with a gas stove use an asbestos mat) for about 10–15 minutes until the bottom of the soufflé begins to set. Then place in a moderate oven for about 30 minutes until well risen and set. Serve immediately.

ALL IN THE COOKING

TO BONE A CHICKEN

There are two kinds of boning :
(a) Partial.
(b) Complete.
A small sharp boning knife is required.

Filling for Boned Chicken.

1 good quality boiling fowl.	2 ozs. butter or margarine.
1 carrot.	2 ozs. flour.
1 onion.	½ pint chicken stock.
1 stick of celery.	2 eggs.
Piece of leek.	Grated lemon rind.
Bouquet garni.	Pinch of nutmeg.
Salt and pepper.	

1. Prepare the fowl and boil with the vegetables for about 2½ hours, skimming constantly. Leave to cool in the chicken stock. Strain off stock and keep aside.

2. Remove the meat from the fowl and mince or chop.

3. Make a white sauce with the butter, flour and the chicken stock. Add the beaten eggs and flavourings, and lastly mix in the meat and seasoning.

To Prepare Fowl for Boning.

Use an undrawn chicken. Singe and cut off head close to the head. Cut skin down the back of the neck, remove crop and windpipe, and cut off the neck close to the body.

Cut a slit on the inside of the leg just below the knee joint, and draw the sinews with a skewer.

Partial Boning.

This is used for Chaudfroid of Chicken and Roast Boned Chicken. The wings and legs are left complete, or, if wished, the thigh bone of the legs may be removed.

1. Place chicken, neck-end towards you, and breast uppermost. Turn back the skin of the neck, cut the flesh from the wish-bone, and remove the bone. Disjoint the wings.

2. Remove the flesh from the back and breast by pressing the knife between the flesh and carcase, working round and round gradually, spiral fashion, and drawing the flesh and skin off. Care must be taken not to pierce the carcase.

3. Disjoint legs, leaving the bones in them, continue until all flesh has been freed from the carcase, right down to the tail, remove carcase.

4. Cut away around the vent and push tail through the hole made.

5. Cut through the ribs of carcase, lift out intestines, keep liver and gizzard for Roast Boned Fowl and use bones for making chicken stock.

Complete Boning.

1. Cut off the tips of the wings and place the fowl on the board with the back uppermost and cut through the skin right down the middle of the back.

2. Remove the wish-bone as for partial boning. Disjoint the wings, take hold of the first joint and cut off the flesh, keeping close to the bone. Remove the bones.

3. Remove the flesh cleanly from the carcase, working down each side towards the breast bone.

4. Disjoint the legs, remove the flesh from the first bone, crack the joint and lift out the top bone. Remove the flesh from the other bone in the same way and take out the bone.

5. Remove the flesh from the carcase right down to the tail and remove the carcase.

6. Turn the legs and wings outside in. Remove any pieces of sinew or gristle. Cut off the vent and tail and any discoloured skin at the neck end.

ROAST BONED CHICKEN

1 undrawn chicken.   Filling for Boned Chicken (page 64).
To serve :—Brown gravy, Bread sauce,
                Rolls of bacon.

1. Partially bone the chicken according to directions (page 64).

2. Put in the filling, shape, truss, weigh, cook and serve as for Roast Chicken, allowing about 1¼ hours according to size.

GALANTINE OF CHICKEN

1 undrawn chicken.   Filling for Boned Chicken (page 64).
Pepper and salt.   1 carrot.
2 celery stalks.   1 onion.
                Bouquet garni.

Meat Glaze (page 223).

To garnish :—Hard-boiled egg, or   Parsley.
                Coloured Savoury Butter (page 223).   Tomatoes.
                Lettuce.

1. Completely bone the chicken (page 65).

2. Spread the chicken out on a board with the skin side downwards, and distribute the flesh evenly over. Sprinkle with salt and pepper, place the filling on the centre and wrap chicken flesh around it.

3. Press into shape, stitch opening and tie in a prepared pudding cloth. Cook in boiling salted water to which the vegetables have been added. Time—about 1¼ hours.

4. When cooked, put between two boards with a light weight on top. Finish as for Beef Galantine, or, if preferred, coat with Chaudfroid Sauce and finish as for Chaudfroid of Chicken.

CHAUDFROID OF FOWL

2 good quality boiling fowl.	1 oz. gelatine.
2 carrots.	½ pint Aspic Jelly (page 221).
2 onions.	Pinch of nutmeg.
2 sticks celery.	A little grated lemon rind.
1 leek.	Pepper and salt.
Bouquet garni.	1 pint cream.

To finish :—Chaudfroid Sauce (page 122).
Chicken Aspic Jelly (page 221).

To decorate :—Truffle, pimento, gherkins, lettuce leaves etc.

1. Prepare the fowl and boil with the vegetables and flavourings for about 2½ hours, skimming constantly. Leave them to cool in the chicken stock.

2. Remove the meat from one fowl and mince it.

3. Cut through the skin attaching the legs to the body of the second fowl, pull back the legs. Hold the vent and back of the fowl with one hand, and with the other hand hold the ventral end of the breast-bone and lift off the breast-bone and wings.

4. Lift off both complete breasts carefully, keeping them whole. Divide each breast into two pieces—they split naturally. Trim the four pieces neatly, making them pear-shaped. Place on a wire tray and put in a cold place.

5. Soak leaf gelatine in a bowl of tepid water, leave until soft, squeeze out of the water when required. If using powdered gelatine mix with 3 tablespoonfuls of water, leave for a short time before use.

6. Add the nutmeg, lemon rind and seasoning to the minced chicken. Have the aspic jelly warm, add the gelatine and stir until dissolved. Half-whip the cream, add the aspic jelly and chicken, mix lightly together.

7. When the filling is almost set, put it into the second bird, and mould to the shape of the fowl. Leave to set in a cold place on a wire tray. Mask with Chaudfroid Sauce and when set give a second coating.

8. Mask the four pieces of breast with Chaudfroid Sauce, and when set give a second coating.

9. Decorate each piece of breast and the fowl with truffle, pimento and gherkin or other similar garnishes.

10. Give a final coating with cold liquid aspic jelly.

11. Arrange the fowl at one end of a large dish with the pieces of breast placed neatly at the other end. Garnish with leaves of lettuce.

FRICASSÉE OF FOWL

1 good quality boiling fowl.	2 ozs. butter or margarine
1 onion.	2 ozs. flour.
1 carrot.	¼ pint milk.
2 sticks of celery.	2 ozs. mushrooms.
Pepper and salt.	1 yolk of egg.
Bouquet garni.	1 tablesp. cream.

Lemon juice.

To garnish :—Grilled rolls of bacon.
Parsley.

1. Prepare and disjoint the fowl, dividing it into about 12 or 14 pieces. Remove as much of the skin as possible.

2. Put the pieces of fowl into a saucepan, add sufficient boiling water to cover. Put in the vegetables and flavourings. Cover, bring to the boil, skim and cook until the fowl is tender. Time— about 1¾ hours.

3. Strain, keeping the stock for the sauce.

4. Make a white sauce with the butter, flour, milk and 1¼ pints of the stock. Boil for 5 minutes, stirring well. Correct consistency and seasoning.

5. Prepare the mushrooms, cut in small pieces and add to the sauce. Cook for about 15 minutes.

6. Cool a little, add the yolk of egg mixed with the cream. Flavour with a little lemon juice. Return the pieces of fowl to reheat gently.

7. Serve in a hot entrée dish garnished with grilled rolls of bacon and parsley.

POACHED FOWL WITH RICE

1 good quality boiling fowl.	2 sticks of celery.
1 carrot.	1 leek.
1 onion.	Bouquet garni.

Savoury Rice :

6 ozs. rice.	1 oz. butter or margarine.
2 ozs. chopped onion.	1 pint chicken stock.

Pepper and salt.

To serve :—1 pint Suprème Sauce (page 123).
To garnish :—Parsley.

1. Prepare the fowl and boil with the vegetables and flavourings for about 2½ hours, skimming constantly. Lift out the fowl and keep hot. Strain off the stock and use for Savoury Rice and Suprème Sauce.

2. Melt the butter for the savoury rice, put in the onion, cover with a round of greaseproof paper. Put the lid on the saucepan and place over a very slow heat for about 10 minutes. Remove the paper, add the rice and mix well. Pour the stock over, season, replace the paper and lid and put the saucepan into a moderate oven for about ½ hour when the rice will have absorbed the stock.

3. Make the Suprème Sauce, using some of the chicken stock.

4. Disjoint and skin the cooked fowl, making about 7–8 portions.

5. Put the savoury rice on a hot dish, arrange the chicken on top and mask with the sauce. Garnish with parsley.

GAME

Game is divided into two classes :
1. Four-footed, *e.g.*, hares, venison.
2. Winged, *e.g.*, pheasant, grouse, plover, woodcock, teal, wild duck.

GAME	IN SEASON
Hares	September to March.
Venison (doe)	October to the end of December.
Venison (buck)	June to the end of September.
Pheasant	1st October to the end of January.
Grouse	12th August to the 9th December.
	(Best during September and October)
Partridge	1st September to the end of January.
Other wild birds	1st August to beginning of March.

Hints on Choosing Game.
As game is usually sold unplucked, it is more difficult to choose than poultry. Young birds are essential for roasting.

To Choose Young Birds.
1. They have smooth, pliable legs, and the male birds have short rounded spurs.
2. The feet are supple and moist and are easily broken.
3. The beaks are pliable.
4. The feathers are soft and even. There is down on the breast and wings. The long wing feathers are pointed, not blunt or rounded. The colours on older birds are usually brighter.

The condition of the bird can be seen by turning back the feathers on the breast.

Older birds should never be roasted.

Hanging of Game.
A bird that has been badly shot or bruised will not hang well. The length of time for hanging game depends :—
1. On individual taste. Most game birds should be hung for a certain length of time or they will taste little different from poultry, and the flesh will be hard and tough.
2. On weather conditions.

Game should not be plucked or drawn before hanging. A piece of string should be tied tightly round the neck of the bird to exclude air, and it should be hung with the feet downwards. If a small piece of charcoal is put inside the vent it will keep longer.

Where several birds are to be hung, there must be a space between each two to allow for the free circulation of air. Where there is danger of flies, sprinkle pepper between the feathers, or put the birds into loose muslin bags.

As a general indication, game birds are ready for cooking when the tail feathers pull out easily. Pheasants require about 5–6 days ; grouse, 3–4 days. If to be eaten " high " they should almost smell disagreeably before cooking.

Water-fowl, on account of the oiliness of their flesh, and small birds, which are not drawn before being cooked, are only hung for one day.

Game : General Preparation for Cooking.

1. Pluck the birds very carefully, especially when well hung, because the flesh is tender.

2. Do not remove the feet, but cut off the toes at the first joint and scald and skin the feet.

3. Draw as for poultry, except in such cases as woodcock and snipe, when the birds are roasted undrawn, as the " trail " is held to add to the flavour.

4. Never wash game, wipe it inside with a damp cloth.

5. Truss as for roast fowl, but cut the wings off at the first joint. These are secured in place with the legs instead of being folded under. The heads of snipe and woodcock are not removed, the heads are plucked and the eyes removed, and the long beaks are used for trussing the birds instead of skewers.

General Rules for Roasting Game.

1. Since the flesh of most game is rather dry, place a piece of fat bacon across the breast. Wrap a piece of greased paper around the feet, as they are liable to burn.

2. It is an improvement to put a piece of seasoned butter into the body cavity.

3. Constant basting with butter or bacon fat is essential to make up for the deficiency in fat. In stoves where fat is not used, cook in a casserole with butter or bacon fat, or cover with greased paper or aluminium foil.

4. Remove the fat bacon from the breast a short time before the bird is cooked. Dredge the breast lightly with flour, and return to the oven to finish the cooking, become brown, and develop the frothy appearance characteristic of roast game.

Accompaniments and Garnish.

(*a*) A well-seasoned gravy—made with stock from the giblets, to which some red wine is added. The gravy must always be served separately, not around the dish.

(*b*) Fried breadcrumbs.

(*c*) Bread sauce.

(*d*) Green Salad ; Orange Salad with Wild Duck.

(*e*) Game Chips.

For garnish—watercress.

Fried Breadcrumbs.

1 cupful breadcrumbs.
1 oz. butter.

Heat the butter in a frying-pan, put in the crumbs and stir over gentle heat until lightly browned, dry and crisp. They should absorb all the fat. Drain on kitchen paper and serve on a dish paper on a small dish.

ROAST GROUSE

Brace of grouse.   Black pepper.
1 oz. butter.   4 slices of fat bacon.
                 A little hot fat.

To garnish :—Watercress.
To serve :—Thin brown gravy to   Green Salad.
          which 1 glass of red   Game Chips.
          wine has been added.   Fried breadcrumbs (page 70).
                 Bread Sauce.

1. Pluck carefully, draw and wipe the birds well inside with a damp cloth.

2. Cream the butter with the pepper, roll it into a ball and place it inside the body with the liver. Truss as for fowl, using thread or fine skewers instead of twine, as large holes will allow the juices to escape.

3. Brush over the grouse with hot fat and place fat bacon over the breasts. Roast, allowing $\frac{1}{2}$ to $\frac{3}{4}$ hour, depending on the size of the birds.

4. Ten minutes before the birds are cooked, remove the fat bacon and dredge the breasts of the birds with flour. Return to oven to brown. When fully cooked, remove thread or skewers and serve birds on a hot dish. Garnish with watercress.

ROAST PARTRIDGE

Prepare, cook and serve as for Roast Grouse. Allow about half an hour to cook.

ROAST PLOVER

2 plovers.   2 slices of fat bacon.

2 oblong croûtes of fried bread.
To garnish :—Watercress.
To serve :—Cut lemon.
          Thin brown gravy.

Prepare and cook in the same way as Grouse. Allow them 15–20 minutes to cook. Serve on croûtes of fried bread, and garnish with watercress and quarters of lemon.

MEAT, POULTRY AND GAME
ROAST PHEASANT

1 pheasant.	Black pepper.
2 ozs. butter.	2 slices of fat bacon.
A little hot fat.	

To garnish :—Watercress.

To serve :—Thin brown gravy to   Green salad.
which 1 glass of red   Game chips.
wine has been added.   Bread sauce.
Fried breadcrumbs (page 70).

1. Pluck bird and reserve the best of the tail feathers. Singe and draw, but do not cut off the feet. Scald and skin them, and cut off the toes.

2. Wipe inside of bird with a damp cloth, put in butter creamed with pepper, and truss as for fowl. Do not use gizzard or liver. Brush over with hot fat. Place slices of fat bacon over the breast.

3. Roast for about 1–1¼ hours, depending on size of bird. A short time before being fully cooked, remove the slices of bacon and dredge the breast with flour.

4. When cooked, remove the twine or skewers and serve the bird on a hot dish. Stick the feathers into the tail-end.

ROAST SNIPE

2 snipe.	2 slices of fat bacon.

2 oblong croûtes of fried bread.
To garnish :—Watercress.
To serve :—Thin brown gravy.   Fried breadcrumbs (page 70).
Green salad.

1. Pluck the birds, being careful not to tear the skin. Do not remove the heads, pluck them and remove the eyes.

2. Do not draw the birds. Cut off the wings at the first joint. Scald and skin the legs and feet and cut off the toes.

3. Use the long beak for trussing instead of a skewer, press the legs and wings together, draw the head around and push the beak through where the legs and wings meet.

4. Cross the leg by slitting the skin of one leg just above the foot and push the other leg through the slit. Place a slice of fat bacon on each bird.

5. Roast, allowing 15–20 minutes. Remove the bacon slices from the breasts a short while before the birds are fully cooked. Allow to brown.

6. Serve on croûtes of fried bread or buttered toast on a hot dish. Garnish with watercress.

ROAST WOODCOCK

Prepare, truss and cook as for Roast Snipe (page 71). Allow 20–25 minutes to cook; care should be taken that it is not over-cooked.

ROAST WILD DUCK

Pair of wild duck.	A little hot fat.
A glass of port wine (if liked).	A little flour.

To garnish :—Watercress.
To serve :—Thickened brown gravy to which the juice of one orange has been added.
Orange Salad (page 87).

1. Prepare and truss in the same way as Roast Duck (page 61).
2. Roast, allowing 30–40 minutes. Wild duck should be served rather underdone.
3. When half-cooked pour the port wine over the duck and baste occasionally with it.
4. Dredge the breasts with flour and return to the oven to brown.
5. When cooked, remove string and serve the birds on a hot dish. Garnish with watercress.

ROAST WIDGEON

Prepare, cook and serve as for Roast Wild Duck, allowing 20–25 minutes.

ROAST TEAL

Prepare, cook and serve as for Roast Wild Duck, allowing 25–30 minutes.

ROAST QUAIL

2 quails.	2 slices of fat bacon.

2 croûtes of fried bread or toast.

To garnish :—Cut lemon.	Watercress.
To serve :—Thin brown gravy.	Fried breadcrumbs.

1. Pluck and remove the head and neck from each bird. Do not remove the legs and feet but scald and skin them and cut off the toes at the first joint.
2. Draw from the neck end. Truss, using fine twine, in the same method as for Roast Fowl. Slit the skin of one leg just above the foot and pass the other leg through the slit. Brush over with hot fat. Put a slice of fat bacon over each breast. Roast, allowing 12–15 minutes. Remove the string and serve each bird on a croûte of fried bread. Garnish with lemon and watercress.

Venison

This is the name given to the flesh of the deer. The flesh of the buck is superior in quality to that of the doe. The flesh should be dark and finely-grained, and the fat firm, clear and white. Animals between four and five years old are in prime condition.

The best joint for roasting is the haunch. The loin and neck may also be roasted.

The shoulder and breast may be stewed.

Hanging of Venison.

Wipe with a clean dry cloth and sprinkle with a mixture of black pepper and ground ginger. Examine the meat and wipe it with a dry cloth every day. In ideal weather and storage conditions, it may be hung for a fortnight. To test for taint, run a skewer down into the joint at the haunch—if it has no unpleasant smell, it is in good condition.

ROAST VENISON

Haunch of venison.   A little melted fat.

Paste :—3 lbs. flour.   Cold water.
To garnish :—Watercress.
To serve :—Thickened brown gravy   Green Salad.
    to which 1 glass of red   Red-currant, Gooseberry,
    wine has been added.   or Cranberry Jelly.

1. Saw off the knuckle bone and wipe the meat with a damp cloth. Rub over with a dry cloth. Brush over with melted fat, and cover with greased paper.

2. Make a stiff paste of flour and water. Roll it out to $\frac{1}{2}$ inch in thickness.

3. Cover the joint completely with the paste. Roll in greased paper and secure with twine. These coverings are necessary to prevent the fat from burning before the lean is cooked—the fat being a great delicacy.

4. Bake—allowing 4–5 hours to cook, depending on the size. Venison requires to be rather underdone.

5. About 20 minutes before the meat is cooked, take out the joint, remove the covering of paste and paper and dredge with flour and return to the oven to brown.

6. Serve on a hot dish, garnish with watercress.

Hares

To Choose.

1. Claws should be smooth, pointed and sharp.

2. The knob under the paws should be well-developed (this disappears as the animal ages).

3. The cleft in the jaw should be narrow.
4. The ears must be soft, thin, and easily torn.
5. The teeth should be small and white.
6. To denote freshness—the flesh should be moist and have a slightly bluish tinge.

Leverets (*Hares in their first year*) should be chosen for roasting, older hares are suitable for soups and Jugged Hare.

Hanging of Hares.
A hare should be well hung, for about one week, under suitable conditions. It should not be paunched or skinned until it has hung for the required amount of time. Hang it by the hind legs, and tie a cup over the mouth to catch any blood. Add a few drops of vinegar to keep the blood from clotting—this may be kept for Hare Soup or Jugged Hare.

To Skin:
Hares, contrary to rabbits, are skinned before being paunched.
1. Slit the skin only on the under side right down to the tail.
2. Continue as for rabbit, but do not remove the tail or ears. The skin is removed from these parts—care being taken that the ears are not torn.
Sometimes one of the hind-legs is slit near the paw, and the hare suspended from a hook while the skinning is being done.

To Paunch and Clean:
1. Hold the hare over a bowl, slit down the abdomen and collect the blood. Add a few drops of vinegar to prevent the blood from clotting. Remove stomach, intestines, liver and kidneys.
2. Break the diaphragm and remove the heart and lungs.
3. Wipe the hare with a clean cloth or wash it quickly in tepid water. Some people hold that washing spoils the flavour of the hare.

ROAST STUFFED HARE

1 hare.	4 ozs. Veal Forcemeat (page 225).
2 slices of fat bacon.	Dripping.

To serve :—Thickened brown gravy.   1 glass port wine.
1 tablesp. red-currant jelly.
To garnish :—Grilled rolls of bacon.   Cut lemon.
Forcemeat balls (page 222).   Parsley.

1. Skin, paunch and clean the hare (page 74). Wipe outside and inside with a clean cloth.
2. Stuff the cavity with forcemeat and sew it up.

3. Truss as for Roast Rabbit, curling the tail over the back. Cover with fat bacon and greased paper.

4. Roast, allowing about one hour for a leveret and 1½–2 hours for a hare. Baste frequently with the dripping.

5. Ten minutes before the hare is cooked, remove the paper and bacon and dredge with a little flour. Put back to finish and become brown.

6. When cooked, remove skewers and thread. Serve on a hot dish. Garnish.

7. Make the gravy and add the wine and red-currant jelly, and serve in a hot sauceboat.

JUGGED HARE

1 hare.	3 onions.
2 tablesps. of brandy.	2 ozs. butter or margarine.
½ bottle red wine.	½ lb. lean bacon.
2 tablesps. of oil.	2 ozs. flour.
Salt and pepper.	Clove of garlic.
	Bouquet garni.

To garnish :—Glazed button onions (page 77).
Glazed mushrooms (page 77).
Croûtes of bread.

To serve :—Red Currant Jelly.

1. Skin and clean the hare, collect the blood. Cut the hare into pieces.

2. Make a marinade by mixing brandy, wine, oil and seasoning and add one onion cut in rings. Put in the hare and leave for 24 hours if possible, turning it occasionally.

3. Melt the butter, add the bacon cut in ½-inch cubes and fry until brown, lift out and keep for garnish.

4. Cut the other onions in quarters, put into the butter and fry until brown. Add the flour and cook slowly until brown.

5. Lift the pieces of hare from the marinade, dry them well, add to the roux and cook for a few minutes.

6. Add the marinade, bring to the boil, skim, add garlic and bouquet garni. Cover and cook gently for about 2 hours.

7. Lift out the hare into a fireproof dish, add the fried bacon and glazed onions and mushrooms. Keep hot.

8. Gradually add the sauce to the blood and heat slowly. Correct seasoning, colour and consistency and strain over the hare.

9. Serve garnished with fried croûtes of bread.

VEGETABLES

ARTICHOKE SOUFFLÉ

½ lb. artichokes.
2 ozs. butter or margarine.
2 ozs. flour.

½ pint milk.
3 eggs.
Salt and pepper.

1. Grease a mould with clarified butter or margarine.
2. Prepare artichokes, and cook until tender. Rub through a fine sieve.
3. Make a white sauce with the butter, flour and milk. Cool a little, add the yolks of eggs one at a time and beat well. Mix in the artichoke purée and seasoning.
4. Beat the whites of eggs stiffly, mix 1 tablespoonful into the sauce, fold in the remainder, and pour into the prepared mould.
5. Put the mould on a baking tin, place over a slow heat (with a gas stove use an asbestos mat) for about 10-15 minutes until the bottom of the soufflé begins to set. Then place in a moderate oven for about 30 minutes until well risen, and set. Serve immediately.

ARTICHOKES AU GRATIN

1 lb. artichokes.
1 oz. butter or margarine.
1 oz. flour.

½ pt. milk.
½ oz. sieved cheese.
Browned crumbs.

Salt and pepper.

1. Make a sauce with the butter, flour and milk. Add salt and pepper.
2. Prepare and cook artichokes, drain well and put into a fireproof dish.
3. Coat with white sauce and sprinkle sieved cheese and browned crumbs over. Brown under the griller or in the oven. Garnish with parsley.

FRIED ARTICHOKES

1 lb. artichokes.

To coat :—Egg and breadcrumbs.
To fry :—Bath of fat.
To garnish :—Parsley.

1. Prepare artichokes. Parboil for 15 minutes, drain well and coat with egg and breadcrumbs.

2. Fry in hot fat and drain well. Serve on a dish paper on a hot dish and garnish with parsley.

FRIED ONION RINGS

½ lb. onions.   About ½ pint milk.
                    Seasoned flour.
To fry :—Bath of fat.

1. Peel the onions and cut into rings, put into the milk and leave for about 20 minutes.

2. Drain well out of the milk and toss in the seasoned flour—shaking off any loose flour.

3. Fry in smoking hot fat until golden brown. Drain well and serve.

NOTE.—The milk in which the onions have been soaked may be used for soup or Béchamel Sauce.

GLAZED ONIONS

Peel some button onions, put them into a shallow saucepan with a little butter or margarine, ¼ pint white stock, a few drops of lemon juice, salt and pepper. Cover with a lid and cook until the onions are soft—about ½ hour. Remove the lid and allow the stock to evaporate. The onions should have a glazed look because the butter remains as a coating on the surface.

GLAZED MUSHROOMS

Remove the stalks and skins from the mushrooms. Cook as for Glazed Onions. Time—about 15 minutes.

BUTTERED CARROTS

1 lb. carrots.   ¼ pint stock.
1 oz. butter or margarine.   Salt and pepper.
A few drops of lemon juice.   Pinch of sugar.
                    Chopped parsley.

1. Prepare the carrots and slice thinly. Put into a saucepan with the stock, lemon juice, sugar, salt, pepper and butter.

2. Bring to the boil, cover and cook gently until the carrots are soft and the liquid evaporated. Time—about ¾–1 hour. Serve garnished with parsley.

BUTTERED PARSNIPS

1 lb. parsnips.   Salt and pepper.
1 oz. butter or margarine.   Chopped parsley.

1. Prepare the parsnips and cut into ½-inch cubes.

2. Cook in boiling salted water until soft. Time—about ¾ hour. Drain well.

3. Melt the butter in a saucepan and toss the parsnips in it. Season and serve garnished with parsley.

BUTTERED SPINACH

1 lb. spinach.   1 oz. butter or margarine.
Salt and pepper.

1. Remove stalks and wash the spinach several times to make sure that all grit and sand are removed.

2. Cook in fast boiling salted water for about 3 minutes with the lid on the saucepan.

3. Drain well, pressing out all the water. Toss in the melted butter, using two forks, season well and serve very hot.

BRAISED CARROTS

1 lb. carrots.   A little clarified fat.
½ pint Thin Brown Sauce (page 120).

Prepare carrots, cut into pieces. Dry and fry until brown in a little hot fat. Place in a fireproof dish or saucepan, pour the sauce over. Cook slowly until tender—about 1–1½ hours. Garnish with parsley.

BRAISED PARSNIPS

1 lb. parsnips.   A little clarified fat.
½ pint Thin Brown Sauce (page 120).

Prepare the parsnips, cut into pieces and cook as for Braised Carrots (page 78).

BRAISED ARTICHOKES

1 lb. artichokes.   A little clarified fat.
½ pint Thin Brown Sauce (page 120).

Prepare the artichokes and cook as for Braised Carrots (page 78).

BRAISED CELERY

1 head celery.   ½ pint Thin Brown Sauce (page 120).

Prepare the celery, cut into 3-inch lengths and cook as for Braised Carrots (page 78) but do not fry.

BRAISED ONIONS

1 lb. onions.   A little clarified fat.
½ pint Thin Brown Sauce (page 120).

Peel the onions and cook as for Braised Carrots (page 78).

CAULIFLOWER AND TOMATO SOUFFLÉ

1 oz. flour.	2 eggs.
1 oz. butter or margarine.	3 tomatoes.
½ pint milk.	1 cooked cauliflower.
1¼ ozs. sieved cheese.	Browned crumbs.

Salt and pepper.

1. Make a white sauce with the butter, flour and milk. Season. Cool a little and add nearly all the cheese.

2. Add the egg yolks and beat well. Beat the whites of eggs stiffly and mix 1 tablespoonful into the sauce, then fold in the remainder.

3. Put layers of the mixture, sliced tomato, cauliflower divided into flowerettes, and seasoning into a greased fireproof dish. Sprinkle the remainder of the cheese and browned crumbs on top.

4. Put the dish on a baking tin, place over a slow heat (with a gas stove use an asbestos mat) for about 10–15 minutes until the bottom of the soufflé begins to set. Then place in a moderate oven for about 30 minutes until well risen and set. Serve immediately.

CAULIFLOWER FRITTERS

1 cauliflower.	2 teasps. vinegar.
1 tablesp. salad oil.	1 slice of finely-chopped onion.
1 teasp. finely-chopped parsley.	Pepper and salt.

To coat :—¼ pint Coating Batter.
To fry :—Bath of fat.
To garnish :—Parsley.

1. Divide the cauliflower into flowerettes and cook in boiling salted water until almost soft.

2. Put the salad oil into a bowl and add the vinegar, onion, parsley, pepper and salt and mix thoroughly.

3. Put the pieces of cauliflower into this marinade and allow to soak for about 30 minutes. Lift out and drain.

4. Dip in batter, fry in hot fat and drain well. Serve on a dish paper on a hot dish and garnish with parsley.

STEAMED CUCUMBER

1 large or 2 small cucumbers.	Salt.

¼ pint Hollandaise Sauce (page 125).

To garnish :—Parsley.

1. Prepare cucumber, cut into 2-inch lengths. Put into a steamer and sprinkle salt over. Steam until tender, about half an hour, and drain well.

2. Put into a hot vegetable dish and coat with Hollandaise Sauce. Garnish with parsley.

SCALLOPED CUCUMBER

Sauce :

1 oz. butter or margarine.	1 oz. flour.
	½ pt. milk.

1 cucumber.	Salt and pepper.
1 oz. chopped cooked onion.	½ oz. butter or margarine.
1 oz. sieved cheese.	Parsley.

1. Peel the cucumber, cut into small pieces and steam.

2. Grease 5 scallop shells and put in the cucumber and onion. Make a sauce with the butter, flour and milk, add the cheese and seasoning, and coat the vegetables with it. Sprinkle with breadcrumbs and put the butter in pieces on top.

3. Bake in a moderate oven until brown. Garnish with parsley and serve.

CASSOLETTES OF CUCUMBER

1 cucumber.	Boiling salted water.
½ teasp. lemon juice.	1 tablesp. seasoned flour.

To coat :—Egg and breadcrumbs.
To fry :—Bath of fat.
To serve :—Green pea purée.   ½ pint Tomato Sauce.
To garnish :—Parsley.

1. Prepare cucumber and cut into slices 1½-inch in thickness. Remove centres by cutting them out with a small round cutter, without breaking the slices.

2. Put the slices into a saucepan, cover with boiling salted water to which the lemon juice has been added. Cook for 10 minutes. Drain, rinse in cold water. Place in the folds of a clean tea cloth until dry.

3. Dip the slices in seasoned flour, and coat with egg and breadcrumbs. Fry in hot fat and drain well.

4. Serve on a hot dish, the centres well filled with pea purée. Pour Tomato Sauce around and garnish with parsley.

STUFFED CUCUMBER

1 cucumber.	½ oz. breadcrumbs.
	½ oz. butter.

Stuffing :

1½ ozs. breadcrumbs.	1 oz. cooked ham or cooked
1 teasp. finely-chopped parsley.	tongue (finely-chopped).
½ oz. melted butter or margarine.	½ teasp. grated lemon rind.
A little stock.	Salt and pepper.

To serve :—½ pint Tomato Sauce.
To garnish :—Parsley.

1. Wash cucumber, notch (page 221) and cut into 2-inch lengths. Remove centres by cutting them out with a small round cutter, without breaking the pieces. Steam gently for 5 minutes. Drain and leave to cool.

2. Prepare stuffing by mixing all the dry ingredients together, moisten with melted butter and a little stock if necessary.

3. Place the pieces of cucumber on a greased tin and fill the centres with stuffing, sprinkle breadcrumbs over and place a small piece of butter on top of each. Cover with greased paper, bake in a moderate oven for about 10–15 minutes.

4. Lift on to a hot dish, pour a little Tomato Sauce around and serve the remainder in a hot sauceboat. Garnish with parsley.

POTATO RIBBONS

2 or 3 potatoes.   Salt.

To fry :—Bath of fat.
To garnish :—Parsley.

1. Prepare potatoes, peel thinly and cut into slices $\frac{1}{2}$-inch in thickness.

2. With a very sharp knife peel each slice into $\frac{1}{2}$-inch wide ribbons, peeling round and round. Have the ribbons so thin that they are transparent, and cut them as long as possible.

3. Leave in strips or tie in bows or knots. Put into cold water until required.

4. Place on a clean tea cloth to dry—the drier they are the lighter they will be when cooked.

5. Fry in hot fat, drain well and leave in a warm place for a few minutes. Sprinkle salt over.

6. Serve on a dish paper in a hot vegetable dish and garnish with parsley.

GAME CHIPS

Wash and peel the potatoes, cut in very thin slices. Put into cold water and leave for about 1 hour. Dry well in a cloth, and fry in smoking hot fat, until brown and crisp.

POTATO FRITTERS

$\frac{1}{2}$ lb. cooked potatoes.   1 oz. butter.
Pepper and salt.   A pinch of nutmeg.
           1 yolk and 2 whites of eggs.

To garnish :—Parsley.

1. Rub the potatoes through a sieve.

2. Melt butter in a saucepan, add potato, pepper, salt, nutmeg,

and beaten yolk of egg. Mix well together. Fold in the stiffly-beaten whites of eggs.

3. Drop dessertspoonfuls of the mixture into smoking hot fat (do not use a frying basket). Fry and drain well. Serve on a dish paper on a hot dish and garnish with parsley.

BAKED POTATO SOUFFLÉS

5 potatoes.	Salt and pepper.
1 oz. butter.	A pinch of nutmeg.
3 tablesps. milk.	1 egg.

½ oz. sieved cheese.

To garnish :—Parsley.

1. Scrub potatoes and dry well. Prick with a skewer and bake in a moderate oven for about 1½ hours, until tender.

2. Cut a piece off each with a sharp knife, scoop out all the inside, and sieve.

3. Heat the butter and milk together, add the sieved potato. Season to taste with pepper and salt, add a pinch of nutmeg.

4. Stir in the beaten yolk of egg, and lastly the stiffly-beaten white of egg.

5. Refill the potato skins with this mixture and sprinkle a little sieved cheese on the top of each.

6. Bake in a moderate oven until lightly browned.

7. Serve on a dish paper on a hot entrée dish and garnish with parsley.

DUCHESSE POTATOES

1 lb. mashed potatoes.	Salt and pepper.
1 oz. butter or margarine.	1 egg

1. Melt the butter, add to the potatoes with salt, pepper and enough beaten egg to bind.

2. Put over the heat for a few minutes to cook the egg.

3. Put into a bag with a rose pipe. Form into large roses on a greased tin by piping round and round in a spiral fashion.

4. Brush with beaten egg and bake in a moderate oven until lightly browned and hot.

POTATO CASSOLETTES

1 lb. mashed potatoes.	1 egg.
1 oz. butter or margarine.	Pepper and salt.

1. Melt the butter, add the potatoes, pepper and salt, and enough beaten egg to bind. Stir over the heat for a few minutes to cook the egg.

2. Using a rose pipe and forcing bag, pipe a circular base about 3 inches in diameter, pipe an edge about 1¼ inches high on this base. Repeat to make 4 or 5 cassolettes.

3. Brush with beaten egg and bake in a moderate oven until hot and lightly browned.

4. Fill the centre with any hot savoury filling as required. Garnish with parsley.

POTATO PURÉE

1 lb. cooked potatoes.	½ gill milk.
1 oz. butter or margarine.	Pepper and salt.

1. Press the potatoes through a sieve without rubbing.

2. Put the milk, butter, salt and pepper into a saucepan. Heat until the butter is melted.

3. Add the potatoes and beat over the heat until very hot.

SPINACH SOUFFLÉ

1 lb. spinach.	2 eggs.
2 ozs. butter or margarine.	1 oz. breadcrumbs.
2 ozs. flour.	A squeeze of lemon juice.
½ pint milk.	A pinch of nutmeg.
Salt and pepper.	

1. Grease a mould with clarified butter or margarine.

2. Prepare the spinach and cook. Sieve.

3. Make a white sauce with the butter, flour, and milk. Cool a little, add the yolks of eggs, one at a time and beat well. Mix in the spinach purée, breadcrumbs, lemon juice, nutmeg, salt and pepper.

4. Beat the whites of eggs stiffly, mix 1 tablespoonful into the sauce, fold in the remainder and pour into the prepared mould.

5. Put the mould on a baking tin, place over a slow heat (with a gas stove use an asbestos mat) for about 10–15 minutes until the bottom of the soufflé begins to set. Then place in a moderate oven for about 30 minutes until well risen and set. Serve immediately.

CREAMED SPINACH

Remove the stalks from the spinach, wash several times in cold water. Put to cook in plenty of boiling salted water and boil for about 3 minutes with the lid on. Drain well. Press through a coarse sieve or put through a fine mincer. Heat thoroughly, add salt, pepper and cream and serve.

STUFFED VEGETABLE MARROW

1 small vegetable marrow.

Stuffing :

6 ozs. minced cooked meat.	1 dessertsp. mushroom ketchup.
6 ozs. breadcrumbs.	1 dessertsp. tomato ketchup.
1 teasp. chopped parsley.	Pepper and salt.
1 dessertsp. chopped onion.	1 oz. melted butter.
	1-2 eggs.

To serve :—½ pint Tomato Sauce.

To garnish :—Parsley.

1. Wash and peel marrow thickly, keeping it whole. Cut out a triangular wedge lengthwise. Scoop out seeds and soft part.

2. Mix all the ingredients for the stuffing together, bind with beaten egg and put into the marrow. Replace the piece which was removed and brush over with melted butter or margarine.

3. Wrap in greased paper and bind firmly with tape, place on a greased tin. Cook in a moderate oven for ¾-1 hour—until quite soft—test with a skewer. Remove string and paper.

4. Serve on a hot dish with Tomato Sauce poured round. Garnish with parsley.

STUFFED SLICES OF VEGETABLE MARROW

½ vegetable marrow.

Stuffing :

½ cup of breadcrumbs.	1 oz. melted butter.
1 tablesp. finely-chopped onion.	1 dessertsp. chopped parsley.
¼ teasp. chopped	Half a beaten egg.
mixed herbs.	2 ozs. cooked ham (chopped).
Salt and pepper.	

To garnish :—Browned crumbs.

To serve :—½ pint Tomato Sauce.

1. Cut marrow into slices about 1 inch in thickness, peel thickly, and remove seeds and soft part. Steam 5-7 minutes.

2. Place slices of marrow on a greased tin, and pile the prepared stuffing into the centre of each slice. Bake in a moderate oven until the marrow becomes quite tender.

3. Serve on a hot dish, sprinkle with browned crumbs. Pour Tomato Sauce around.

SALADS

BEAN SALAD

6 sticks of celery.　　1 lb. cooked butter beans or haricot beans.
½ onion.　　Mayonnaise.
To decorate :—Chopped parsley.　Sliced tomato.　Curled celery (p. 223).

1. Prepare celery, curl a little of it and cut the remainder into ½-inch pieces. Prepare onion and chop finely.
2. Mix celery, onion and cooked beans, add mayonnaise and mix well. Pile into a polished glass dish. Sprinkle finely-chopped parsley over and decorate with celery tops, sliced tomato and curled celery.

FRENCH BEAN SALAD

1 head lettuce.　　　½ lb. cooked French beans.
French dressing.

1. Prepare lettuce. Shred finely, keeping back a few of the centre leaves. Toss shredded lettuce and French beans in French dressing.
2. Line a glass bowl with the lettuce leaves. Pile the dressed vegetables in the centre.

BEETROOT AND POTATO SALAD

4 cooked beetroots.　　　2 hard-boiled eggs.
1 bunch spring onions.　　5 cooked potatoes.

To serve :—French dressing **or** Mayonnaise.

1. Peel beetroot and slice thinly. Prepare onions, and chop. Slice hard-boiled eggs, and peeled potatoes.
2. Arrange all the ingredients in layers in a glass dish having a layer of sliced hard-boiled eggs on top.

CAULIFLOWER SALAD

1 cauliflower.　　　½ teasp. chopped **parsley.**
Mayonnaise.　　　A little cress.
Lettuce.　　　1 hard-boiled egg.

1. Divide the cauliflower into flowerettes and cook. Put the saucepan under the cold tap and allow the water to run until the cauliflower is cold. Drain well.

85

2. Line a glass dish with some lettuce leaves, arrange cauliflower on the lettuce, coat with mayonnaise and sprinkle finely-chopped parsley over. Garnish the salad with cress and decorate it with sections of hard-boiled egg.

CARROT AND RAISIN SALAD

2 or 3 young carrots.	A little watercress.
1 head lettuce.	4 ozs. seedless raisins.

Mayonnaise.

1. Prepare the carrots and grate them, shred lettuce and cress. Clean the raisins. Mix carrot and raisins in a bowl, pour mayonnaise over and mix carefully.
2. Make a bed of lettuce in a glass dish and pile dressed carrots and raisins in the centre. Decorate with watercress.

CELERY AND BANANA SALAD

4 or 5 sticks of celery.	1 large apple.
Bunch of watercress.	1 tablesp. sherry.
Small cress.	1 tablesp. water.
1 or 2 bananas.	Mayonnaise.

2 ozs. chopped walnuts.

1. Prepare celery and cress. Cut 2 sticks of celery into 3-inch lengths, shred to within 1 inch of one end. Place in cold water for 15 minutes to curl. Chop the remainder of the celery.
2. Peel, core and slice the apple. Cut into matchlike strips. Steep in sherry and water. Drain.
3. Peel and split banana in two lengthwise, and then across in six.
4. Make a bed of watercress in a glass dish. Mix the prepared fruit, chopped celery and nuts with mayonnaise and pile in the centre of the dish. Decorate with curled celery and small cress.

DANDELION SALAD

Young dandelion leaves.	Nasturtium flowers.
French dressing.	Bunch of cress.

Wash dandelion leaves and tear into small pieces. Separate petals of nasturtium flowers. Toss leaves and petals in French dressing and pile into a polished glass dish. Garnish with some cress and petals of nasturtium flowers.

DANISH SALAD

Diced cooked beetroot.	Salt and pepper.
Chopped onion.	Diced boiled potatoes.
Lettuce.	Mayonnaise.

Mix the diced beetroot and potatoes, add onion, pepper and salt. Prepare and shred lettuce. Mix all together. Put into a glass dish, coat with mayonnaise. Garnish with a few dice of beetroot and potatoes.

EGG MAYONNAISE

4 hard-boiled eggs.	Mayonnaise.
Lettuce leaves.	Paprika or tomato.
Parsley.	

Cut the eggs in halves. Arrange on lettuce leaves. Coat with mayonnaise and decorate with paprika or strips of tomato and parsley.

ORANGE SALAD

2 oranges.	1 teasp. tarragon vinegar.
1 dessertsp. castor sugar.	Cayenne.
1 dessertsp. salad oil.	½ teasp. chopped parsley.

Peel oranges, removing all the pith. Slice them thinly, crosswise. Arrange in a shallow glass dish. Mix sugar, salad oil, vinegar and cayenne. Pour over orange slices. Sprinkle chopped parsley over.

PINEAPPLE AND CELERY SALAD

1 small head celery.	1 head lettuce.
½ tin sliced pineapple.	

To serve :—Mayonnaise.

Prepare celery and lettuce. Shred large lettuce leaves and chop celery. Put lettuce into a polished glass dish and place sliced pineapple on top. Sprinkle chopped celery over.

TOMATO SALAD

6 tomatoes.	French Dressing.
1 teasp. chopped onion.	Pepper and salt.

To garnish :— Chopped parsley.

Skin the tomatoes and cut in slices. Put into a bowl with the onion and seasoning. Dress with French Dressing and arrange in a glass dish. Sprinkle a little chopped parsley on top.

BELGIAN TOMATO SALAD

2 tomatoes.	1 onion.
2 hard-boiled eggs.	Lettuce.

To serve :—Mayonnaise.

Prepare vegetables. Slice onion, hard-boiled eggs and tomatoes. Lay slices overlapping in a circle around a shallow glass dish. Place a few lettuce leaves in the centre of the dish.

TOMATO AND ORANGE SALAD

5 tomatoes.	3 oranges.
1 head lettuce.	French dressing.

1. Prepare tomatoes and lettuce. Slice tomatoes thinly, shred lettuce. Peel oranges, removing all the pith, and divide into segments.
2. Toss salad ingredients in French dressing. Arrange alternate rings of orange and tomato on a bed of lettuce in a glass dish.

TOMATO AND CELERY SALAD

1 head lettuce.	Mayonnaise.
½ head of celery.	1 oz. cream cheese.
½ lb. tomatoes.	1 oz. chopped walnuts.

Cayenne pepper.

1. Prepare lettuce, and line a glass dish with it.
2. Prepare celery, cut into ½-inch lengths ; prepare tomatoes, and cut into thin slices. Put celery and tomatoes into a bowl, pour mayonnaise over. Mix well and pile in the centre of the dish.
3. Cut cheese into ½-inch dice and arrange in a ring around the dressed vegetables. Sprinkle the walnuts over and a little cayenne pepper on top.

MIXED VEGETABLE SALAD

Cabbage.	Lemon juice.
Carrot.	Salt and pepper.
Beetroot.	Lettuce.

To serve :—Mayonnaise.

Cut the heart part of a crisp white cabbage into fine shreds, wash in salted water and then drain well. There should be about 2 breakfast-cupfuls of these. Mix 1 breakfast-cupful of finely-grated raw carrot and 1 breakfast-cupful diced cooked beetroot with the shredded cabbage. Sprinkle the mixture with lemon juice and season. Line a glass dish with some prepared crisp lettuce leaves, pile the mixture in the centre. Serve mayonnaise separately.

CRAB SALAD

1 radish.	1 crab.
1 gherkin.	1 tablesp. of French dressing or Mayonnaise.
1 tomato.	A little lettuce or cress.

1. Prepare all vegetables. Slice radish and gherkin. Skin tomato and cut into quarters or eighths according to size.

2. Remove meat from shell of crab (page 35) and chop. Mix crab meat, radish, gherkin and tomato (keep back a little tomato for garnish) in a bowl, add dressing and mix again.

3. Arrange one or two prepared lettuce leaves on individual dishes, put a spoonful of mixture on top. Garnish with cress and tomato.

FISH SALAD

½ lb. cold cooked fish.	2 gherkins.
Salt and pepper.	1 head of lettuce.
1 teasp. lemon juice.	2 hard-boiled eggs.
6 capers.	Cress.

To serve :—Mayonnaise.

1. Skin, bone and flake fish, season and sprinkle lemon juice, chopped capers, and chopped gherkins over.

2. Prepare lettuce, line a glass bowl with it.

3. Cut eggs in halves, remove yolks carefully and sieve them. Add sieved yolks to fish mixture, mix well and pile into the centre of the dish. Decorate with rings of egg white and prepared cress.

PRAWN SALAD

6 cooked prawns.	1 head of endive or a bunch of watercress
1 dessertsp. capers.	Mayonnaise.
1 head of lettuce.	Cayenne.
½ teasp. salt.	

1. Take the meat from the prawns including the creamy part lying along the back of the shell.

2. Cut meat into pieces, season, keep back a few of the best pieces to go on top of the salad.

3. Prepare lettuce and endive. Shred the lettuce and pull the endive to pieces.

4. Put a layer of lettuce in the bottom of a salad bowl, next a layer of prawn meat. Continue in layers until all the ingredients have been used up. Coat with mayonnaise. Garnish with pieces of prawn meat, lettuce and endive. Sprinkle capers over.

CHICKEN SALAD

1 head of lettuce.	2 hard-boiled eggs.
½ head of celery.	¼ lb. cooked chicken.

Mayonnaise.

1. Prepare lettuce and celery. Chop celery. Line a glass dish with some lettuce leaves, shred remainder.

2. Cut each hard-boiled egg into 4 sections and cut chicken into ½-inch dice.

3. Put chicken, celery and shredded lettuce into a bowl, add mayonnaise and mix well. Pile into the glass dish on to the bed of lettuce. Decorate with hard-boiled egg.

FRUIT AND LETTUCE SALAD

Pears.	Bananas.
Apples.	Lemon juice.
Pineapple.	Chopped walnuts.
Grapes.	Lettuce leaves.

Dressing :

¼ pint cream.	1 saltspoonful curry powder.

1 dessertspoonful sherry.

1. Prepare the fruit, cut into pieces and mix with the lemon juice and chopped nuts.

2. Arrange lettuce leaves on individual plates, put some of the mixed fruit on the lettuce.

3. Half whip the cream, add curry powder and sherry and mix together. Put a spoonful on top of the fruit.

COLE SLAW

Shred some cabbage finely, wash it and drain well. Toss in Vinaigrette Dressing and serve in a salad bowl.

NOTE.—Raisins, sultanas, chopped apple, shredded celery or chopped pineapple may be mixed with the cabbage if liked.

PUDDINGS AND SWEETS

CHANCELLOR PUDDING

2 ozs. macaroon biscuits.	1 oz. mixed peel (chopped).
5 ozs. cake crumbs.	1 oz. angelica (chopped).
3 ozs. glacé cherries.	Rind and juice of 1 lemon.

½ glass sherry.

Custard: ¾ pint milk. 3 eggs. 1 oz. sugar.

To serve:—Sabayon Sauce (page 125).

1. Crush the macaroons, and put them into a bowl with the cake crumbs. Add chopped cherries, mixed peel, angelica, grated lemon rind, lemon juice and the sherry. Mix well.
2. Make the custard and pour it over the ingredients in the bowl. Leave to soak for about half an hour.
3. Pour into a greased mould and cover with greased paper. Steam gently for about 1¼ hours.
4. Remove the paper and turn the pudding on to a hot dish. Dredge with castor sugar.

DELAWARE PUDDING

Suet Pastry:

6 ozs. flour.	½ teasp. baking powder.
2 ozs. chopped suet.	¼ teasp. salt.

Cold water.

Filling:

1 lb. apples.	2 ozs. butter.
3 ozs. currants.	4 ozs. Demerara sugar.
2 ozs. candied peel.	½ teasp. mixed spice.

Rind and juice of ½ lemon.

To serve:—Lemon Sauce.

1. Peel, core and chop the apple finely. Clean the currants and chop the peel.
2. Cream the butter, add the sugar, grated lemon rind, spice, fruit and lemon juice. Mix well.
3. Make suet pastry, roll out thinly, and cut out a small round to fit bottom of bowl. Put this round of pastry into a greased pudding bowl, then put in a spoonful of filling.

91

4. Cut another round of pastry a little larger than the first one, put into bowl on top of filling. Place another spoonful of filling on top of round of pastry.

5. Continue in this way until the bowl is three-quarters full, finishing with a round of pastry. Cover with greased paper and steam from 2-2½ hours. Remove paper and turn the pudding on to a hot dish.

VIENNOISE PUDDING

Caramel :

1 tablesp. sugar.	2 tablesp. water.

Custard :

½ pint milk.	2 eggs.

¼ lb. bread (cut into ¼-inch dice).	Grated rind of ½ lemon.
3 ozs. sultanas.	2 ozs. brown sugar.
1 oz. chopped mixed peel.	½ glass sherry.
1 oz. whole almonds.	

To serve :—Sabayon Sauce or Caramel Sauce.

1. Put the sugar and water into a saucepan, stir until the sugar is dissolved. Bring to the boil and cook until it becomes a good brown colour, but do not allow to burn. Add a dessertspoonful hot water to stop further cooking.

2. Add the milk and stir over the heat until the caramel is mixed with the milk. Beat the eggs and pour the caramelled milk on to them. Mix well.

3. Put bread, cleaned sultanas, peel, blanched and chopped almonds, grated lemon rind and sugar into a bowl. Pour the custard over them, add the sherry and leave to soak for about half an hour.

4. Stir and pour into a greased pudding bowl. Cover with greased paper and steam gently for about 1¼ hours.

5. Remove the paper and turn the pudding on to a hot dish. Dredge with castor sugar.

REDESDALE PUDDING

6 ozs. brown breadcrumbs.	Grated nutmeg.
3 ozs. chopped suet.	¼ teasp. cinnamon.
2 ozs. brown sugar.	Pinch of salt.
2 ozs. chopped peel.	½ teasp. baking powder.
2 ozs. sultanas.	1 glass sherry.
1 dessertsp. dessicated coconut	2 eggs.

To serve :—Sabayon Sauce.

1. Mix all dry ingredients together in a bowl.

2. Add sherry and beaten eggs and mix well.

3. Pour into a greased mould or bowl, cover with greased paper and steam for about 2 hours.

4. Remove the paper and turn the pudding on to a hot dish dredge with castor sugar.

PUDDINGS AND SWEETS

ALMOND PUDDING

4 ozs. breadcrumbs.
2 ozs. sugar.
2 ozs. suet (finely-chopped).
2 ozs. macaroon biscuits (crushed).
2 ozs. ground almonds.

Pinch of salt.
½ teasp. baking powder.
1 egg and 2 yolks of eggs
2 drops of almond essence.
About ¾ gill milk.

Meringue :—1 white of egg.

2 ozs. castor sugar.

To decorate :—Cherries and angelica.
To serve :—Italian Meringue Sauce.

1. Mix all dry ingredients together in a bowl.

2. Beat the egg and yolks with the almond essence and pour on to the dry ingredients, add sufficient milk to moisten.

3. Put into a greased mould or bowl, cover with greased paper, and steam for about 2 hours.

4. Remove paper and turn the pudding on to a hot dish.

5. Make meringue and pipe on to the pudding. Decorate with cherries and angelica. Put into a cool oven until lightly browned.

BURDAGE PUDDING

3 ozs. breadcrumbs.
3 ozs. finely-chopped suet.
3 ozs. macaroon biscuits (crushed).
1 oz. brown sugar.
¼ teasp. powdered cinnamon.

1 tablesp. strawberry jam.
Rind and juice of ½ lemon.
2 eggs.
A little milk.
¼ teasp. bread soda.

To decorate :—Cherries and angelica.
To serve :—Sabayon Sauce or Italian Meringue Sauce.

1. Mix all the dry ingredients, except bread soda, together in a bowl.

2. Add jam, rind and juice of lemon, the beaten eggs and milk, and mix well.

3. Dissolve the bread soda in 1 dessertspoonful of milk, add to the other ingredients, and mix well through them.

4. Pour into a greased mould or bowl, cover with greased paper and steam for about 2 hours.

5. Remove paper and turn the pudding on to a hot dish and decorate with cut cherries and angelica.

93

APPLE FRITTERS

1 lb. apples.

Batter :—
4 ozs. flour.   1 egg.
Pinch of salt.   ¼ pint milk.

*To fry :—*Bath of fat.
*To serve :—*Castor sugar.

1. Make batter, and leave in a cool place for about an hour.
2. Peel and core the apples. Cut into rings about ½-inch in thickness.
3. Dip the apple rings into the batter, lift out with a skewer, allow any surplus batter to drain off, then drop into hot fat. Do not put too many fritters into the fat at one time. Fry until golden brown, drain well.
4. Toss each fritter in castor sugar. Serve on a d'oyley on a hot dish.

BANANA FRITTERS

Split the bananas, cut each piece in two, sprinkle with lemon juice and finish as for Apple Fritters (page 94).

ORANGE FRITTERS

Peel the oranges, divide into sections and remove any pith and pips, and continue as for Apple Fritters (page 94).

SWEDISH PANCAKES

Batter :—
6 ozs. flour.   1 oz. melted butter.
3 yolks of eggs.   ¾ pint milk.
¼ pint cream.   Pinch of salt.

2-3 tablesps. raspberry jam.

*Meringue :—*3 whites of eggs.
6 ozs. castor sugar.
1 oz. almonds (shredded).

1. Make the batter. Pour into a jug. Cook as for Pancakes, but fry on one side only.
2. Spread each pancake with jam and pile one on top of the other in a hot fireproof pie-plate.
3. Beat the whites of eggs stiffly, fold in the sugar and spread over the top and sides of the pile of pancakes. Stick almonds all over the meringue, put into a cool oven to set—about 20–30 minutes. Serve hot.

PUDDINGS AND SWEETS

APPLE MERINGUE PUDDING

4 ozs. cake crumbs.

Custard :—2 yolks of eggs.
½ pint milk.

½ oz. sugar.
A few drops of lemon juice

Apple Pulp :—1½ lbs. apples.
Grated lemon rind

Sugar to sweeten.
A little water.

Meringue :—2 whites of eggs
4 ozs. castor sugar.

To decorate :—½ oz. shredded almonds

1. Make Custard Sauce with yolks of eggs and milk, add sugar and flavouring.
2. Crumble the sponge cake into a pie-dish and pour the custard over.
3. Stew the apples to a thick pulp with sugar, water and lemon rind, and put on top of the sponge cake.
4. Beat the whites of eggs stiffly fold in the castor sugar and pile roughly on top of apples. Decorate with shredded almonds.
5. Bake in a cool oven until the meringue is set and very lightly browned.

WALNUT PUDDING

1 oz. chocolate powder.
⅛ pint milk or water
4 ozs. butter.
4 ozs. sugar.

5½ ozs. flour.
2 eggs.
Vanilla essence.
¼ teasp. baking powder.

2 ozs. chopped walnuts.

To serve :—Chocolate Foam Sauce.

1. Put the chocolate powder into a small bowl, add the milk or water and place over a saucepan of hot water until the chocolate melts and the mixture becomes quite smooth. Allow to cool.
2. Make madeira cake mixture, adding the chocolate to the creamed butter and sugar. Mix in the walnuts after adding the flour.
3. Put into a greased pudding bowl or mould, cover with greased paper and steam for about 1½ hours.
4. Remove the paper, turn the pudding on to a hot dish and dredge with castor sugar.

BEN RHYDDING PUDDING

Sponge cake.
1 lb. apples.

Sugar.
½ pint cornflour custard.

¼ pint whipped and sweetened cream

1. Line a pudding bowl, about 6 inches in diameter, with a layer of sponge cake.
2. Stew the apples with a very little water and sweeten. Cool, pour into the lined bowl and cover with a layer of sponge cake,

3. Put a plate over the bowl with a weight on top and leave for 1-2 hours.

4. Turn on a glass dish, pour the custard around and decorate with roses of cream.

PUFFED SWEET OMELET

2 eggs.	Vanilla essence.
½ oz. castor sugar.	½ oz. butter.
	1 tablesp. jam.

1. Put the jam in warm place to heat.

2. Beat the yolks of eggs and sugar until creamy. Add the vanilla essence.

3. Beat the whites of eggs stiffly, pour the yolks over, and fold them through the whites.

4. Put the butter on a seasoned omelet pan and allow to become sizzling hot. Pour on the omelet mixture and flatten out on the pan.

5. Cook until set and lightly browned underneath. Brown the top of the omelet under a griller or in front of a radiant fire.

6. Turn on to a d'oyley on a hot dish or plate, allowing half of the omelet to rest on the palm of the left hand, having the fried side up.

7. Crease the centre with a knife. Spread the hot jam over one-half of the omelet, and fold the other half over. Dredge the top with castor sugar and serve immediately.

RUM OMELET

2 eggs.	1 tablesp. milk.
	½ oz. butter.
To serve :—2 tablesps. apricot jam.	3 tablesps. rum.
Castor sugar.	

1. Make an omelet.

2. Heat the jam, then add 1 tablesp. rum and use this for filling the omelet.

3. Serve on a hot dish, dredge with castor sugar. Pour remainder of the rum over and light just before serving.

PEAR AND BANANA PUDDING

2 cooking pears.	¼ lb. sugar.
2 bananas.	¼ pint water.

Custard mixture :—
1 oz. butter or margarine.	½ pint milk and syrup.
1 oz. flour.	½ oz. sugar.
	2 yolks of eggs.

Meringue :—
2 whites of eggs.	4 ozs. castor sugar.

1. Make a syrup with the sugar and water. Wipe the pears, cut in two, remove the core, peel and cook gently in the syrup Lift out of the syrup.

2. Make a thick white sauce with the butter, flour, milk and syrup left after cooking the pears. Add the sugar, cool a little and beat in the yolks of eggs.

3. Skin the bananas and cut in slices. Cut the pears in pieces. Arrange both in layers in a greased fireproof dish and pour the custard mixture over.

4. Beat the whites of eggs stiffly, fold in the sugar, and pile roughly on top of the custard mixture.

5. Bake in a very moderate oven until the meringue is set and lightly browned.

APPLE AND RICE MERINGUE PUDDING

2 ozs. rice.	2 yolks of eggs.
1 pt. milk.	1 oz. sugar.
Grated lemon rind.	
Apple pulp :—	
1 lb. apples.	Sugar to sweeten.
A little water.	Grated lemon rind.
Meringue :—	
2 whites of eggs.	4 ozs. castor sugar.

1. Wash the rice and put into a saucepan with the milk, cook until soft and thick.

2. Cream the yokes of eggs with the sugar and lemon rind, add the rice and mix well. Put into a greased pie-dish.

3. Stew the apples to a thick pulp with sugar, a little water and lemon rind, and spread on top of the rice mixture.

4. Beat the whites of eggs stiffly, fold in the castor sugar and pipe or spread roughly over the apples. Put into a cool oven until the meringue is set and lightly browned.

OMELETTE SOUFFLÉE

2 yolks of eggs.	Vanilla essence.
1½ ozs. castor sugar.	3 whites of eggs.
1 teasp. cornflour.	1 tablesp. apricot jam.

1. Cream the yolks of eggs and castor sugar in a bowl, using a wooden spoon. Stir in the cornflour and the vanilla essence.

2. Beat the whites of eggs stiffly and fold through the creamed yolks and sugar. Pour half into a buttered soufflé dish, then put in the jam, and fill up with the remainder of the mixture. With the blade of a knife make a pattern on the surface.

3. Dredge the top with castor sugar. Bake in a moderate oven for about 10-12 minutes until well-risen and golden brown in colour. Serve immediately with a folded table-napkin around the dish.

PINEAPPLE PUDDING

3 ozs. butter.	4 ozs. brown sugar.
	1 small tin pineapple.

Cake Mixture :—

2 ozs. butter or margarine.	6 ozs. flour.
3 ozs. castor sugar.	¾ gill milk.
1 egg.	¼ teasp. baking powder.

1. Put the butter into a cake tin about 7 inches in diameter. Heat until the butter is melted, add the brown sugar and stir until dissolved.
2. Drain the slices of pineapple and arrange in the tin. Cool.
3. Cream the butter and sugar, beat in the egg. Stir in the milk and flour alternately. Add the baking powder and spread over the pineapple.
4. Bake in a very moderate oven for about ¾ hour. Turn out on to a hot dish and serve.

BANANA AND ICE CREAM CRUNCH

1½ ozs. butter or margarine.	2 bananas.
1 tablespoonful golden syrup.	1 block ice cream.
1½ cups cornflakes.	¼ pint cream.

1. Melt the butter in a saucepan, add the golden syrup and cornflakes. Stir over a low heat until the cornflakes are well coated with the mixture. Put into a glass dish.
2. Peel and slice the bananas, place on top of the cornflakes.
3. Slice the block of ice cream and cover the bananas with it.
4. Half whip the cream, sweeten and flavour it. Pour over the ice cream, sprinkle a few cornflakes on top and serve immediately.

BAKED ALASKA

Sponge Mixture :—

2 eggs.	2 ozs. flour.
2 ozs. castor sugar.	Vanilla essence.

A block of ice-cream.
Fruit juice, sherry or liqueur.

Meringue : 2 whites of eggs.　　4 ozs. castor sugar.

1. Make the sponge mixture and bake in a prepared oblong cake tin about 4 ins. × 8 ins.
2. Put the cake on a flat fireproof dish and soak it while it is still warm with fruit juice, sherry or liqueur. Leave until cold.
3. Beat the whites of eggs stiffly. Sprinkle in half of the sugar and continue beating until the mixture stands in points. Fold in the remainder of the sugar.

4. Place the ice cream on the soaked sponge cake and cover completely with the meringue.

5. Bake in a hot oven 7–10 minutes. Serve at once.

OMELETTE SOUFFLÉE EN SURPRISE

Sponge Mixture :—

2 eggs.	2 ozs. flour.
2 ozs. castor sugar.	Vanilla essence.

Fruit juice.	Sherry or liqueur.
A block of ice-cream.	

Soufflé Mixture :—

2 yolks of eggs.	1 teaspoonful cornflour.
2 ozs. castor sugar.	Vanilla essence.
3 whites of eggs.	

1. Make the sponge mixture and bake in a prepared oblong cake tin about 4 ins. × 8 ins.

2. Put the sponge cake on a flat fireproof dish and soak it while it is still warm with fruit juice, sherry or liqueur. Leave until cold.

3. Cream the yolks of eggs with the sugar until thick and creamy, add the vanilla essence and cornflour. Mix well. Beat the whites of eggs stiffly and fold through the yolk mixture.

4. Place the ice-cream on the soaked cake and cover completely with the omelet mixture. Dredge with castor sugar and put into a hot oven for about 7–10 minutes. Serve at once.

BAKED LEMON PUDDING

5 ozs. Short Pastry.

Filling :

4 ozs. cake crumbs.	3 ozs. butter.
Grated rind and juice of 1 lemon.	3 ozs. sugar.
1 gill milk.	2 yolks of eggs.

*Meringue :—*2 whites of eggs.	4 ozs. castor sugar.

1. Line a greased pie-plate with the pastry. Flake and decorate the edges.

2. Soak the crumbs in the lemon juice and milk.

3. Cream the butter and sugar. Add the grated lemon rind and yolks of eggs and beat well. Mix in the cake crumbs and lemon juice.

4. Put into the lined pie-plate and bake in a moderate oven until set—about 35–40 minutes.

5. Beat the whites of eggs stiffly, fold in the castor sugar and pile roughly on top of the pudding. Put into a cool oven until the meringue is set and very lightly browned. Serve on a d'oyley on a hot dish.

WINDSOR TART

8 ozs. Rough Puff Pastry.

Filling :

1 lb. apples.	1 oz. currants.
Sugar to sweeten.	A little grated nutmeg.

Make as for Apple Cake, sprinkling the currants and nutmeg between the apples.

BEIGNETS SOUFFLÉS

Choux Pastry (page 155).
To fry :—Bath of fat.
To serve :—Castor sugar. Fruit Sauce.

1. Make the choux pastry and put into a forcing bag fitted with a plain eclair pipe.

2. Have the fat hot but not smoking. Pipe 1-inch strips (cut off with a sharp knife) into the fat and fry until a golden brown colour, when they should have puffed out to about three times their original size. Do not put too many beignets into the fat at one time.

3. Lift the beignets out of the fat and drain well. A well-made beignet soufflé should be well puffed out with a hollow in the centre and just a little of the paste adhering to the crust, which should be crisp and dry.

4. Dredge with castor sugar and pile high on a hot dish with a d'oyley.

FLAN CASES

Pastry Flan Case

4 ozs. flour.	1 yolk of egg.
2 ozs. butter or margarine.	Pinch of salt.
1 oz. castor sugar.	Cold water.

1. Sieve the flour and salt into a bowl. Rub in the butter.

2. Cream the yolk of egg and sugar together, add a little cold water. Mix with the flour to form a stiff dough.

3. Turn on to a floured board and knead lightly.

4. Roll out the pastry about 1 inch larger than the flan ring. Lift the pastry into the greased ring and press into shape.

5. Make a roll on the edge by pressing back the pastry and trim off the surplus pastry by running the rolling pin over the top. Bring up the edge to rest on the top of the ring.

6. Finish the edge as desired, lift the flan ring on to a greased tin and continue as required.

Sponge Flan Case

2 eggs.	2 ozs. flour.
2 ozs. castor sugar.	Vanilla essence.
¼ teasp. baking powder (if liked).	

1. Grease a flan cake tin and dust with a mixture of castor sugar and flour.
2. Make the sponge mixture and put into the prepared tin. Bake in a fairly moderate oven for about 10 minutes.
3. Turn on to a wire tray and leave until cool. Use as required.

FRUIT FLAN

1 Pastry Flan Case (page 100).

Filling :
1 small tin of fruit.   ¼ oz. gelatine.
½ glass sherry.   1 gill syrup from fruit.
Colouring.

To decorate : Whipped and sweetened cream.

1. Soak leaf gelatine in a bowl of tepid water, leave until soft, squeeze out the water when required. If using powdered gelatine, mix with 3 tablespoonfuls of water, leave for a short time, and use.
2. Make the flan case, put a piece of greased paper in the centre with some beans on it to prevent the pastry from rising.
3. Bake in a moderate oven for about 20 minutes, remove the beans and paper, and return the flan case to the oven to dry out for about 5 minutes.
4. Leave to cool for about 10 minutes on the baking tin, then lift the flan on the left hand and let the ring slide off over the arm.
5. Arrange the fruit neatly in the pastry case.
6. Heat the syrup, add the gelatine and stir until dissolved. Add sherry and colouring. Leave until beginning to set, pour over the fruit and when set decorate with whipped and sweetened cream.

PEAR FLAN

1 Pastry Flan Case (page 100).   Apricot Jam.

Pastry Cream :
1 egg.   ½ pint milk.
1 oz. flour.   1 oz. sugar.
Flavouring.

___

4 half pears (cooked or tinned).
Apricot Glaze (page 224).

1. For the pastry cream mix the flour and sugar together, break in the egg, add flavouring and beat well together.
2. Add the heated milk, return to the saucepan and stir until it boils for about 1 minute. Leave to cool.
3. Make the flan case and lift on to a greased baking tin. Spread a thin layer of apricot jam in the bottom, then three-quarter fill with the pastry cream.
4. Cut the pears in thin slices and arrange them spiral fashion on the pastry cream.

5. Bake in a moderate oven for about 35 minutes. Leave to cool for about 15 minutes on the baking tin, then lift the flan on to the left hand and let the ring fall off over the arm.

6. Brush the top of the flan with apricot glaze.

NOTE.—Any other fruit may be used instead of pears.

APPLE FLAN

1 Pastry Flan Case (page 100).	Sugar.
1½ lbs. apples.	Apricot glaze (page 224).

1. Peel, core and slice 1 lb. apples, stew with 1 tablespoonful water until soft. Beat to a pulp, sweeten to taste, and leave until cold.

2. Put the apple purée in the flan case and spread evenly.

3. Peel, quarter and core the remaining apples. Cut in very thin slices and arrange these spiral fashion on the apple purée. Fill the centre with a second spiral of apple. Sprinkle a little castor sugar over these apple slices.

4. Bake in a moderate oven for about ½ hour. Leave to cool for about 10 minutes on the baking tin, then lift the flan on the left hand and let the ring fall off over the arm.

5. Brush the top of the flan with apricot glaze.

APRICOT FLAN

1 Pastry Flan Case (page 100).

Franzipan :

2 ozs. butter or margarine.	1½ ozs. ground almonds.
2 ozs. castor sugar.	1 oz. flour.
1 egg.	Almond essence.
1 tin apricots.	Apricot glaze (page 224).

1. Cream the butter and sugar, beat in the egg, then mix in the flour, almonds and flavouring.

2. Make the flan case and lift on to the greased baking tin. Spread the franzipan mixture in it.

3. Arrange the apricots, cut side up, over the surface, and bake in a moderate oven for about ½ hour.

4. Leave to cool for about 15 minutes on the baking tin, then lift the flan on the left hand and let the ring fall off over the arm.

5. Brush the top with apricot glaze.

RASPBERRY FLAN

1 Sponge Flan Case (page 100).	½ pint cream.
1 lb. raspberries.	Castor sugar.

1. Pick over the raspberries carefully, put aside about 12 raspberries for decoration, sprinkle the remainder with castor sugar and leave for about 1 hour.

2. Put the flan case on a large flat round dish and fill the centre with the raspberries and juice.

3. Whip the cream, sweeten and flavour it, spread on top of the flan. Decorate with the whole raspberries.

DARMSTADT PUDDING

5 ozs. Rough Puff Pastry.

Filling :

2 ozs. butter.	2 yolks of eggs.
1½ ozs. sugar.	2 ozs. cake-crumbs.

2 tablesps. marmalade.

Meringue :—2 whites of eggs.   4 ozs. castor sugar.

1. Line a fireproof plate with the pastry. Roll out the trimmings, cut into small rounds. Use to decorate the edge.

2. Cream the butter and the sugar, add the yolks of eggs and beat well. Mix in the cake crumbs and the marmalade and spread over the centre of the pastry.

3. Bake in a hot oven for the first 10 minutes, then reduce the heat until the pudding is cooked—about 30–35 minutes.

4. Beat the whites of eggs stiffly, fold in the castor sugar and pile roughly on top of the pudding. Return to a cool oven to set and lightly brown the meringue.

5. Remove the pudding carefully from the plate and serve on a d'oyley on a plate.

PARIS TART

4 ozs. Flaky Pastry.

Filling :

1 lb. apples.	Sugar to sweeten.

A little water.

Custard Mixture :

½ pint milk.	2 strips lemon rind.
2 teasps. cornflour.	2 yolks of eggs.

1 oz. sugar.

Meringue :—2 whites of eggs.   4 ozs. castor sugar.

1. Line a fireproof plate with the pastry. Flake and decorate edges. Prick centre with a fork and place a piece of greased paper over with some beans on it to prevent the pastry from rising.

2. Bake in a hot oven for the first 10 minutes, then reduce the heat until the pastry is cooked—about 20 minutes. Remove beans and paper and put back into the oven for a further five minutes to allow the pastry to dry out.

3. Stew the apples with a little water and sufficient sugar to sweeten.

4. Make custard mixture as for Cornflour Custard Sauce.

5. Loosen pastry case from plate, put in the stewed apples and cover with the custard.

6. Beat the whites of eggs stiffly and fold in the castor sugar. Pile roughly on top of the custard.

7. Put into a cool oven until the meringue is set and very lightly browned. Lift tart on to a d'oyley on a plate.

HOT VANILLA SOUFFLÉ

2 ozs. butter or margarine.	3 eggs.
2 ozs. flour.	1 oz. sugar.
½ pt. milk.	½ teasp. vanilla essence.

To serve :—Sabayon Sauce (page 125).

1. Grease a mould or 6 dariole moulds, and dust them out with castor sugar.

2. Melt the butter, add the flour and cook for a few minutes without colouring. Add the milk, bring to the boil, stirring all the time.

3. Add the sugar and vanilla essence, cool a little, and add the yolks of eggs one at a time, and beat well.

4. Beat the whites of eggs stiffly and mix 1 tablespoonful into the sauce, fold in the remainder.

5. Half-fill the prepared mould and place a piece of greased paper on top. Put the mould in a deep tin threequarters full of hot water, put the tin on top of the stove and cook over a gentle heat until the soufflé has reached to the top of the mould—about 20 minutes.

6. Place the deep tin in a moderate oven and cook until the soufflé is set—about 20–25 minutes more.

7. Remove the paper, lift the soufflé mould out of the water. Turn the soufflé on to a heated dish, lifting the mould carefully from the soufflé. Pour a little sauce over and serve immediately.

HOT CHOCOLATE SOUFFLÉ

2 ozs. butter or margarine.	3 eggs.
2 ozs. flour.	1 oz. sugar.
½ pint milk.	¼ teasp. vanilla essence.
1 oz. chocolate powder.	

To serve :—Chocolate Foam Sauce (page 124) *or* Sabayon Sauce (page 125)

Make as for Hot Vanilla Soufflé, adding the chocolate powder to the sauce.

CHARLOTTE RUSSE

1 pkt. lemon jelly.	Cherries and angelica.
5 ozs. boudoir biscuits.	

Filling :

½ oz. gelatine.	1 oz. castor sugar.
½ lb. strawberry jam.	1 tablesp. rum.
1 gill milk.	½ gill water.
Juice ½ lemon.	½ pint cream.

1. Soak leaf gelatine in a bowl of tepid water, leave until soft, squeeze out of the water when required. If using powdered gelatine mix with 3 tablespoonfuls of water, leave for a short time and use.

2. Line the bottom of a plain pint-size tin with jelly and decorate with cherries and angelica as on page 224.

3. Trim the ends of the biscuits and straighten the sides. Arrange them closely around the sides of the tin, with the sugared side of the biscuit next the tin. There must be no space between the biscuits.

4. Sieve the jam into a bowl with the milk, add the lemon juice, sugar and rum. Heat the ½ gill water, put in the gelatine, stir until dissolved and add to the sieved jam, mix well.

5. Leave until just beginning to set, whip for a few minutes. Add the half-whipped cream, fold through the mixture, then pour into the prepared tin.

6. Unmould as on page 224 on to a glass dish. Arrange chopped jelly around.

COLD PINEAPPLE SOUFFLÉ

1 pkt. lemon jelly.	1 tablesp. sherry.
1 small tin pineapple.	1 oz. castor sugar.
¼ oz. gelatine.	½ pint cream.

1. Soak leaf gelatine in a bowl of tepid water, leave until soft, squeeze out of the water when required. If using powdered gelatine mix with 3 tablespoonfuls of water, leave for a short time and use.

2. Prepare a soufflé mould by tying a band of paper 4-5 inches deep around the outside.

3. Dissolve the jelly, using the pineapple juice and enough hot water to make up to ¾ pint. Add the gelatine, sugar and sherry, stir until the gelatine is dissolved. Leave until beginning to set, then whip until light and frothy.

4. Fold in the half-whipped cream and lastly the shredded pineapple, keeping back 4 cubes of the pineapple for decoration.

5. Brush the mould and paper with cold water and pour in the mixture. It should come about 1½ inches above edge of mould. Leave until set.

6. Remove the band of paper carefully. Decorate the top with the pineapple, chopped jelly or chopped pistachio nuts. Place mould on a d'oyley on a dish.

NOTE.—Peaches, apricots or other fruits may be used instead of pineapple.

BANANA CHARTREUSE

1 pkt. lemon jelly.	2 bananas.

Filling :

6 bananas.	1 tablesp. rum.
½ gill milk.	½ oz. gelatine.
1½ ozs. castor sugar.	½ gill water.
	½ pint cream.

1. Soak leaf gelatine in a bowl of tepid water, leave until soft, squeeze out of the water when required. If using powdered gelatine, mix with 3 tablespoonfuls of water, leave for a short time and use.

2. Line the mould with jelly as on page 224 and decorate with bananas cut in ⅛ inch slices, page 224.

3. Sieve the bananas with the milk, and add the sugar and rum.

4. Heat the water, add the gelatine, stir until dissolved. Add to the sieved bananas and leave until beginning to set. Whip for a few minutes.

5. Fold in the half-whipped cream and pour into the prepared mould and leave until set.

6. Unmould as on page 224. Arrange chopped jelly around.

ORANGE CHARTREUSE

1 pkt. orange jelly.	1 orange.

Filling :

½ pint milk.	2 ozs. sugar.
2 eggs.	½ oz. gelatine.
Rind and juice of 1 orange.	¼ pint cream.

1. Soak leaf gelatine in a bowl of tepid water, leave until soft, squeeze out of the water when required. If using powdered gelatine mix with 3 tablespoonfuls of water, leave for a short time and use.

2. Line a plain mould with jelly (page 224).

3. Peel one orange, divide into segments, split each segment in two lengthwise and use to decorate the bottom and the sides of the mould (page 224).

4. Make custard with the milk and yolks of eggs, add grated orange rind, juice and sugar and mix well.

5. Add the gelatine, stir until dissolved. Leave until beginning to set.

6. Fold in the half-whipped cream and the stiffly-beaten whites of eggs, pour into the prepared mould and leave until set.

7. Unmould as on page 224 on to a glass dish. Arrange chopped jelly around.

MUSHROOM GÂTEAU

Meringue :
2 whites of eggs.   4 ozs. castor sugar.

Sponge Cake :
2 eggs.   2 ozs. flour.
2 ozs. castor sugar.   ¼ teasp. baking powder.

To soak sponge :
¼ pint liquid lemon jelly.   2 tablesps. sherry.

To decorate :
½ pint whipped and sweetened cream. Angelica.
Chopped lemon jelly.   Chopped pistachio nuts.
½ oz. chocolate powder.

1. Make meringue mixture. Put the mixture into a forcing bag fitted with a plain pipe. Force on to an oiled tin in rounds about the size of a half-crown and in strips about 1½ inches in length. Dust over with castor sugar and cook in a cool oven for about 2½ hours, until well dried out.

2. Make the sponge mixture and bake in one sandwich tin about 7 inches or 8 inches in diameter. Leave until cold.

3. Place the sponge cake on a flat dish. Prick with a fork, soak with the liquid jelly and sherry, leave until set.

4. Spread with the cream and put chopped jelly over the cream.

5. Rub the undersides of the meringues in the chocolate powder, make a hole in the centre and stick in the stalks.

6. Stand the " mushrooms " in the cream. Put a few blades of grass made from angelica here and there. Sprinkle chopped pistachio nuts over.

NOTE.—Do not put meringues on top until just before serving the gâteau.

PEAR GÂTEAU

1 sponge cake (page 172).

1 square of jelly ⎱
¾ pint water   ⎰   1 tin pears.
                               Carmine.
½ pint cream.   Cloves.
1 teasp. castor sugar.   Angelica.
A few drops of vanilla essence.

To decorate :—1 oz. almonds.   5 cherries.

1. Cut out the centre of the cake, leaving one inch on the bottom and sides.

2. Dissolve the jelly in the water. When cold pour over the cake and leave until set.

3. Whip the cream, add the sugar, flavouring, and half the pears cut into pieces. Put this mixture into the centre of the cake.

4. Brush the round surface of the pears with a little carmine, put a clove to represent the calyx, and a small piece of angelica to represent the stalk in each pear. Arrange these around the cream.

5. Blanch the almonds and cut into strips. Stick these into the side of the cake. Decorate the top with the cherries.

VANILLA BAVAROIS

Lemon jelly.	Cherries and angelica.
½ pint milk.	¼ oz. gelatine.
2 yolks of eggs.	¼ pint cream.
2 ozs. sugar.	2 whites of eggs.

½ teaspoonful vanilla essence.

1. Soak leaf gelatine in a bowl of tepid water, leave until soft, squeeze out of the water when required. If using powdered gelatine, mix with 3 tablespoonfuls of water, leave for a short time and use.

2. Line a mould or 8 dariole moulds with jelly and decorate with small pieces of cherry and angelica (page 224).

3. Heat the milk, cream the yolks of eggs and sugar, add the vanilla essence, pour the milk on to them and return to the saucepan. Cook until the custard coats the back of the spoon.

4. Add the gelatine, stir until it is dissolved, leave until the custard begins to set.

5. Fold in the half-whipped cream and stiffly-beaten whites of eggs. Pour into the prepared mould.

6. When set, unmould as on page 224 on to a glass dish.

CHOCOLATE BAVAROIS

½ pint milk.	¼ oz. gelatine.
2 yolks of eggs.	¼ pint cream.
2 ozs. sugar.	2 whites of eggs.
1 oz. chocolate powder.	¼ teasp. vanilla essence.

To decorate :—Whipped and sweetened cream.

Make as for Vanilla Bavarois, adding chocolate powder to the custard. Put into a mould or glass dish to set. Decorate with roses of cream.

COFFEE BAVAROIS

1 pkt. lemon jelly.	Violets and angelica.

Filling :	
½ pint milk ⎱ Custard.	¼ oz. gelatine.
2 yolks of eggs ⎰	¼ pint cream.
1½ ozs. sugar.	2 whites of eggs.
1 dessertsp. coffee essence.	1 dessertsp. rum.

1. Soak leaf gelatine in a bowl of tepid water, leave until soft, squeeze out of the water when required. If using powdered gelatine, mix with 3 tablespoonfuls of water, leave for a short time and use.

2. Line a plain mould with lemon jelly (page 224) and decorate with violets and angelica (page 224).

3. Make the custard, and add sugar, coffee essence and rum. Add the gelatine and stir until dissolved. Leave until beginning to set.

4. Fold in the half-whipped cream and the stiffly-beaten whites of eggs. Pour into the prepared mould, and leave until set.

5. Unmould as on page 224 on to a glass dish. Arrange chopped jelly around.

CARAMEL BAVAROIS

1 pkt. lemon jelly.	Cherries or violets and angelica.

Filling :

½ pint milk ⎱ Custard.	3 tablesps. water ⎱ Caramel.
2 yolks of eggs ⎰	2 tablesps. sugar ⎰
2 ozs. sugar.	¼ oz. gelatine.
1 tablesp. brandy.	2 whites of eggs.

¼ pint cream.

1. Soak the leaf gelatine in a bowl of tepid water, leave until soft, squeeze out of the water when required. If using powdered gelatine mix with 3 tablespoonfuls of water, leave for a short time.

2. Line and decorate a plain mould (page 224).

3. Make custard and add sugar and brandy. Add the gelatine and stir until dissolved.

4. Put sugar and two tablespoonfuls of water for caramel into a saucepan. Stir until the sugar is dissolved. Boil until a brown colour, then add the other tablespoonful of hot water and mix well over the heat. Cool a little and add to the custard. Leave until beginning to set.

5. Fold in the half-whipped cream and the stiffly-beaten whites of eggs and fill into the prepared mould. Leave until set.

6. Unmould as on page 224 on to a glass dish. Arrange chopped jelly around.

VENETIAN CREAM

1 pkt. jelly.	Cherries and angelica.

Cake Crumb Mixture :

2 ozs. macaroon biscuits.	1 oz. castor sugar.
3 ozs. cake crumbs.	Vanilla essence.

½ glass sherry.

Cream Mixture :

½ pint cream.	¼ oz. gelatine.
1 oz. sugar.	½ gill water.

Vanilla essence.

To decorate :—½ oz. whole almonds.

1. Soak the leaf gelatine in a bowl of tepid water, leave until soft. Squeeze out of the water when required. If using powdered gelatine mix it with 3 tablespoonfuls of water, leave for a short time and use.

2. Line the bottom of a plain mould with jelly and decorate with cherries and angelica (page 224).

3. Crush the biscuits, put them with the cake crumbs into a bowl, pour the sherry over and leave until well soaked.

4. Half-whip the cream, add sugar and vanilla essence. Heat the ½ gill of water, add the gelatine and stir until dissolved and it has cooled a little. Add to the cream and fold it through. Use when beginning to set.

5. Pour ½-inch layer of the cream mixture into the prepared mould. Leave until set, and then put in ½-inch layer of cake-crumb mixture.

6. Continue in this way until all the mixture is used up, and finish with a layer of cream. Leave until set.

7. Unmould as on page 224, on to a glass dish. Blanch the almonds and cut in strips. Stick these into the sides of the sweet and arrange chopped jelly around.

GINGER CREAM

1 pkt. lemon jelly.			Cherries and angelica.

Filling :

½ pint milk			¼ teasp. ginger. essence.
2 teasps. cornflour	Cornflour		2 ozs. preserved ginger.
1 egg		Custard	1 dessertsp. sherry.
1 oz. sugar			¼ oz. gelatine.
	¼ pint cream.		

1. Soak leaf gelatine in a bowl of tepid water, leave until soft, squeeze out of the water when required. If using powdered gelatine mix with 3 tablespoonfuls of water, leave for a short time and use.

2. Line a border mould with lemon jelly. Decorate with cherries and angelica (page 224).

3. Make Cornflour Custard. Add ginger essence, sherry and gelatine and stir until dissolved. Leave until beginning to set, whip for a few minutes.

4. Fold in the half-whipped cream and lastly the chopped ginger, turn into the prepared mould and leave until set.

5. Unmould as on page 224, on to a glass dish. Arrange chopped jelly around.

VACHERIN CHANTILLY

Meringue :

3 whites of eggs.	6 ozs. castor sugar.

Filling :

½ pint cream.	Castor sugar.

Flavouring.

To decorate :—Cherries and angelica.

1. Prepare baking sheets by rubbing very lightly with oil or butter and mark three rounds of about 8 inches diameter on them.

2. Beat the whites of eggs stiffly, sprinkle in half the sugar and continue beating until the mixture stands in points at the end of the beater. Fold in the remainder of the sugar.

3. Put the meringue mixture into a forcing bag, fitted with a rose pipe, and completely cover two of the marked rounds by commencing in the centre and piping in a spiral fashion.

4. For the third round, pipe a trellis pattern and complete by piping a circle around the outside.

5. Bake in cool oven for about 2 hours until well dried out. When cooked leave on the baking tin for a few minutes to shrink.

6. Whip the cream, sweeten and flavour it. Spread about half of the cream on one of the rounds of meringue, place the second round on top, then spread more cream on this layer.

7. Place the trellis layer on top and decorate with roses of cream and small pieces of cherry and angelica.

SAVARIN AU RHUM

¼ lb. flour.	2 tablesps. tepid milk and water (mixed)
Pinch of salt.	2 eggs.
¼ oz. yeast.	2 ozs butter.
½ teasp. castor sugar.	

Rum Syrup :

¼ lb. granulated sugar.	Rind of ½ lemon.
¼ pint water.	½ glass of rum.

Apricot glaze (page 224).

To decorate :—Whipped Cream, Cherries and angelica.

1. Grease a border mould and dust out with equal quantities of castor sugar and flour.

2. Sieve the flour and salt into a warm bowl and put in a warm place to heat.

3. Cream yeast and sugar, add the tepid milk and water. Make a well in the centre of the flour and pour the yeast liquid into it. Cover the yeast with a little flour and leave in a warm place until the yeast bursts through the flour.

4. Break an egg into the flour and work in with the fingers. Repeat with the second egg. Beat to introduce air and to make the batter quite smooth.

5. Soften the butter a little and beat into the batter. Continue beating until the batter comes thick in one lump from the bowl.

6. Put the batter into the prepared mould, cover with a damp cloth and leave in a warm place until it has risen to the top of the tin—about 1 hour.

7. Bake in a moderate oven for about 30–40 minutes until nicely browned and cooked.

8. Put the sugar and water for the rum syrup into a saucepan with the thinly-peeled rind of the lemon. Stir until the sugar is dissolved. Boil quickly for 5 minutes. Add rum and strain.

9. Turn the savarin on to a dish, pierce in several places with a skewer, soak with rum syrup. Brush with apricot glaze. Decorate with whipped cream, cherries and angelica.

SAVARIN AUX FRUITS

Make as for Savarin au Rhum but use liqueur instead of rum in the syrup and fill the centre with fresh fruit salad.

BABA AU RHUM

¼ lb. flour.	2 tablesps. tepid milk and water (mixed)
Pinch of salt.	2 eggs.
¼ oz. yeast.	2 ozs. butter.
½ teasp. castor sugar.	

Rum Syrup:
¼ lb. sugar.   ¼ pint water.
                ½ glass rum.
To decorate:—Jam.   ¼ pint whipped and sweetened cream.

1. Make mixture as for Savarin (page 111).

2. Half-fill well-greased patty tins or dariole moulds with the mixture. Cover with a damp cloth and leave to rise in a warm place until the dough reaches the top of the moulds.

3. Bake in a moderate oven until nicely browned and firm to the touch. Turn upside down on a deep dish. Prick with a skewer.

4. To make rum syrup, put the sugar and water into a saucepan, stir until the sugar is dissolved. Bring to the boil and boil for 3–4 minutes, add rum. Dip each baba into the syrup for about 1 minute.

5. When cold make a circle of whipped cream on top, and put a little jam in the centre and serve.

VOL AU VENT OF FRUIT

8 ozs. puff pastry.

Filling :
Strawberry jam.	¼ pint cold liquid jelly.
1 banana or any fruit liked.	¼ pint cream.
Icing sugar.	

To make Vol au Vent Case.

1. Roll the pastry out very evenly to ½ inch in thickness and leave for 10 minutes before cutting to help to prevent shrinkage.

2. Cut out with a large cutter, keeping the cutter half an inch from the edge of the pastry on all sides. Mark the centre of each piece with a cutter of smaller size, cutting half-way through the pastry.

3. Place on a baking tin and bake in a hot oven for about 10 minutes, reduce the heat and bake for about 45 minutes until the pastry is cooked.

4. Leave to cool on a wire tray. Remove the centre carefully and keep for the top.

To Fill Case.

1. Put a little strawberry jam into the centre of the case, cover with sliced banana, then pour the jelly, which should be just beginning to set, over.

2. When set, decorate with whipped and sweetened cream. Put the small round of pastry on top to form a lid. Dredge the top of the pastry with icing sugar and serve.

TIPSY CAKE

1 large sponge cake.	½ pint milk ⎫
Raspberry jam.	2 eggs ⎬ Custard.
1-2 glasses sherry	½ oz. sugar ⎭

To decorate :—1 oz. shredded almonds.
½ pint whipped, sweetened and flavoured cream.

1. Split the sponge cake several times, spread each slice with jam, then put back in their original position. Prick with a fork.

2. Place on a glass dish, pour the sherry over the cake and leave to soak.

3. Make custard. Cool, and then coat the cake with it.

4. Stick shredded almonds over the cake at intervals. Decorate with roses of cream.

APRICOT EGGS

Genoese slab (page 172).	Cream.
Lemon jelly.	Tinned apricots.

1. Dissolve the jelly in the apricot syrup, adding water to make up to correct amount. Leave until almost cold.

2. Cut the cake into rounds and soak them with the jelly.

3. Half-whip the cream, sweeten and flavour. Put a spoonful on each round of sponge, and place an apricot in the centre.

NOTE.—If liked the apricots may be glazed with jelly before placing on the cream.

RHUBARB TRIFLE

Sponge Cake.

2 eggs.	2 ozs. flour.
2 ozs. sugar.	¼ teasp. baking powder.

1 lb. rhubarb.	Sugar to sweeten.
A little water.	

½ pint Cornflour Custard.

To decorate :— ¼ pint whipped and sweetened cream.
1-inch pieces of cooked rhubarb.

1. Make sponge cake, and cook in a 7-inch tin.

2. Stew the rhubarb, drain off the juice and beat the fruit to a pulp.

3. Split the sponge cake and prick with a fork. Put lower half in a glass dish. Pour a little rhubarb juice over and spread with the rhubarb pulp.

4. Place the second half on top, pour the remainder of the juice over. Coat with Cornflour Custard.

5. Decorate with the whipped cream and pieces of rhubarb.

FRUIT SALAD

Syrup :— ¼ lb. sugar.	2 tablesps. sherry.
1 gill water.	Juice of half a lemon.
	Colouring.

2 oranges.	¼ lb. green grapes.
2 bananas.	¼ lb. red cherries.
2 pears.	1 small tin of pineapple.
¼ lb. black grapes.	1 oz. chopped walnuts.

To serve :— ½ pint cream.

1. Put the sugar and water into a saucepan. Allow the sugar to dissolve, then bring to the boil. Boil for 3-4 minutes. Add sherry, lemon juice and colouring. Cool a little.

2. Peel the oranges and cut into small pieces.

3. Peel the bananas and cut into slices. Peel pears, cut in eighths, core, then cut each piece across in two.

4. Cut the grapes in halves and remove the stones. Remove the stalks and stones from the cherries. Cut the pineapple into small pieces.

5. Put all the fruit into a large bowl, add the chopped nuts, then pour the syrup over and leave until cold. Serve in a glass dish.

FRUIT IN JELLY

1 pkt. jelly.	1 orange.
¾ pint boiling water.	1 banana.
2 tablesps. sherry.	A few grapes.
Small tin pineapple.	

1. Dissolve jelly in boiling water. Add sherry and leave until cold.

2. Pour ½-inch layer of jelly into a wet mould, leave until set.

3. Arrange a layer of banana slices on top of the layer of jelly. Pour a little cold liquid jelly over and leave until set.

4. Next put in a layer of orange segments, pour some cold liquid jelly over and allow to set.

5. Continue in this way until all the fruit and jelly are used up.

6. When set, dip the mould quickly into boiling water, lift out and allow to stand for a few seconds; turn out on to a well-polished glass dish.

FRUIT FLUFF

1 pkt. jelly.	8 oz. tin evaporated milk.
¼ pint water.	1 oz. castor sugar.
	Fruit.

1. Dissolve the jelly in the hot water and leave until beginning to set.

2. Whisk well and add the evaporated milk and sugar. Keep whisking until it has doubled in size and is almost set.

3. Have the fruit prepared and fold through the jelly mixture. Pour into a glass dish. When set decorate with cream if liked.

ORANGE BASKETS

Oranges.	1 pkt. orange jelly.
Sugar.	Water.

To decorate :—Whipped and sweetened cream. Cherries. Angelica.

1. Wipe the oranges with a damp cloth, cut them in halves and scoop out the inside with a silver spoon.

2. Strain and measure the juice, make up to 1 pint with water. Bring to the boil and dissolve the jelly in it. Sweeten and pour into the orange cases. Leave until set.

3. Decorate with roses of cream, place a piece of cherry on each rose. Steep the angelica in warm water, cut into long strips and arrange as handles across the baskets.

ITALIAN MOUSSE

2 eggs.	¼ oz. gelatine.
2 ozs. castor sugar.	Strawberry jam.
1 dessertsp. cold water.	Rum.
Rind and juice of 1 lemon.	

To decorate :—¼ pint whipped and sweetened cream.
1 oz. browned chopped almonds.
Angelica.

1. Soak leaf gelatine in a bowl of tepid water, leave until soft, squeeze out of the water when required. If using powdered gelatine mix with 3 tablespoonfuls of water, leave for a short time and use.

2. Separate yolks from whites of eggs, put the yolks into a bowl, add sugar and cold water. Whisk over hot water until thick and creamy. Add grated rind and strained juice of the lemon. Add the gelatine and stir until dissolved.

3. Fold in stiffly-beaten whites of eggs.

4. Put 2 teasps. jam and 2 teasps. rum in each individual glass. Fill glasses with the mousse mixture. Leave until set.

5. Put a rose of cream on top of each mousse, decorate with angelica and almonds.

APRICOT MOUSSE

½ pint sieved apricots.	¾ oz. gelatine.
3 eggs.	½ gill apricot syrup.
2 ozs. sugar.	A few drops of carmine.
Juice of ¼ lemon.	¼ pint cream.

To decorate :—¼ pint whipped and sweetened cream.
1 oz. browned almonds.
½ oz. chopped pistachio nuts.

1. Soak leaf gelatine in a bowl of tepid water, leave until soft, squeeze out of the water when required. If using powdered gelatine mix with 3 tablespoonfuls of water, leave for a short time and use.

2. Put the apricot purée into a bowl with yolks of eggs and sugar. Whisk over hot water until thick and creamy.

3. Heat the apricot syrup, add the gelatine and stir until dissolved. Remove bowl to the table and add lemon juice and syrup. Colour with a few drops of carmine. Beat for a few minutes.

4. Fold in the stiffly beaten whites of eggs and half-whipped cream.

5. Pour into a glass dish, leave until set and sprinkle with chopped browned almonds. Put roses of cream on top, and decorate with chopped pistachio nuts.

STRAWBERRY MOUSSE

1 lb. tin of strawberries.	4 whites of eggs.
1 pkt. jelly.	2 ozs. castor sugar.
½ pint cream.	

1. Heat the syrup from the tin of strawberries, add the packet of jelly and stir until dissolved. Leave until cold.

2. Beat the whites of eggs until stiff, then whisk in the cold jelly.

3. Beat the cream with the sugar and fold into the jelly mixture. Sieve the strawberries and fold lightly through.

4. Serve in a glass dish or in individual dishes and decorate with extra whipped cream if liked.

MERINGUED APPLES

¼ lb. sugar.	1 teasp. lemon juice.
¼ pint water.	6 even-sized apples.
Meringue :—3 whites of eggs.	6 ozs. castor sugar.

To serve :—Whipped and sweetened cream or Custard Sauce.

1. Put sugar, water and lemon juice into a saucepan, allow to dissolve, bring to the boil and boil 2–3 minutes. Peel and core the apples, cook them in the syrup. They should be slightly underdone. Put the apples on an oiled baking tin, keeping them well part.

2. Beat the whites of eggs stiffly, fold in the castor sugar and put meringue mixture into a forcing bag fitted with a rose pipe. Pipe the meringue over each apple, covering it completely.

3. Sprinkle castor sugar over and place in a cool oven until the meringue is crisp and of a pale biscuit colour—about ½ hour.

CRÊPE SUZETTE

Batter :	4 ozs. flour.	1 oz. castor sugar.
	Pinch of salt.	½ oz. butter.
	1½ gills milk.	½ gill cream.
	2 eggs.	Clarified fat or oil.
Sauce :	4 ozs. butter.	2 glasses Orange Curaçao.
	8 lumps sugar.	Brandy.

Orange and lemon.

1. Sieve the flour and salt into a bowl. Make a bay in the centre of the flour, drop the eggs into it, add half of the milk gradually, stirring with a wooden spoon. Allow the flour to fall in gradually from the sides.

2. Beat for 5 minutes, add the remainder of the milk, the sugar, melted butter and cream. Stand the batter in a cold place for at least one hour.

3. Heat a 5-inch frying-pan. Add a little melted fat, and heat. Pour enough batter into the pan to cover the bottom thinly. Cook until set and lightly browned. Turn and cook the second side.

4. Keep the pancakes hot on a plate over a saucepan of boiling water, until required.

5. Rub the lump sugar on the rinds of the lemon and orange.

6. Heat a silver-lined copper pan. Put half the butter on the pan and heat over a low flame. Add half the sugar and crush with a fork. Squeeze a little lemon and orange juice over. Add half the Orange Curaçao.

7. Put in four pancakes, heat, turn over, fold each pancake in half and then across in half again.

8. Pour brandy over, turn up the flame, tilt the pan to ignite the brandy.

9. Have two dessert plates hot. Lift two pancakes on to each plate, spoon the sauce from the pan over the pancakes, dredge with castor sugar and serve immediately. Repeat with the remainder of the pancakes.

VANILLA ICE CREAM I

1½ pints milk ⎫	4 ozs. castor sugar.
2 eggs ⎬ Custard.	2 teasps. vanilla essence.
1½ ozs. cornflour ⎭	½ pint cream.

1. Make Cornflour Custard. Add sugar and vanilla essence. Allow to dissolve.

2. Leave until cold, then add half-whipped cream and mix well. Pour into the freezing can (follow instructions for using freezing machine). Serve plain or with cream or fruit.

VANILLA ICE CREAM II

1 pint milk.	1 tablesp. cornflour.
2 eggs.	1 small tin of condensed milk.
1 teasp. vanilla essence.	3 tablesps. sugar.

1. Make Cornflour Custard with the milk, eggs and cornflour. Add the sugar and allow to cool.

2. Place in the freezing tray until almost firm. Remove and beat well with a rotary beater, adding the flavouring and tinned milk.

3. Return to the freezing tray and freeze to correct consistency.

LEMON WATER ICE

2 lemons.	1 pint water.
4 ozs. sugar.	1 white of egg.

1. Wipe the lemons, peel off the rind very thinly and put into a basin.

2. Put the sugar and water into a saucepan. Allow to dissolve slowly, bring to the boil and boil for 10 minutes. Remove any scum. Pour over the rind, cover and leave until cold.

3. Add the juice of the lemons and strain all through muslin. Put into the freezing can.

4. When half frozen, mix in the stiffly-beaten white of egg. Continue freezing until sufficiently stiff.

CHOCOLATE ICE CREAM

½ pint custard.	2 ozs. sugar.
2 tablesps. milk.	½ pint cream.
2 ozs. chocolate powder.	Vanilla essence.

Dissolve the chocolate powder in the milk. Add to the custard with the sugar and flavouring. Half-whip the cream and mix into other ingredients. Freeze and serve as required.

ICES

STRAWBERRY OR RASPBERRY CREAM ICE

1 lb. raspberries or strawberries.	4 ozs. castor sugar.
2 tablesps. lemon juice.	½ pint cream.

1. Put raspberries into a bowl and sprinkle with the castor sugar and lemon juice. Leave for about ½ hour. Rub through a sieve, using a wooden spoon.

2. Whip the cream, and stir it lightly into the raspberry purée. Freeze and serve as required.

NOTE.—Strawberry or raspberry jam may be used instead of the fresh fruit—if so, no sugar is required.

CHOCOLATE ICE PUDDING

3 ozs. macaroon or boudoir biscuits.	2 ozs. castor sugar.
1 pint Cornflour Custard.	1 teasp. vanilla essence.
1 oz. chocolate powder ⎫	1 tablesp. sherry.
1 tablesp. milk ⎭	½ pint cream (half-whipped).

1. Crush the biscuits and add to the custard. Add the chocolate dissolved in the milk, the sugar, vanilla essence and sherry to the custard. Mix well together, leave until cold, then add the cream. Pour into a perfectly dry mould.

2. Put into the ice box and leave until frozen. Dip the mould in cold water, turn out on to a glass dish.

APRICOT OR PEACH CREAM ICE

1 small tin of apricots or peaches.	½ pint cream.
2-3 ozs. castor sugar.	2 teasps. lemon juice.
2 or 3 drops of carmine.	

1. Make the apricot or peach purée by rubbing the fruit through a sieve, using a little of the syrup as the purée should not be too thick.

2. Half whip the cream and mix with the purée. Add sugar and lemon juice and enough colouring to make an apricot colour. Freeze and serve as required.

MERINGUES GLACÉS

Meringue cases (page 177).	Ice cream.
Whipped and sweetened cream.	Cherries and angelica.

Fill the meringue cases with ice cream and decorate with cream, cherries and angelica.

SAUCES

BÉCHAMEL SAUCE

½ pint of milk.
1 blade of mace.
1 bayleaf.
½ small onion.
2 cloves.

1 oz. butter or margarine.
1 oz. flour.
Salt and pepper.
1 tablesp. of cream (if liked).

1. Put the milk, mace, washed bayleaf, and onion stuck with the cloves, into a saucepan. Cover and infuse for 20 minutes. Bring to the boil and strain.
2. Melt the butter, draw aside and add the flour. Stir well and cook until dry and sandy.
3. Remove the saucepan to the side of the fire or to the table and allow to cool for a few minutes. Add the flavoured milk slowly, stirring all the time and making sure to blend out all the lumps.
4. Return to the fire and bring to the boil, stirring all the time. Boil for 5 minutes. Season with pepper and salt. Just before serving add cream. Do not re-boil.

THIN BROWN SAUCE

2 ozs. lean beef.
1 oz. chopped onion.
1 oz. chopped carrot.
¼ oz. margarine.
1 teasp. cornflour.

½ pint brown stock.
1 teasp. tomato purée.
Bouquet garni.
Salt and pepper.

1. Cut the meat in small pieces.
2. Melt the margarine, and when hot put in the meat. Fry quickly until well browned so that the juice will not run out of the meat. Add carrot and onion and fry until brown.
3. Add stock, bring to the boil, skim, add tomato purée, bouquet garni and seasoning. Simmer gently for about ½ hour.
4. Strain and return to the rinsed saucepan. Add the blended cornflour and boil for about 5 minutes until cooked. The sauce should be of the consistency of olive oil and should just mask the back of a spoon. Correct for colour and flavour.

SAUCES

ESPAGNOLE SAUCE

1 oz. fat.
1 oz. flour.
1 carrot.
1 small onion.
½ oz. bacon rind.
Bouquet garni.

1 teasp. tomato purée or 2 tomatoes.
A few mushroom stalks and skins
(if available).
½ pint brown stock.
Salt and pepper.

1. Chop the carrot and onion. Cut the bacon rind in small pieces.

2. Extract the fat from the bacon rind in a heavy saucepan, add the fat, put in the vegetables and fry until golden brown. Add the flour and cook slowly until it becomes sandy and light brown.

3. Add the tomato and cook for a few minutes. Work on the stock, bring to the boil, skim, add other ingredients and cook gently for about 30 minutes, skimming occasionally to remove fat. Replace liquid as it boils away.

4. Strain, correct for colour, consistency and flavour.

CHASSEUR SAUCE

½ pint Demi-Glace or
Espagnole Sauce.
2–3 ozs. mushrooms.
½ oz. butter.
1 large tomato.

1 teasp. chopped onion.
Salt and pepper.
1 teasp. lemon juice.
1 tablespoonful of wine.

1. Remove the stalks and skins from the mushrooms and slice them thinly. Remove the skin from the tomato, cut in two and scoop out the seeds. Chop the flesh roughly.

2. Melt the butter, add onion, mushrooms, tomato flesh, seasoning and lemon juice, cover with a round of greaseproof paper and a lid and cook gently for about 10 minutes.

3. Add the Demi-Glace or Espagnole sauce, boil up and cook for about 10 minutes. Add wine and correct for consistency and flavour.

MUSHROOM SAUCE

2 ozs. mushrooms.
½ oz. butter or margarine.
1 tablesp. white stock.

½ pint Béchamel Sauce.
1 teasp. lemon juice.
Salt and pepper.

1. Remove the stalks and skins from the mushrooms. Slice them thinly. Put them into a small saucepan with the butter, stock, lemon juice and seasoning. Cover and cook on top of the stove or in an oven for about 10 minutes.

2. Heat the Béchamel Sauce and add the mushrooms and cooking liquor to it. Correct for consistency and seasoning.

DEMI-GLACE SAUCE (Half-Glaze Sauce)

½ pint Espagnole Sauce.   1 teasp. tomato purée or 2 tomatoes.
1¼ pints brown stock.

Put the Espagnole Sauce and stock into a saucepan and bring to the boil. Skim and add the tomato. Boil gently until reduced to ½ pint, skimming constantly to remove fat which rises to the top. When the fat is discarded the sauce has a high gloss. Strain and use.

PIQUANTE SAUCE

1 oz. finely-chopped shallots.	1 oz. gherkins.
½ gill vinegar.	½ oz. capers.
½ gill wine.	½ teasp. chopped parsley.
½ pint Demi-Glace Sauce.	¼ teasp. chopped tarragon.

¼ teasp. chopped chervil.

1. Put the shallots, vinegar and wine into a heavy saucepan. Reduce to half. Add the Demi-Glace Sauce. Bring to the boil, skim and continue to boil gently for about 20 minutes.
2. Chop the gherkins and capers and add with the herbs to the sauce. Correct for flavour and serve with pork or meat which needs a " spicy " flavouring.

SAUCE DIABLE (Devil Sauce)

1 small shallot.	Salt.
4 peppercorns.	1 tablesp. brown vinegar.

½ pint Demi-Glace Sauce (page 122).

1. Chop the shallot finely. Crush the peppercorns and put with the vinegar and shallot into a small saucepan. Reduce until a teaspoonful remains.
2. Add the Demi-Glace Sauce and simmer gently for about 10 minutes. Strain and serve.

WHITE CHAUDFROID SAUCE

½ pint Chicken Velouté Sauce (page 124).	½ gill cream.
½ oz. gelatine.	Salt and pepper.

1. Soak leaf gelatine in a bowl of tepid water, leave until soft, squeeze out of the water when required. If using powdered gelatine mix with 3 tablespoonfuls of water, leave for a short time and use.
2. Heat the Velouté Sauce, add the gelatine and stir until dissolved. Correct seasoning.
3. Keep nearly half of the sauce warm in a bain-marie, allow the remainder to cool on ice, stirring well until it is sufficiently set to coat the back of the spoon.
4. Mix in the cream and use to coat as required, add some of the warm sauce when necessary to keep it at coating consistency.

SAUCES

BROWN CHAUDFROID SAUCE

1 pt. Thin Brown Sauce (p. 120) *or* 1 pt. Demi-Glace Sauce (p. 122).
1 oz. gelatine.   ½ glass sherry or Madeira.
Salt and pepper.

1. Soak leaf gelatine in a bowl of tepid water, leave until soft, squeeze out of the water when required. If using powdered gelatine mix with 3 tablespoonfuls of water, leave for a short time and use.
2. Heat the sauce, add the gelatine and stir until dissolved. Add the wine and correct seasoning.
3. Keep nearly half of the sauce warm in a bain-marie, allow the remainder to cool on ice, stirring well until it is sufficiently set to coat the back of the spoon.
4. Use to coat as required, adding some of the warm sauce when necessary to keep it at coating consistency.

RÉFORME SAUCE

Make as for Sauce Diable and add 1 teaspoonful of Red Currant Jelly. Serve with strawlike strips of cooked egg white, beetroot, ham, tongue and gherkin in the sauce.

CARDINAL SAUCE

½ pint Béchamel Sauce.   1 tablesp. cream.
¼ pint fish stock.   1 oz. Lobster Butter (page 37).

Add fish stock to the Béchamel Sauce, bring to the boil and cook until reduced by ¼ pint. Add the cream and Lobster Butter. Mix well but do not boil. Correct consistency and seasoning.

SHRIMP SAUCE

1 oz. butter or margarine.   Salt and pepper.
1 oz. flour.   ½ gill picked shrimps *or*
¾ pint milk.   1 small tin shrimps.

Make a sauce with the butter, flour and milk. Chop the shrimps and add to the sauce. Season, bring to the boil, and boil for 7 or 8 minutes.

SAUCE SUPRÊME

¾ pint Velouté Sauce (page 124).   1 yolk of egg.
1 tablespoonful white wine *or*   ½ oz. butter.
1 teaspoonful lemon juice.   1 tablespoonful cream.
Salt and pepper.

1. Add wine or lemon juice to the Velouté Sauce.
2. Cream the butter, add the yolk of egg and cream, mix well. Add a little sauce and then remainder until well mixed. Re-heat but do not allow to boil.
3. Correct seasoning and the consistency by adding a little stock or milk if necessary.

HOT TARTARE SAUCE

½ pint White Sauce (pouring)	Salt and pepper.
1 teasp. chopped parsley.	1 teasp. chopped gherkin.
1–2 yolks of eggs.	1 teasp. chopped capers.
1 tablesp. cream.	1 tablesp. lemon juice *or* white vinegar.

1. Beat the yolks with the cream and add the sauce carefully, taking care not to let the mixture curdle. Season.
2. Cook a little, stirring all the time. Do not boil. Mix in the parsley, gherkins, capers and lemon juice slowly.

VELOUTÉ SAUCE (Chicken, Veal or Fish)

1 oz. butter or margarine.	¾ pint chicken, veal or fish stock.
1 oz. flour.	½ oz. chopped onion.
Salt and pepper.	

1. Melt the butter, add the onion, cover with a round of greased paper and a lid and cook over a slow heat for about 5 minutes.
2. Add the flour and cook slowly until dry and sandy without colouring.
3. Add the stock, bring to the boil and skim. Boil gently for about 10-15 minutes.
4. Strain and add seasoning. Correct consistency and use as required.

CHOCOLATE SAUCE

½ pint milk.	½ oz. cocoa.
1½ teasps. cornflour.	2 ozs. sugar.
A little vanilla essence.	

1. Mix the cornflour and the cocoa together. Blend with a little of the milk, bring the remainder of the milk to the boil.
2. Add the blended cornflour and cocoa and boil for about 5 minutes, stirring all the time. Add the sugar and a little vanilla essence.

CHOCOLATE FOAM SAUCE

½ pint milk.	½ oz. sugar.
1 teasp. cornflour.	½ oz. chocolate powder.
1 egg.	1 teasp. rum.
Vanilla essence.	

1. Make as for Cornflour Custard, but use yolk of egg instead of whole egg.
2. Blend chocolate with 1 tablespoonful water. Heat until the chocolate is melted. Add to sauce with the sugar and vanilla essence and mix well. Add rum and mix in the stiffly-beaten white of egg.

124

SAUCES

GLOSSY HOT CHOCOLATE SAUCE

4 ozs. chocolate couverture.
2 ozs. sugar.
1 oz. butter.
½ gill water.
Vanilla essence.

1. Put the sugar and water into a saucepan, allow to dissolve over a slow heat. Bring to the boil and boil for 3 minutes.

3. Melt the chocolate in a saucepan in a bain-marie. Add the syrup slowly, stirring well. Add a few drops of vanilla essence and butter. Mix well.

SABAYON SAUCE

2 eggs.
2 ozs. icing sugar.
1 gill white wine *or*
½ gill sherry and ½ gill water.

Put eggs and sugar into a bowl and whip until creamy. Add wine and place the bowl into a saucepan of hot water. Whisk until the sauce is thick and frothy. Care must be taken to cook without overheating.

CARAMEL SAUCE

1 oz. sugar ⎫ Caramel.
2 tablesps. water ⎰
1½ gills of milk.
1 egg.
1 teasp. sugar.

1. Put sugar and water into a saucepan, and stir until the sugar is dissolved, bring to the boil, and boil until it turns a brown colour. Add 1 dessertspoonful hot water to stop further cooking.

2. Add milk, and mix well. Beat the egg and pour milk and caramel on to it taking care not to let it curdle. Cook in a bain-marie until it coats the back of the spoon. Add sugar and stir until dissolved.

WHIPPED BRANDY SAUCE

2 yolks of eggs.
1 oz. sugar.
½ gill water.
½ gill brandy.
½ gill cream.

Put yolks and sugar into a bowl and whip slightly. Add the other ingredients, whipping while doing so. Place the bowl over a saucepan of boiling water and whisk until thick and frothy. Serve at once.

HOLLANDAISE SAUCE

3 tablesps. water.
3 tablesps. white vinegar.
Salt and pepper.
1 egg or 2 yolks.
2 ozs. butter.

1. Put water and vinegar into a saucepan, reduce a little and cool slightly.

2. Beat the egg and pour this liquid on to it, taking care not to let it curdle. Add half of the butter cut into small pieces.

3. Stand bowl in a saucepan of boiling water, stir with a wooden spoon, and cook until the sauce is thick enough to coat the back of the spoon. Season, and add remainder of butter cut into small pieces, mix well.

SAUCE MOUSSELINE

Make Hollandaise Sauce and add 2 tablespoonfuls of half-whipped cream.

BÉARNAISE SAUCE

¼ teasp. finely-chopped shallots.	½ gill vinegar.
¼ oz. chopped tarragon stalks.	2-3 yolks of eggs.
¼ oz. chervil stalks.	3 ozs. butter.
4 peppercorns.	1 teasp. chopped chervil.
Cayenne pepper and salt.	1 teasp. chopped tarragon.

1. Put the shallots, chopped tarragon and chervil stalks, peppercorns, a pinch of salt and the vinegar into a heavy saucepan.

2. Reduce by two-thirds, remove from the heat and allow to cool a little. Beat the yolks of eggs and pour on the liquid slowly whisking well.

3. Stand the saucepan in hot water over a gentle heat and whisk in the butter in small pieces.

4. Rub the sauce through a tammy cloth or fine strainer, add chopped chervil and tarragon. Correct seasoning with a little cayenne pepper and salt.

MAYONNAISE

1 yolk of egg.	¼ teaspoonful made mustard.
Pinch of salt, sugar and pepper.	1 tablespoonful white vinegar.
	2 tablespoonfuls olive oil.

1. Put the yolk of egg into a bowl, add salt, sugar, mustard, pepper and 1 teaspoonful of the vinegar.

2. Warm the oil slightly by placing the bottle in hot water, then add it drop by drop to the yolk of egg, mixing well all the time. The sauce should become very thick as the yolk of egg absorbs the oil.

3. Thin down to required consistency with remainder of vinegar —if too sharp in flavour use tepid water or lemon juice. Half-whipped cream may also be added at the end to make it richer and smoother in texture.

SAUCES

RÉMOULADE SAUCE

¼ pint mayonnaise.
1 teasp. chopped gherkin.
1 teasp. chopped capers.
½ teasp. chopped parsley.
½ teasp. chopped tarragon.

Add chopped gherkin, capers, parsley and tarragon to the mayonnaise and mix well.

TARTARE SAUCE

¼ pt. mayonnaise. 1 teasp. chopped onion. 1 teasp. chopped chives.
Blanch the onion and add with the chives to the mayonnaise.

GINGER SYRUP SAUCE

¼ pint water.
3 ozs. sugar.
½ teasp. ground ginger.
2 or 3 strips of lemon rind.
2 tablesps. brandy.
1 tablesp. lemon juice.

Put the water, sugar, ground ginger and lemon rind into a saucepan. Allow the sugar to dissolve, then bring to the boil and simmer gently for about 15 minutes.

Strain, then return to the saucepan. Add brandy and lemon juice. Re-heat.

CRANBERRY SAUCE

1 lb. cranberries.
¼ lb. brown sugar.
½ pint water.

1. Pick over the cranberries, removing stalks, and wash them.

2. Put them into a saucepan with the water. Stew slowly until reduced to a pulp, pressing the fruit against sides of saucepan occasionally with the back of a wooden spoon to help to get the juice out.

3. Rub through a sieve and return to the saucepan, add sugar and allow it to dissolve. Re-heat thoroughly.

FRUIT SAUCE (for Game)

1 lb. red plums or damsons.
½ lb. brown sugar.
1-inch piece of cinnamon stick.
1 oz. butter
2 cloves.
1 glass port wine.
2 tablesps. red-currant jelly.

1. Wash the fruit, pick over and remove any stalks. Put into a saucepan with sugar, cloves and cinnamon. Stew slowly until reduced to a pulp.

2. Rub through a sieve and return to rinsed saucepan. Add red-currant jelly and port wine and bring to the boil. Draw the saucepan to the side of the fire, and mix in the butter in small pieces. Use either hot or cold.

FRUIT SAUCE

¼ lb. red plums or other fruit.	2 ozs. sugar.
½ pint water.	1 teasp. lemon juice.
1 dessertsp. arrowroot.	A few drops of carmine.

1. Stew the plums in a little water. Rub through a sieve.

2. Blend the arrowroot with a little water, heat remainder of water, and pour on to the blended arrowroot. Return to the saucepan, bring to the boil and stir until clear. Add the sugar and lemon juice.

3. Lastly add sieved plums and simmer all together for a few minutes. Add enough carmine to make a nice red colour. Serve either hot or cold.

ITALIAN MERINGUE SAUCE

¼ lb. sugar.	1 white of egg.
¼ gill cold water.	Carmine.
	1 tablesp. sherry.

1. Put the sugar and water into a saucepan, and stir until the sugar is dissolved. Bring to the boil and boil until the syrup forms a thread between finger and thumb. (215°F.)

2. Beat the white of egg stiffly and pour the syrup on to it, continue beating until thick and frothy. Add sherry. If liked, add a few drops of carmine to make a pale pink colour.

PEPPERMINT CREAM SAUCE

2 or 3 marshmallows.	1 egg white.
1 tablesp. sugar.	2 or 3 drops of peppermint
¼ gill water.	essence.

1. Put the sugar and water into a saucepan and stir until dissolved. Bring to the boil and add the marshmallows. Boil to a thread.

2. Beat the white of egg stiffly and pour the syrup on to it, whisk thoroughly until thick and foamy, add peppermint essence.

BLACK BUTTER

2 ozs. unsalted butter.	1 dessertsp. chopped parsley.
Pepper and salt	1 tablesp. lemon juice.

1. Melt the butter and allow to brown without burning. Cool a little. Add lemon juice, parsley, pepper and salt. Mix all well together and re-heat.

SAUCES

ANCHOVY BUTTER

4 or 5 anchovies.	Seasoning.
2 ozs. butter	A few drops of carmine

Pound the anchovies in a mortar or rub through a sieve. Cream butter and mix in anchovies and seasoning. Colour a light pink colour with a few drops of carmine. Set on ice or in a cool place until required.

NOTE.—Anchovy essence may be used instead of anchovies.

DEVIL BUTTER

2 ozs. butter.	Cayenne pepper.
¼ teasp. curry paste.	½ teasp. lemon juice.
	½ teasp. chutney.

Beat butter until creamy. Add all other ingredients and mix well. Rub through a sieve. Set on ice or in a cold place until required. Arrange in small pats.

BRANDY BUTTER

2 ozs. unsalted butter.	1 tablesp. brandy.
	4 ozs. castor or icing sugar.

1. Cream the butter in a bowl. Add sieved sugar to the butter and continue beating until white and creamy. Add brandy and beat until well mixed.

2. Set the sauce on ice or in a very cold place to harden. Pile up in a small fancy dish and sprinkle a little grated nutmeg on top, or make into flat pats and place on a lace d'oyley on a small plate.

BRANDY SAUCE

½ pint water.	2 ozs. butter.
¾ oz. cornflour.	1 oz. sugar.
	½ glass brandy.

1. Bring the water to the boil, add the cornflour blended with cold water. Boil for 5 minutes, stirring all the time.

2. Mix the butter and sugar together and stir into the sauce. Add the brandy, mix well and serve.

SAVOURIES AND SUPPER DISHES

SAVOURIES

Savouries are small well-flavoured dishes which may be used for the Savoury Course, for Buffets, and some for Hors d'Oeuvre. They are usually served on one of the following :—

CROÛTES—which are slices of fried bread or toast.

CANAPÉS—which are rounds or fancy shapes of thin toasted bread or small plain or savoury biscuits.

BRIDGE ROLLS—small bread rolls about 2½ inches in length.

CASSOLETTES—potato cases (see page 82).

CROUSTADES—bread cases. To make—cut slices of bread ¾-inch thick then cut into 1½-inch squares. Cut out the centres with a round cutter, leaving ¼ inch on the bottom and sides ; then soak the bread in beaten egg to which a little milk and seasoning have been added. Fry in smoking hot fat until golden brown in colour, and drain on kitchen paper.

PASTRY CASES—

(a) Puff Pastry Cases—called Bouchées—Make as for Vol au Vent Cases, using 2-inch cutter.

(b) Short or Cheese Pastry Cases—Line some flat patty tins or barquette moulds with the pastry and prick with a fork or skewer. Put some greased paper and beans in each to prevent the pastry from rising. Bake in a moderate oven for about 10 minutes, reduce the heat, remove beans and paper and put back into the oven for a short time to dry out the pastry.

(c) Choux Pastry Cases—Prepare in the same way as Eclair Cases, using a narrow pipe and cutting into 2-inch lengths.

Suggestions for Savoury Fillings.

Chicken, ham, lobster, crab, prawn, salmon, sardine, mushroom, tomato, egg, cheese.

ANCHOVY TWISTS

Cheese pastry.   Tin of anchovy fillets.
                Cayenne pepper.

1. Cut each anchovy fillet into 2 or 3 strips.

2. Roll out the pastry thinly and cut into strips about 3 inches in length and ½ inch in width. Place a strip of anchovy on top of each strip of pastry, and sprinkle with pepper.

3. Twist each strip, corkscrew fashion, place on a tin and bake in a hot oven until lightly browned.

4. Serve on a dish paper on a hot dish and garnish with parsley.

BEEF SNACKS

8 ozs. minced raw beef.   2 teasps. chopped gherkins.
2 ozs. breadcrumbs.   ½ gill cream or milk.
2 teasps. chopped capers.   Pepper and salt.
                3 slices of white bread.

To fry :—2 ozs. butter.
To garnish :—Parsley.

1. Mix the beef, breadcrumbs, capers, gherkins and cream together and season.

2. Cut the bread in fingers about 3 inches by 1 inch and fry on one side.

3. Pile the mixture on the fried side of the bread. Put back on the pan and fry the other side. Turn them over and fry the meat mixture until cooked and browned. Drain well.

4. Serve on a dish paper on a hot dish and garnish with parsley.

CHEESE AIGRETTES

1½ ozs. butter or margarine.   Cayenne pepper and salt.
1½ ozs. flour.   ½ teasp. made mustard.
¼ pint water.   1½ ozs. sieved hard cheese.
                2 eggs.

To fry :—Bath of fat.
To garnish :—Parsley.

1. Make a sauce with the butter, flour and water, and cook well. Cool, add the pepper, salt, mustard and cheese, and beat in the yolks of eggs. Beat the whites stiffly and fold through the mixture.

2. Drop small spoonfuls of the mixture into smoking hot fat and fry. Drain well. Serve on a dish paper on a hot dish. Garnish with parsley.

BENGAL SAVOURY

½ oz. butter or margarine.   1 teasp. lemon juice.
1 teasp. chutney.   1 oz. shredded almonds.
½ teasp. curry paste or powder. Salt.
1 egg.

To serve :—Small rounds of buttered toast.
To garnish :—Chilli rings. Parsley.

1. Melt the butter in a saucepan and add the chutney, curry, lemon juice, shredded almonds and salt. Mix and add the beaten egg. Stir over the heat until thick and creamy.
2. Pile on the toast and serve on a dish paper on a hot dish. Garnish with chilli rings and parsley.

CHEESE CHOUX

¼ pint water.   3 eggs.
2 ozs. butter or margarine.   2 ozs. sieved hard cheese.
4 ozs. flour.   ¼ teasp. made mustard.
Cayenne pepper and salt.

To fry :—Bath of fat.
To garnish :—Parsley.

1. Make Choux Pastry (page 155), and add the cheese, mustard and seasonings. Put into a forcing bag with a plain pipe.
2. Force into hot fat and cut off at 1-inch intervals. Fry until golden brown, lift out and drain well.
3. Serve on a dish paper on a hot dish and garnish with parsley.

CHEESE FINGERS

4 ozs. Rough Puff Pastry.
Filling :
2 ozs. sieved hard cheese.   Cayenne pepper and salt.
1 egg.

To garnish :—Parsley.

1. Roll out pastry into a square ¼-inch in thickness.
2. Mix the cheese and seasonings with the beaten egg, keeping a little cheese and egg for finishing. Spread the mixture on half the pastry, fold the other half over and press lightly together.
3. Brush over with beaten egg and sprinkle with the rest of the cheese. Cut into fingers and place on a tin. Bake in a fairly hot oven for about 25 minutes.
4. Serve on a dish paper on a hot dish and garnish with parsley.

CHEESE FLAN

4 ozs. Cheese Pastry.

Filling :

1 oz. butter **or** margarine.	2 ozs. sieved hard cheese.
1 oz. flour.	½ teasp. made mustard
½ pint milk.	Cayenne pepper and salt.

2 **eggs**.

To garnish :—Parsley.

1. Make a flan case with the pastry (page 33) and bake.
2. Make a sauce with the butter, flour and milk. Add the cheese (keeping back a little for sprinkling over), mustard and seasonings to the sauce, and beat in the egg yolks. Fold in the stiffly-beaten whites.
3. Pour the mixture into the flan case. Sprinkle cheese over the top and put into moderate oven until lightly browned.
4. Garnish with parsley and serve on a dish paper on a hot dish.

CHEESE PATTIES

3 ozs. Short Pastry.

Filling :

½ oz. butter **or** margarine.	1½ ozs. sieved hard cheese.
½ oz. flour.	½ teasp. made mustard.
¼ pint milk	Cayenne pepper and salt.

1 **egg**.

To garnish :—Parsley.

1. Line patty tins with the pastry.
2. Make a sauce with the butter, flour and milk. Add three-quarters of the cheese, mustard and seasonings and mix well. Mix in the beaten egg yolk and fold in the stiffly-beaten white.
3. Half-fill the lined patty tins with the mixture and sprinkle the rest of the cheese on top. Bake in a moderate oven 20-30 mins.
4. Serve on a dish paper on a hot dish and garnish with parsley.

CHEESE RAMEQUINS

1 oz. butter or margarine.	Cayenne pepper and salt.
1½ gills milk.	½ teasp. made mustard.
2 ozs. breadcrumbs.	2 ozs. sieved hard cheese.

1 **egg**.

To garnish :—Parsley.

1. Heat the butter and milk together and add the breadcrumbs. Leave aside until the breadcrumbs swell.
2. Add the seasonings, mustard and cheese, keeping back 1 teaspoonful of cheese for the top. Add the beaten egg yolk, and lastly fold in the stiffly-beaten white of egg.

3. Pour the mixture into greased ramequin cases. Sprinkle the remainder of the cheese on top. Bake in a moderate oven 15–20 minutes.

4. Serve the cases on a dish paper on a hot dish and garnish with parsley.

CHEESE SOUFFLÉ

2 ozs. butter or margarine.	3 eggs.
2 ozs. flour.	Salt.
½ pt. milk or tomato juice.	Cayenne pepper.
3–4 ozs. hard cheese (grated).	A little mustard.

1. Grease a fireproof dish with clarified fat.

2. Make a sauce with butter, flour and milk or tomato juice. Cool for 10 minutes.

3. Add the yolks of eggs one at a time, beat well. Mix in most of the cheese and seasonings.

4. Beat the whites of eggs stiffly, mix in one tablespoonful into the sauce, fold in the remainder, and half-fill the prepared dish with the mixture. Sprinkle the remainder of cheese on top.

5. Put the dish on a baking tin, place over a slow heat (with a gas stove use an asbestos mat) for about 10-15 minutes, until the bottom of the soufflé begins to set.

6. Place in a fairly moderate oven for about 40 minutes until well risen, browned and set. Serve immediately.

CHEESE COCKTAIL SAUSAGES

3 heaped tablesps. breadcrumbs	¼ teasp. mustard.
2 ozs. sieved hard cheese.	Cayenne pepper and salt.
1 tomato, *or*	1 oz. butter or margarine
1 teasp. tomato sauce.	½ egg

To coat :—Beaten egg and breadcrumbs
To fry :—Bath of fat.
To garnish :—Parsley.

1. Mix the breadcrumbs, cheese, skinned and chopped tomato, mustard, cayenne pepper and salt together. Add the melted butter and sufficient beaten egg to bind.

2. Turn on to a lightly-floured board, knead until smooth. Form into a roll, and divide equally into 16 pieces. Form each piece into a small sausage-shaped roll.

3. Coat with egg and crumbs, fry in smoking hot fat and drain well.

4. Put a cocktail stick into each sausage, and arrange on a dish paper, on a hot dish. Garnish with parsley.

CHICKEN LIVER SAVOURIES

4 chicken livers.	2 ozs. butter or margarine.
2 teasps. finely-chopped onion.	Cayenne pepper and salt.

To serve :—4 small rounds of toast or fried bread.

Chop the livers finely. Fry with the onion in hot butter until thoroughly cooked—about 3–4 minutes. Season, pile on toast. Serve on a dish paper on a hot dish.

EGG AND CUCUMBER SAVOURY

1 cucumber.

Filling :

2 eggs.	1 oz. sieved hard cheese.
2 tablesps. milk.	Pepper and salt.

1 oz. butter or margarine.

To garnish :—Cress or parsley.
To serve :—Tomato Sauce.

1. Cut the cucumber into six pieces 1½ inches in length. Peel and remove the centres with a cutter. Steam the cucumber until tender. Time—15–20 minutes.

2. Make scrambled egg mixture and mix in the cheese.

3. Arrange the pieces of cucumber on a hot dish, fill the centre of each with the mixture, piling it high in the centre. Pour Tomato Sauce around and garnish with cress.

PORTUGUESE EGGS

2 eggs.	Finely-chopped parsley.

To serve :—¼ pint Tomato Sauce

Grease two dariole moulds and line with parsley. Break an egg into each one. Stand in boiling water and poach until set. Turn out on to a hot dish and pour Tomato Sauce around.

CURRIED EGGS

1 oz. butter or margarine.	Pepper and salt.
1 teasp. curry powder.	½ onion (finely-chopped).
1 oz. flour.	½ apple (finely-chopped).
¾ pint stock or milk.	1 tomato or 1 teasp. tomato purée.
1 dessertsp. chutney.	4 hard-boiled eggs.

Border of rice :—6 ozs. boiled rice.

To garnish :—Paprika.   Parsley.

1. Melt the butter in a saucepan, add the onion and fry until golden brown.
2. Put in the flour and curry powder and cook all together for a few minutes. Remove from the heat and cool slightly.
3. Add the stock or milk gradually stirring all the time, bring to the boil and skim.
4. Add the chutney, apple, tomato and salt, cover and simmer for about ¾ hour, stirring frequently. Strain.
5. Remove the shells from the eggs and cut each in two. Add to the sauce and reheat for about 10 minutes.
6. Make a border of rice in a hot entrée dish. Put the eggs and sauce in the centre. Garnish with a little paprika and parsley.

CROUSTADES OF SMOKED HADDOCK

6 croustades (page 130).

Filling :

3 ozs. cooked smoked haddock.	Salt.
½ oz. butter or margarine.	Cayenne pepper.
1 tablesp. cream.	

Remove skin and bone from the fish, flake and add to the melted butter in a saucepan. Heat thoroughly. Season, add the cream and fill into the hot croustades. Serve on a dish paper on a hot dish and garnish with parsley.

CROÛTES IVANHOE

4 ozs. cooked smoked haddock.	Pepper and salt.
1 oz. butter or margarine.	1 egg.
1 teasp. chopped parsley.	1-2 tablesps. cream or milk.
1 teasp. lemon juice.	6 mushrooms.
6 rounds of buttered toast.	

To garnish :—Parsley.

1. Remove all skin and bone from fish. Flake and add it to the melted butter in a saucepan with the flavourings and seasonings.
2. Add the beaten egg, and enough cream to make the mixture soft. Stir over a gentle heat until thick and creamy.
3. Prepare the mushrooms and fry them in a little butter.
4. Pile mixture on the rounds of toast, put a mushroom on each, and garnish with parsley. Serve on a dish paper on a hot dish.

SALMON CASSEROLE

1 oz. butter or margarine.	6 cooked potatoes.
1 oz. flour.	¼ lb. cooked peas.
¾ pint milk.	1 lb. tin salmon.
Pepper and salt.	½ oz. sieved hard cheese.

1. Make a sauce with the butter, flour and milk, add seasoning.
2. Grease a fireproof dish, put in a layer of sliced potato, cover with the peas. Spread the flaked salmon over. Put the remainder of the sliced potatoes on top.
3. Pour in the sauce and sprinkle with the sieved cheese.
4. Bake in a moderate oven until piping hot and lightly browned.

HAM SCRAMBLE

1 egg.	1 teasp. chutney.
1 tablesp. milk.	Pepper.
½ oz. butter or margarine.	¼ teasp. made mustard.
¼ lb. chopped cooked ham.	6 squares of buttered toast.

To garnish :—Parsley.

Scramble the egg with the milk and butter. Add the ham, chutney, mustard, pepper, and mix together. Pile on top of the toast and garnish with parsley. Serve on a dish paper on a hot dish.

SPAGHETTI NIÇOISE

¼ lb. spaghetti.	1 oz. butter or margarine.
½ lb. tomatoes.	1 oz. finely-chopped onion.
Pepper and salt.	Clove of garlic.

To serve :—2 ozs. sieved hard cheese.
To garnish :—Parsley.

1. Cook the spaghetti in boiling salted water until tender—about 15 minutes.
2. Remove the eyes from the tomatoes, skin them, cut in two and remove the seeds. Cut the flesh into small pieces.
3. Melt the butter in a large saucepan, put in the onion, cover with a round of greased paper and a lid and cook slowly for about 5 minutes. Add the tomato and cook for a further 5 minutes. Season and add chopped garlic.
4. Drain the spaghetti and add to the tomato and onion mixture. Mix well, using two forks to avoid breaking the spaghetti.
5. Serve very hot in a heated entrée dish. Sprinkle with sieved cheese and garnish with parsley.

SPAGHETTI BOLOGNAISE

6 ozs. spaghetti.	Pepper and salt.
¼ lb. tomatoes.	Juice of ¼ lemon.
1 oz. butter or margarine.	3 ozs. chopped raw or cooked meat.
1 oz. finely-chopped onion.	⅛ pt. Thin Brown Sauce (page 120)

To serve :—2 ozs. sieved hard cheese.   Parsley.

1. Cook the spaghetti in boiling salted water until tender—about 15 minutes.

2. Remove the eyes from the tomatoes, skin them, cut in two and remove the seeds.   Cut the flesh into small pieces.

3. Melt the butter in a large saucepan, put in the onion. Cover with a round of greased paper and a lid and cook slowly for about 5 minutes.   Add the meat and fry quickly for about 3 minutes, then add tomato and cook for further few minutes.   Lastly add lemon juice, seasoning and sauce.   Cook for about 5–10 minutes with the lid on the saucepan.

4. Drain the spaghetti and add to the other ingredients.   Mix well, using two forks to avoid breaking the spaghetti.

5. Serve very hot in a heated entrée dish.
Sprinkle with sieved cheese and garnish with parsley.

GNOCCHI ROMAINE

1 pint milk.	Pepper and salt.
4 ozs. semolina.	1½ ozs. sieved hard cheese.
Pinch of nutmeg.	1 oz. butter or margarine.

1 yolk of egg.

To serve :—½ oz. sieved hard cheese.
To garnish :—Parsley.

1. Put the milk into a saucepan, bring to the boil, sprinkle in the semolina, stirring well.

2. Add nutmeg, pepper and salt, cover and cook gently for about 10–15 minutes.

3. Add cheese, butter and yolk of egg and mix well.   Cook on the side of the stove for a few minutes to cook the egg.

4. Grease a plate and spread out the mixture on it to about ½ inch in thickness.   Cover with a piece of buttered paper and leave until cold.

5. Cut into 12 triangles, or if liked use a fancy cutter.   Arrange neatly in a buttered fireproof dish, sprinkle with sieved cheese and reheat in a quick oven.   Serve garnished with parsley.

VEAL LIVER LYONNAISE

1 lb. veal liver.	Juice of ¼ lemon.
½ lb. onions.	½ pt. Thin Brown Sauce (page 120)
1 oz. butter or margarine.	Salt and pepper.

To fry :—Clarified fat.
To garnish :—Parsley.

1. Peel the onions and cut into shreds. Melt the butter in a heavy saucepan, put in the onions with seasoning. Cover with a round of greased paper and a lid and cook slowly until soft—about 20 minutes.

2. Cut the liver into $\frac{1}{2}$ inch slices. Pass through seasoned flour and fry in hot fat for about 2 minutes. Lift on to a hot dish and keep hot.

3. Pour any excess fat off pan, add onions and lemon juice. Cook for a few minutes and add the Thin Brown Sauce. Boil up and mask over the liver. Garnish with parsley.

KIPPER PUFFS

6 ozs. Rough Puff Pastry or Flaky Pastry.

2 kippered herrings.	$\frac{1}{2}$ gill milk.
$\frac{1}{2}$ oz. butter or margarine.	1 dessertsp. Tomato Sauce.
$\frac{1}{2}$ oz. flour.	1 teasp. Mushroom Ketchup.

Pepper and salt.

To glaze :—Beaten egg.
To garnish :—Parsley.

1. Cook the herrings, remove the bone and skin, flake the flesh finely with two forks.

2. Make a sauce with the butter, flour and milk. Add the herrings, tomato sauce, mushroom ketchup, salt and pepper.

3. Roll pastry into a thin oblong shape. Spread the mixture on one half, fold the other half over and press down lightly. Cut into fingers, brush over with beaten egg and bake in a hot oven for 20–25 minutes.

4. Serve on a dish paper on a hot dish and garnish with parsley.

HERRING ROE SAVOURY

$\frac{1}{4}$ lb. streaky rashers (cut thinly).	3 tomatoes.
4 herring roes.	Pepper and salt.

To coat :—Rich coating batter.
To fry :—Bath of fat.
To garnish :—Parsley and cut lemon.

1. Remove rind and bones from rashers and divide each in two.

2. Wash the roes in cold water and dry them.

3. Skin and slice the tomatoes.

4. Place a piece of roe on a slice of tomato, season, roll up in a half rasher, and continue until all are used up.

5. Dip each in batter and fry in smoking hot fat. Drain well. Serve on a dish paper on a hot dish and garnish with parsley and cut lemon.

KIPPER SAVOURY

Pastry cases :   4 ozs. Short Pastry.
Filling :
2 kippered herrings.   1 teasp. Tomato Sauce.
1 teasp. Mushroom Ketchup.   1 egg.
                      2 tablesps. milk.
To garnish :—Wafer paper.

1. Line some small boat-shaped tins with the pastry.
2. Cook, skin, bone, and flake the fish finely, add the ketchup, milk, tomato sauce and beaten yolk of egg and mix well. Fold in the stiffly-beaten white of egg and put into the cases.
3. Cook in a hot oven until lightly browned. Reduce heat and cook for 20 minutes.
4. Make sails out of wafer paper and garnish the savouries with them. Serve on a dish paper on a hot dish.

SAUSAGE AND HAM BARQUETTES

Cheese pastry (page 154).   Chopped cooked ham.
Sausage meat.   Mayonnaise.
              Chopped parsley.

1. Line some boat-shaped tins with the cheese pastry, half-fill them with sausage meat.
2. Bake in a moderate oven for about 20 minutes. Cool on a wire tray.
3. Mix the chopped ham with a little mayonnaise and put on top of the sausage meat. Garnish with chopped parsley.

MUSHROOM PATTIES

        5 ozs. Puff Pastry or Rough Puff Pastry.
Filling :
6 ozs. mushrooms.   ¼ pint milk.
½ oz. butter or margarine.   Pepper and salt.
½ oz. flour.   Pinch of nutmeg.

1. Make and bake puff patties as for Vol au Vent (page 112) using a 3-inch cutter.
2. Prepare mushrooms and cut in halves or quarters according to size. Stew them in the milk, remove the mushrooms. Cream the butter with the flour and add gradually to the milk, whisking while doing so. Boil up and return the mushrooms. Season and add the nutmeg.
3. Put a little of the mushroom mixture into each patty case and put on pastry lid. Serve hot.

MUSHROOM TOAST

4 ozs. mushrooms.	¼ pint milk.
½ oz. butter or margarine.	Pepper and salt.
¼ oz. flour.	Pinch of nutmeg.

To serve :—6 rounds of buttered toast.
To garnish :—Parsley.

1. Prepare the mushrooms and cut into small pieces.
2. Stew them in the milk, remove the mushrooms, cream **the** butter with the flour and add to the milk gradually, whisking while doing so. Boil up and return the mushrooms, season **and** add the nutmeg.
3. Serve on the toast and garnish with parsley.

GRILLED MUSHROOMS

½ lb. mushrooms.	Pepper.
Salt.	1 oz. melted butter.
1 teasp. lemon juice.	4 pieces of buttered toast.

To garnish :—Parsley.

1. Prepare mushrooms, place on a plate, sprinkle with salt, pepper and lemon juice. Pour melted butter over, leave to soak for a few minutes, basting well.
2. Put on to a hot greased griller and grill, turning when half cooked. Serve on rounds of hot buttered toast. Garnish with parsley. Serve on a dish paper on a hot dish.

STEWED MUSHROOMS

½ lb. mushrooms.	1 oz. butter.
Pepper.	¼ pint milk.
Salt.	½ oz. cornflour.
1 teasp. lemon juice.	1 tablesp. cream.

To garnish :—Parsley.

Prepare mushrooms. Sprinkle with salt, pepper and lemon juice. Melt butter in a saucepan, put in mushrooms and add the milk. Cook for about 15 minutes. Lift mushrooms on to a hot dish. Add blended cornflour to the milk, bring to the boil and boil for a few minutes. Add cream and mushrooms, reheat and serve in a hot entrée dish. Garnish with parsley.

STUFFED MUSHROOMS

8 large mushrooms.

Stuffing :

½ oz. butter.	½ oz. breadcrumbs.
½ oz. finely-chopped cooked ham.	Salt and pepper.
1 teasp. finely-chopped parsley.	¼ teasp. lemon juice.
½ oz. finely-chopped onion.	1 teasp. tomato sauce.
½ teasp. Worcester sauce.	

To serve :—8 rounds of buttered toast.
To garnish :—Parsley.

1. Prepare mushrooms, place on a greased tin—cup uppermost.
2. Melt butter, add chopped ham, parsley, onion, breadcrumbs, salt, pepper and lemon juice. Cook until piping hot, add tomato sauce and Worcester sauce. Mix well.
3. Pile into the mushroom cups. Cover with greased paper. Bake in a moderate oven for about 15 minutes.
4. Lift each mushroom on to a round of buttered toast. Serve on a plain dish paper on a hot dish, garnish with parsley.

DEVILLED MUSHROOMS

4 large mushrooms.	1 oz. boiled rice.
1 dessertsp. vinegar.	1 teasp. Worcester sauce.
1 dessertsp. water.	½ teasp. tomato ketchup.
1 oz. Devil Butter (page 128).	A few drops of lemon juice.

To serve :—4 small squares of buttered toast.
To garnish :—Parsley.

1. Prepare the mushrooms, removing the stalks. Place them on a small baking tin, cup side up, and pour vinegar and water over.
2. Divide the Devil Butter in four and put a piece into each mushroom. Bake in a fairly hot oven for 10 minutes.
3. Add the Worcester sauce, ketchup and lemon juice to the hot rice and mix.
4. Place a mushroom on each square of toast, and pile some of the rice mixture into each mushroom. Return to the oven for a few minutes.
5. Serve on a dish paper on a hot dish and garnish with parsley.

NUT CUTLETS

1 oz. butter or margarine.	3 ozs. brown breadcrumbs.
1 oz. flour.	1 dessertsp. Tomato Sauce.
¼ pint milk.	1 teasp. chutney.
3 ozs. mixed nuts.	Pepper and salt.
1 stick macaroni.	

To coat .—Beaten egg and breadcrumbs.
To fry :—Bath of fat.
To garnish :—Parsley.
To serve :—Tomato sauce.

142

1. Make a sauce with the butter, flour and milk. Add the chopped nuts, breadcrumbs, Tomato Sauce, chutney, pepper and salt. Mix well together.

2. Turn the mixture on to a wet plate, and smooth over with a wet knife, making the mixture about 1 inch in thickness. Leave it aside to become cold and firm, then cut into 8 triangular pieces.

3. Shape each piece like a cutlet on a lightly-floured board, coat with egg and breadcrumbs and put a piece of macaroni into the narrow end of each to represent bone of cutlet.

4. Fry in smoking hot fat until golden brown in colour. Drain well. Serve on a dish paper on a hot dish and garnish with parsley.

NUT SAUSAGES

1 oz. butter or margarine.	4 ozs. chopped mixed nuts.
1 oz. flour.	¼ teasp. mixed herbs.
¼ pint milk.	½ cooked onion (chopped).
2 ozs. white breadcrumbs.	Pepper and salt.
2 ozs. brown breadcrumbs.	1 egg.

To fry :—1 oz. butter.
To garnish :—Parsley.

1. Make a sauce with the butter, flour and milk.

2. Mix the breadcrumbs, nuts, herbs and onion together and season. Bind with the sauce and yolk of egg. Form into a roll on a lightly-floured board and divide into 12 equal pieces. Shape each piece like a sausage and coat with slightly-beaten white of egg.

3. Fry in sizzling hot butter. Drain, serve on a dish paper on a hot dish and garnish with parsley.

NUT SOUFFLÉ

1 oz. breadcrumbs.	1 teasp. finely-chopped parsley.
1½ gills milk.	½ stick of celery (finely-chopped).
3 ozs. finely-chopped nuts.	Pepper and salt.
	2 eggs.

1. Put the breadcrumbs and milk into a saucepan and heat until the breadcrumbs swell. Add the nuts (keeping a little for the top), parsley, celery, seasonings, yolks of eggs and mix well.

2. Beat the whites of eggs stiffly and fold them lightly through the mixture. Pour into a greased soufflé mould or fireproof dish and sprinkle the top with nuts.

3. Bake in a moderate oven until well risen and set. Time about 30 minutes. Serve immediately.

TOMATO OMELET

Omelet :

2 eggs.	1 teasp. chopped parsley.
Cayenne pepper.	1 tablesp. water or milk.
Salt.	½ oz. butter.

Filling :

2 tomatoes.	
½ teasp. chopped onion.	½ oz. butter.
Pinch of sugar.	Pepper.
	Salt.

To fry :—½ oz. butter.

1. Dip the tomatoes in boiling water, remove the skin and slice the tomatoes thinly. Cook gently with the onion in ½ oz. butter, add the sugar and seasoning. Mix and keep hot.

2. Make the omelet as for French Savoury Omelet, put the filling in the centre and fold over.

FRENCH SAVOURY OMELET

2 eggs	½ teasp. finely-chopped onion.
Pepper and salt.	1 tablesp. tepid water or milk.
1 teasp. finely-chopped parsley.	½ oz. butter.

To fry :—½ oz. butter.

1. Beat the eggs sufficiently to mix yolks and whites together, but do not beat to a froth.

2. Add the seasonings, flavourings and water and mix. Add ½ oz. butter cut into two or three pieces.

3. Heat the butter in a seasoned omelet pan. When sizzling, pour in the omelet mixture.

4. Using a knife, break the cooked surface in several places quickly, so that the liquid may run from the top to the bottom to cook, *or*, cook the mixture in layers by tilting the pan and folding over the layers of cooked mixture—the layers must be thin.

5. When the mixture is almost set, but still soft and creamy, turn each side of the omelet in towards the centre, fold in two, and turn on to a hot dish. Serve immediately.

KIDNEY OMELET

Omelet :

2 eggs.	Salt.
1 teasp. chopped parsley.	1 tablesp. water or milk.
Pepper.	½ oz. butter.

Filling :

1 mutton kidney.	
1 shallot.	½ oz. butter.
	Cayenne pepper.

Salt.

To fry :—½ oz. butter.

1. Prepare and chop the kidney and shallot and sauté in ½ oz. butter for about 10 minutes. Season.

2. Make the omelet as for French Savoury Omelet, put the filling in the centre and fold over.

MUSHROOM OMELET

Omelet :

2 eggs.	Salt.
Cayenne pepper.	1 tablesp. water or milk.
	½ oz. butter.

Filling :

2 ozs. mushrooms.	Salt and pepper.
½ oz. butter.	1 dessertsp. cream.

*To fry :—*½ oz. butter.

1. Prepare and chop the mushrooms and cook them in ½ oz. butter. Remove half of them, add cream, pepper and salt to the remainder and keep hot.
2. Prepare omelet and add half of the mushrooms to it. Cook as for French Savoury Omelet, put the creamed mushrooms in the centre and fold over.

CHEESE OMELET

2 eggs.	1 tablesp. sieved hard cheese.
Cayenne pepper.	1 tablesp. water or milk.
Salt.	½ oz. butter.

*To fry :—*½ oz. butter.

Make as for French Savoury Omelet, substituting cheese for the other flavourings.

HAM OMELET

2 eggs.	1½ ozs. chopped cooked ham.
Cayenne pepper.	1 tablesp. water or milk.
	½ oz. butter.

*To fry :—*½ oz. butter.

Make as for French Savoury Omelet, substituting ham for the other flavourings.

FISH OMELET

2 eggs.	1 teasp. chopped parsley.
Cayenne pepper.	1½ ozs. flaked cooked fish.
Salt.	1 tablesp. water or milk.
	½ oz. butter.

*To fry :—*½ oz. butter.

Make as for French Savoury Omelet, adding the prepared fish.

SARDINE SNACKS

3 ozs. Rough Puff Pastry.	1 small tin of sardines.

To coat :—Beaten egg and breadcrumbs.
To fry :—Bath of fat.
To garnish :—Parsley.

1. Roll pastry very thinly and evenly and cut into strips 3 inches in width.

2. Place a sardine on end of strip of pastry, damp the edges, double the pastry over and cut off. Press the edges together firmly. Repeat with the rest of the sardines.

3. Coat with beaten egg and breadcrumbs. Cook in hot fat and drain well.

4. Serve on a plain dish paper on a hot dish and garnish with parsley.

SALMON CROUSTADES

6 croustades (page 130).

Filling :

2 ozs. cooked salmon.	1 teasp. lemon juice.
½ oz. butter or margarine.	Pepper and salt.
Pinch of nutmeg.	1 tablesp. breadcrumbs.
1 teasp. chutney.	2 tablesps. milk.

To garnish :—Parsley.   Cut lemon.

1. Remove skin and bone from the fish and flake.

2. Melt the butter, add the fish, flavourings, seasonings, breadcrumbs and milk. Stir over the fire until very hot.

3. Pile into the hot croustades. Garnish with lemon and parsley. Serve on a dish paper on a hot dish.

VEGETABLE FLAN

4 ozs. Cheese Pastry. (page 154).

Filling :

1 oz. butter or margarine	1¼ ozs. sieved hard cheese.
1 oz. flour.	Pepper and salt.
½ pint milk.	½ lb. diced cooked vegetables (mixed).

To garnish :—Parsley.

1. Make and bake a small flan case with the pastry as on page 33.

2. Make a sauce with the butter, flour and milk. Add the cheese (keeping back a little), pepper, salt and vegetables. Reheat but do not boil.

3. Put into the flan case and sprinkle cheese on top. Brown under the griller or in the oven. Serve on a dish paper on a hot dish and garnish with parsley.

VEGETABLE SAUSAGES

2 tablesps. cooked peas.	2 tablesps. cooked beans.
2 tablesps. cooked carrot.	1 tablesp. mashed potatoes.
1 tablesp. cooked celery.	2 tablesps. chopped nuts.
4 tablesps. breadcrumbs.	½ egg.

Pepper and salt.

To coat :—Beaten egg and breadcrumbs.
To fry :—Bath of fat.
To garnish :—Parsley

Sieve all the vegetables. Mix with the other ingredients and bind with beaten egg. Finish as for Cheese Cocktail Sausages (page 134).

SALTED ALMONDS

¼ lb. whole almonds.	2 tablesps. salad oil.
	Fine salt.

1. Blanch the almonds and dry them.

2. Put the oil into a frying pan, heat it and fry almonds slowly until crisp and golden brown. Lift them on to a sheet of kitchen paper, and toss them in fine salt. Put on to a tin and dry off in a cool oven.

3. Leave until cold, and serve, or keep until required in a glass jar covered with a tightly-fitting lid.

PRINCESS SAVOURY

2 ozs. cooked chicken.	Pinch of nutmeg.
1 tablesp. white sauce.	Pepper and salt.
1 tablesp. thick cream.	

To serve :—6 cheese biscuits.
To garnish :—Tomato.

Mince the chicken and mix with the white sauce, nutmeg and seasonings. Sieve, add the cream and pipe on to the biscuits. Garnish with tomato and serve on a dish paper on a dish.

ANCHOVY SAVOURIES

Pastry :

3 ozs. flour.	1 teasp. anchovy essence.
Pepper and salt.	½ teasp. lemon juice.
1½ ozs. butter or margarine.	Cold water.
1 yolk of egg.	Carmine.

Anchovy Butter :

1 oz. butter	1 teasp. anchovy essence.
1 teasp. lemon juice.	

Anchovy fillets.

1. Sieve flour and seasonings, rub in the butter and mix to a stiff paste with yolk of egg, anchovy essence, lemon juice and water. Colour with a few drops of carmine.

2. Turn on to a floured board, knead lightly. Roll out, cut into fingers and place on a lightly-greased tin. Prick them well and bake in a hot oven for 12–15 minutes. Cool on a wire tray.

3. Cream the butter, add anchovy essence and lemon juice and mix well.

4. Place an anchovy fillet down centre of each strip of pastry and decorate with anchovy butter and parsley.

CHEESE BUTTERFLIES

4 ozs. Cheese Pastry. (page 154).

Filling :
½ gill cream.   Cayenne pepper.
½ oz. sieved cheese.   Salt.

To garnish :—Parsley.

1. Roll out the pastry to about ⅛-inch in thickness and stamp into rounds with a small fluted cutter. Prick well. Cut the trimmings into crescents (2 for each round).

2. Place on a lightly-greased tin. Bake in a moderate oven for about 10 minutes until a pale biscuit colour. Allow to cool.

3. Whip the cream, add the cayenne pepper and salt and fold in the cheese. Pile on top of the pastry.

4. Arrange the crescents on top to resemble a butterfly. Garnish with parsley. Serve on a dish paper on a dish.

CHEESE STRAWS

4 ozs. flour.   1 oz. sieved hard cheese.
Pinch of salt.   ¼ teasp. made mustard.
2 ozs. butter.   Beaten egg.
                    Cayenne pepper.
To garnish :—Parsley.

1. Sieve flour and salt into a bowl. Rub in the butter with the tips of the fingers. Add the cheese, mustard and pepper, and mix to a stiff paste with beaten egg. Turn on to a floured board, and knead lightly until smooth.

2. Roll out evenly to ¼-inch in thickness and cut into strips about 3 inches by ½ inch wide.

3. Place on a lightly-greased tin and bake in a moderate oven for about 10–15 minutes until a pale biscuit colour.

4. Arrange them on a dish paper on a dish and garnish with parsley.

SARDINE EGGS

3 hard-boiled eggs.   Mayonnaise or salad dressing.
6 or 8 sardines.   Pepper and salt.

To serve :—Lettuce leaves.

1. Cut the eggs in halves, remove the yolks, and cut a small piece from the bottom of each white to make it stand firmly. Notch the edge with a scissors.

2. Pound the yolk of egg, sardines, pepper and salt together. Mix with a little mayonnaise or salad dressing. Pipe into the egg whites. Serve on lettuce leaves.

STUFFED EGGS

2 hard-boiled eggs.	½ oz. sieved hard cheese.
Mayonnaise.	Pepper and salt.

To garnish :—Tomato.　　Parsley.　　Lettuce leaves.

1. Cut eggs in halves, remove the yolks, and cut a small slice from the bottom of each white to make it stand firmly. Notch the edges with a scissors.
2. Sieve the yolks of eggs, add the cheese and seasoning. Bind with a little mayonnaise or salad dressing.
3. Fill the centre of the egg-whites with the mixture, using a bag and pipe. Decorate with tomato and sprigs of parsley and place on lettuce leaves on a dish.

HAM EGGS

3 hard-boiled eggs.	1½ ozs. chopped cooked ham.
Mayonnaise or salad dressing.	Pepper.

To serve :—Lettuce leaves.

1. Cut eggs in halves, remove yolks, and cut a small slice from the bottom of each white to make it stand firmly. Notch the edges with a scissors.
2. Sieve the yolks of eggs, add the ham and pepper. Bind with a little mayonnaise or salad dressing.
3. Fill the centres of the egg-whites with the mixture and serve on lettuce leaves on a dish.

PYRAMIDS PARMESAN

4 ozs. Cheese Pastry (page 154).	3 tomatoes.

Cheese Cream :

¼ pint cream.	1 teasp. vinegar.
½ oz. grated Parmesan cheese.	Pepper and salt.

To garnish :—Finely-chopped parsley.

1. Roll out the pastry evenly and thinly. Cut into rounds, prick them with a fork and place on a lightly-greased tin. Bake in a moderate oven until pale fawn in colour, about 10 minutes. Allow to cool.
2. Skin the tomatoes and slice across. Place a slice on each cheese biscuit.
3. Whip the cream and fold in the sieved cheese. Add the vinegar and seasoning and pipe on top of the tomato. Garnish with parsley and serve on a dish paper on a dish.

FARCED OLIVES

6 queen olives.

Anchovy Cream :
¼ gill whipped cream.   ¼ teasp. anchovy essence.
Pepper and salt.

To serve :—Lettuce leaves.

Cut a small piece of the stalk end off the olive to make it stand evenly.   Remove the stone by peeling in a spiral fashion and keeping the knife close to the stone.   Put back into its original shape, fill with the Anchovy Cream.   Serve on a few lettuce leaves on a dish.

PRUNE SAVOURY

6 prunes.   2 tablesps. cream.
6 salted almonds (page 147).   Pepper and salt.
6 small cheese biscuits.

To garnish :—Cress.

1. Wash the prunes and soak for some hours, dry, slit along the sides and remove the stones.   Insert a salted almond into each prune.
2. Half-whip the cream, season and whip until stiff enough for piping.
3. Pipe a circle of cream around the edge of each biscuit. Place the prune in the centre and pipe the remainder of the cream on top of each prune.
4. Garnish with cress and serve on a dish paper on a dish.

SARDINES TARTARE

6 sardines.   6 fingers of toasted bread.
Tartare Sauce.

To garnish :—Strips of tomato.   Parsley.   Lettuce leaves.

Remove tails and skin from sardines, and place on the fingers of toast.   Coat with Tartare Sauce and garnish with strips of tomato and sprigs of parsley.   Serve on lettuce leaves on a dish.

SARDINE CROÛTES

6 sardines.   Pepper and salt.
Mayonnaise or salad dressing.   4 small rounds of toasted bread
1 hard-boiled egg.   ½ tomato (cut in four sections).
Finely-chopped parsley.

1. Remove tails and skin from sardines.   Mix sardines, yolk of hard-boiled egg and seasonings together.   Mix with a little mayonnaise or salad dressing and rub through a sieve.   Pipe on to the toast.
2. Decorate with chopped white of egg, pieces of tomato and parsley.   Serve on a dish paper on a dish.

SAVOURY CROUSTADES

6 large croustades (page 130).

Filling :
2 tomatoes.	1 egg.
1 oz. butter.	½ oz. breadcrumbs.
1 teasp. finely-chopped onion.	½ oz. sieved hard cheese.

Pepper and salt.

To garnish :—Parsley.

1. Skin the tomatoes and slice them. Melt the butter, add the tomatoes and onion and fry to a pulp.
2. Add the beaten egg, breadcrumbs, cheese and seasonings and stir until thick and creamy. Pile into the hollows in the croustades. Garnish with parsley and serve on a dish paper on a hot dish.

COLD STUFFED TOMATOES

6 tomatoes.

Filling :
Mixture of vegetables cut in small dice, *e.g.*, celery, cucumber, cooked carrot, cooked French beans, cooked green peas, cooked potatoes, etc.	Diced pineapple (if liked). Raw apple (shredded). Chopped nuts (if liked). Mayonnaise.

To serve :—Lettuce leaves.

1. Wash and dry the tomatoes. If large, cut in halves. If small, remove a cap from the round side. Scoop out the centres.
2. Mix the vegetables, pineapple, apple and nuts with the mayonnaise. Fill into the tomato cups. Serve on lettuce leaves.

WALNUT SAVOURY

Savoury biscuits.	Walnuts.
Cream cheese.	Savoury butter.

To garnish :—Cress.

Spread the biscuits with cream cheese. Place a walnut on each and pipe a little savoury butter on top of each walnut. Serve on a dish paper on an entrée dish and garnish.

Sandwiches

Sandwiches are provided for picnics, parties and journeys because they are easy to pack and are ready for use without further preparation. They should be neatly cut, garnished and served, having each variety labelled.

Preparation of Bread.

Use pan loaves one day old, they are best and most economical for making sandwiches. Spread the bread with creamed butter. Cut the slices evenly and thinly.

NOTE.—For large quantities it will be found economical to cream ½ lb. butter in a bowl and gradually work in ¼ pint tepid milk or White Sauce.

TO MAKE HAM SANDWICHES

Cooked ham, sliced thinly.	Creamed butter.
Bread.	Made mustard.

To garnish :—Parsley.

1. Mix a little mustard with the butter, spread on the bread and slice thinly.

2. Place a slice of ham on a slice of bread. Cover with a second slice of bread and press together.

3. When about six sandwiches are made, pile them one on top of the other, press well together, cut off the crusts with a sharp knife, cut the sandwiches into triangles, squares or fingers.

4. Serve on a plain dish paper and garnish with parsley.

NOTE.—It is often preferable to mince the ham as it is more economical ; and if liked, a ham paste may be made by mixing the minced ham with cold Béchamel Sauce.

SANDWICH FILLINGS

Beef.

Thinly sliced—roast beef, pressed beef or pressed spiced beef. Or minced beef mixed with horseradish sauce and cress.

Chicken.

Sliced or chopped chicken mixed with salt and pepper.

Chicken and Ham.

2 ozs. minced cooked chicken.	1 tablesp. Béchamel Sauce.
1 oz. minced cooked ham.	½ teasp. finely-chopped parsley
	Pepper.

Mix all the ingredients together.

Tongue.

Slice cooked tongue thinly.

Cheese.

Mix creamed cheese with chopped chives or watercress and season with cayenne pepper and salt, or mix with celery and nuts.

Cucumber.

Slice peeled cucumber thinly, then soak it in lemon juice or vinegar and seasonings for half an hour.

Tomato.

Peel, slice or chop the tomatoes and season. A little finely-chopped onion may be added if liked.

Tomato Mixture.

½ oz. butter or margarine.	4 tomatoes.
½ teasp. chopped onion.	Pepper and salt.
2 eggs.	

1. Heat the butter in a small saucepan. Add the onion. Cover with a round of greaseproof paper and a lid. Cook over a gentle heat for about 5 minutes.

2. Remove the paper, add the skinned, sliced tomatoes and seasoning. Cook until soft.

3. Add the beaten eggs and stir over a gentle heat until the mixture thickens. Leave to cool.

Lettuce and Cress.

Shred lettuce finely and chop cress, mix both, adding a little mayonnaise and season.

Sardines.

Sieve sardines, mix with mayonnaise or salad dressing.

Kippered Herrings.

Cook, bone, skin and flake a kippered herring, mix with mayonnaise, salad dressing or cold Béchamel Sauce.

Egg.

Hard-boil and chop egg. Mix with mayonnaise, salad dressing or cold Béchamel Sauce and seasoning. As a variation chopped cress or celery may be added.

Sweet Fillings.

Preserves, jam, honey and lemon curd are the usual kinds.

Date

Stone dates, chop and mix with chopped nuts. Use a brown loaf.

Apple.

Mix grated raw apple with finely-chopped nuts or grated chocolate. Use a brown loaf.

Banana.

Mashed bananas mixed with a little sugar. If liked, a little raspberry or strawberry jam may be added. Use a brown loaf.

To Pack Sandwiches.

Use Polythene containers or cover with a damp table napkin.

PASTRY

SUET PASTRY

6 ozs. flour.
2 ozs. beef suet.
½ teaspoonful baking powder.
Pinch of salt.
Cold water.

1. Sieve flour, salt and baking powder into a bowl. Add finely-chopped suet, mix well. Mix to a fairly stiff paste with cold water.

2. Turn out on to a lightly-floured board. Knead with the tips of the fingers until smooth. Roll into the required shape.

CHEESE PASTRY

4 ozs. flour.
2 ozs. butter or margarine.
A little salt.
1 oz. hard cheese.
1 yolk of egg.
A little water.
Pinch of cayenne pepper.

1. Sieve flour and salt into a bowl, rub in the butter. Put the cheese through a sieve. Add it with the pepper to the flour and butter, mix well.

2. Beat the yolk of egg with 1 tablespoonful cold water. Add this to the dry ingredients in the bowl and mix all to a stiff paste, using a little more water if necessary.

3. Turn out on to a lightly-floured board. Knead lightly until smooth. Roll into required shape.

ROUGH PUFF PASTRY

5 ozs. flour.
3 ozs. butter or margarine.
1 teasp. lemon juice.
Cold water.
Pinch of salt.

1. Sieve flour and salt into a bowl. Put in butter, cut into pieces about the size of a walnut, and mix well through the flour.

2. Mix to a paste with cold water and lemon juice. Turn out on to a lightly-floured board. Roll into a long strip with a floured rolling-pin.

3. Fold evenly in three and turn the fold to the left-hand side. Press edges of the pastry lightly with the rolling-pin.

4. Roll again into a long strip, fold and repeat four times. Leave the pastry in a cool place between rollings.

5. When rolling for the last time roll into required shape. Leave in a cool airy place until required.

PASTRY

HASTY PASTRY

5 ozs. flour.   3 ozs. butter or margarine.
Pinch of salt.   Cold water.
1 teasp. lemon juice.

1. Sieve flour and salt into a bowl. Put in the butter and cut into pieces about the size of a hazel nut.
2. Mix to a paste with water and lemon juice, turn out on to a floured board and knead lightly with the tips of the fingers.
3. Roll into a long strip, fold evenly in three.
4. Turn the fold to the left hand side and roll out again into a long strip. Fold each end to the centre and then fold in two. Roll into the required shape.

BISCUIT PASTRY

4 ozs. flour.   Pinch of salt.
2 ozs. butter or margarine.   Cold water.
1 oz. castor sugar.   1 yolk of egg.

1. Sieve flour and salt into a bowl. Rub in the butter with the tips of the fingers until the mixture looks like fine breadcrumbs. Add sugar to the flour and mix well.
2. Beat yolk of egg with a little cold water. Add to the dry ingredients and mix to a stiff dough with beaten yolk, adding a little more water if necessary.
3. Turn out on to a lightly-floured board. Knead with the tips of fingers until smooth. Roll into required shape.

CHOUX PASTRY

½ pint water.   4 ozs. flour.
2 ozs. butter.   3 eggs.

1. Put water and butter into a saucepan, bring to the boil.
2. Have the flour sieved on to a piece of paper. Draw the saucepan to side of fire. Toss all flour into the saucepan, mix together quickly with a wooden spoon. Beat until smooth.
3. Return to quick heat and cook for a few seconds until the mixture leaves the sides of the saucepan.
4. Remove to the table and drop in one egg. Beat until the mixture is of the same consistency as it was before adding the egg. Repeat with the other two eggs, beating well.

PUFF PASTRY

10 ozs. flour.   8 ozs. butter or pastry margarine.
Pinch of salt.   1 teasp. lemon juice.
Cold water.

1. Sieve the flour and salt into a bowl. Cut off about 2 ozs. of the butter and rub it into the flour with the tips of the fingers.
2. Mix to a fairly stiff paste with cold water and lemon juice. Turn on to a lightly-floured board and knead until pliable.

3. Cut a cross on top (*diagram a*). Open up cuts and pull out the corners. Cover with a cloth and leave in a cold place to relax for about 20 minutes.

4. Roll out the four corners until about quarter the thickness of the centre (*diagram b*).

5. Work the butter until of the same consistency as the dough, form it into a square and put in the centre of the dough (*diagram c*).

6. Fold the corners over the butter (*diagrams d* and *e*). Press into a square shape with the hand, leave to relax for about 15 minutes, then roll into a long strip.

7. Fold evenly in three (*diagram f*) and leave in a cold place for about ½ hour.

8. Turn the fold to the left-hand side, roll out again, fold each end to the centre (*diagram g*) and then fold in two.

9. Roll again into a long strip, fold evenly in three (diagram f). Wrap in greaseproof paper and a damp cloth, and leave until required for use.

10. Repeat Number 8 and roll out to the required thickness.

FLAKY PASTRY

4 ozs. flour.	1 teasp. lemon juice.
3 ozs. butter or margarine.	Cold water.
Pinch of salt.	

1. Sieve flour and salt into a bowl. Divide the butter into four portions, and rub one portion into the flour.

2. Mix to a stiff paste with cold water and lemon juice. Turn out on a lightly-floured board. Knead lightly with the tips of the fingers. Roll into a long strip.

3. With a sharp knife, spread one portion of butter in small flakes evenly over two-thirds of the pastry, and in even rows to within 1 inch from edge of pastry. Shake a little flour over this butter and then fold pastry evenly in three, first folding up the third without any butter, so that there is an alternate layer of butter and paste.

4. Turn the fold to the left-hand side. Roll out again and repeat with the other two portions of the butter. Roll into required shape.

RAISED PIE CRUST

½ lb. of flour.	¼ pt. water.
3 ozs. lard.	Salt and pepper.

1. Put the water and fat into a saucepan and bring slowly to the boil.

2. Sieve the flour and salt into a bowl. Make a well in the centre and pour in the water and fat. Mix well. Leave to rest until firm enough to knead.

3. Knead lightly and mould as required. If not used immediately keep in a warm place.

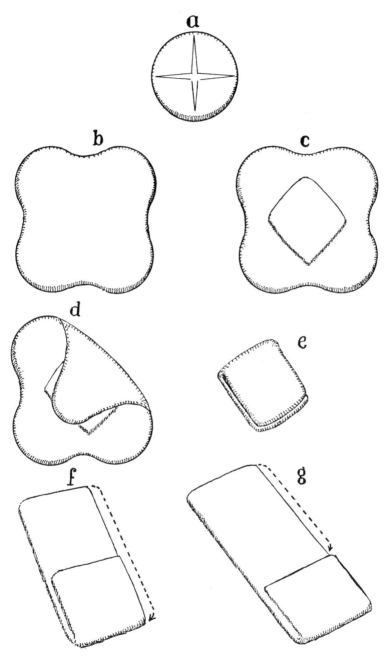

FANCY BREAD AND CAKES

CROISSANTS

½ lb. flour.
Pinch of salt.
¼ oz. yeast.

1 egg.
About ½ gill milk or water
2 ozs. butter or margarine.

1. Sieve the flour and salt into a bowl and leave in a warm place for a short time.

2. Cream the yeast with ½ teaspoonful sugar and 1 tablespoonful of tepid water. Make a well in the centre of the flour, pour in the creamed yeast, about two-thirds of the beaten egg and enough tepid milk or water to mix to a fairly loose dough.

3. Turn on to a very lightly floured board and knead until pliable, using as little flour as possible. Place in a floured bowl, cover with a damp cloth and leave in a warm place until it has doubled its size—about 1 hour.

4. Turn on to a lightly floured board and knead lightly for a few minutes to redistribute the yeast throughout the dough.

5. Roll into an oblong strip. Spread the softened butter over two-thirds of the dough.

6. Fold the dough evenly in three, first folding up the third without any butter, so that there is an alternate layer of butter and paste.

7. Turn the fold to the left-hand side. Roll into a long strip and fold again in three. Repeat this process once.

8. Roll into a strip about 8 inches wide and 12 inches long. Divide down the centre and cut across in three to make six 4-inch squares. Cut diagonally across each square.

9. Roll up each triangle, starting at the base and rolling towards the tip. Brush the tip with egg and seal in position. Form into crescent shapes and place on a greased tin.

10. Put to prove for about 15 minutes. Brush with beaten egg and put into a fairly hot oven. Time—about 25–30 minutes. Cool on a wire tray.

FANCY BREAD AND CAKES

AUSTRIAN BREAD

¾ lb. flour.	1 egg.
½ teasp. salt.	About ¼ pt. of milk.
2 ozs. butter or margarine.	3 or 4 ozs. prepared fruit.
1¼ ozs. castor sugar.	1½ ozs. chopped almonds
½ oz. yeast.	

To ice :—3 ozs. Glacé Icing (page 189).

1. Sieve the flour and salt into a bowl. Rub in the butter and add the sugar.

2. Cream the yeast with ½ teaspoonful of sugar and 1 tablespoonful of tepid water. Make a well in the centre of the flour, pour in the creamed yeast, beaten egg and enough tepid milk to mix to a fairly-loose dough. Knead until pliable.

3. Place in a floured bowl, cover with a damp cloth and leave in a warm place until it has doubled its size—about 1 hour.

4. Knead lightly for a few minutes to redistribute the yeast throughout the dough. Sprinkle in the chopped almonds and fruit, mixing them through the dough.

5. Divide in two and shape into rolls about 8 inches long. Place on a greased baking tin and put to prove for about 20 minutes.

6. Brush with beaten egg and bake in a fairly hot oven. Time— about ½ hour.

7. Lift on to a wire tray. When beginning to cool brush with thin Glacé Icing.

CHERRY LUNN

½ lb. flour.	¼ oz. yeast.
½ teasp. salt.	About ½ gill milk.
1½ ozs. butter or margarine	1 egg.
½ oz. castor sugar.	2–3 ozs. cherries.
Grated lemon rind.	4 strips of short pastry ¾″ × 5″.

1. Sieve the flour and salt into a bowl. Rub in the butter. Add sugar and lemon rind.

2. Cream the yeast with ½ teaspoonful of sugar and 1 tablespoonful of tepid water. Make a well in the centre of the flour, pour in the creamed yeast, beaten egg (keeping back a little for glazing), and enough tepid milk to mix to a fairly ⌐se dough. Knead well.

3. Cover with a damp cloth and leave in a warm place until it has doubled its size—about 1 hour.

4. Turn on to a lightly-floured board and knead lightly for a few minutes to redistribute the yeast throughout the dough. Knead in chopped cherries.

5. Form into a long narrow roll about 8 inches by 2 inches. Damp the strips of pastry and place, trelliswise, on top. Leave in a warm place to prove for about 20 minutes.

6. Brush over with beaten egg and place half a cherry in each diamond. Bake in a fairly hot oven. Time—about $\frac{1}{2}$ hour. Brush with syrup and return to the oven for 2 or 3 minutes. Cool on a wire tray.

SALLY LUNN

Make as for Cherry Lunn but omit cherries, forming into two round cakes. Omit pastry strips.

SWISS BREAD

$\frac{3}{4}$ lb. flour.	$\frac{1}{2}$ oz. yeast.
$\frac{1}{4}$ teasp. salt.	$1\frac{1}{2}$ ozs. castor sugar.
$1\frac{1}{2}$ gills tepid milk and water.	$1\frac{1}{4}$ ozs. butter or margarine.

1. Sieve the flour and salt into a bowl and leave in a warm place for a short time.

2. Cream the yeast with $\frac{1}{2}$ teaspoonful of sugar and 1 tablespoonful of tepid water. Make a well in the centre of the flour, pour in the creamed yeast and enough tepid milk and water to mix to a fairly-loose dough. Knead until pliable.

3. Place in a floured bowl, cover with a damp cloth and leave in a warm place until it has doubled its size—about 1 hour.

4. Knead in the sugar and melted butter, dipping the fingers in warm flour. Turn on to a floured board. Knead.

5. Roll out to $\frac{1}{4}$ inch in thickness. Cut into rounds with a floured cutter. Damp the edges and fold in two.

6. Prove for about 15 minutes on a greased baking tin.

7. Bake in a fairly hot oven. Time—about 25 minutes.

8. Dissolve 2 teaspoonfuls of sugar in 1 tablespoonful of water. Boil for 1 minute and brush over the bread.

ALMOND RINGS

8 ozs. flour.	$\frac{1}{4}$ teasp. salt.
2 ozs. butter or margarine.	$\frac{1}{4}$ oz. yeast.
1 oz. castor sugar.	Beaten egg.
About $\frac{3}{4}$ gill milk.	

Almond paste :

2 ozs. ground almonds.	2 teasps. lemon juice.
2 ozs. castor sugar.	A few drops of almond essence.
A little beaten egg.	

2 ozs. prepared sultanas.	1 oz. chopped peel.

Water icing :

2 ozs. icing sugar.	Boiling water.

1 oz. browned almonds.

1. Rub 1 oz. of butter into the flour, add sugar and salt.
2. Cream the yeast with ½ teaspoonful sugar and 1 table-spoonful of tepid water. Make a well in the centre of the flour, pour in the creamed yeast, a little more than half the beaten egg and sufficient tepid milk to mix to a loose dough. Knead.
3. Cover with a damp cloth and leave in a warm place until it has doubled its size—about 1 hour.
4. Turn on to a lightly-floured board and knead a little. Roll out into an oblong shape.
5. Spread the remainder of the butter over two-thirds of the dough. Fold the dough evenly in three, first folding up the third without any butter, so that there is an alternate layer of shortening and paste. Turn the fold to the left-hand side. Roll into a long strip and fold again in three. Repeat this process once.
6. Cut into two pieces. Roll each piece into an oblong strip about 14 ins. by 5 ins. Spread with soft almond paste and sprinkle the prepared fruit and chopped peel over. Roll up diagonally, starting at one corner.
7. Damp ends, form into a ring and press ends together.
8. Place on a warm greased baking sheet. Cover and leave in a warm place to prove for about ½ hour.
9. Bake in a fairly hot oven for about ½ hour. Cool on a wire tray.
10. Pour a little water icing over the top and sprinkle with chopped browned almonds.

BATH BUNS

1 lb. flour.	1½ gills tepid milk.
½ teasp. salt.	1½ ozs. castor sugar.
3 ozs. butter or margarine.	4 ozs. prepared sultanas.
¾ oz. yeast.	4 ozs. prepared chopped peel.
1–2 eggs.	Grated rind of 1 lemon.
A little coarse sugar.	

1. Sieve the flour and salt into a bowl. Rub in the butter.
2. Cream the yeast with ½ teaspoonful sugar and 1 table-spoonful tepid water. Make a well in the centre of the flour, pour in the creamed yeast, beaten egg (keeping back a little) and enough tepid milk to mix to a fairly-loose dough. Knead until pliable, place in a floured bowl.
3. Cover with a damp cloth and leave in a warm place until it has doubled its size—about 1 hour.
4. Add sugar, sultanas, peel and lemon rind. Mix well.
5. Turn on to a floured board, divide into buns and mould into rounds.
6. Place on a greased tin, cover and leave in a warm place to prove for about 15 minutes.
7. Brush over with beaten egg, sprinkle a little coarse sugar over.
8. Bake in a fairly hot oven for about 20 minutes.

NUT AND ORANGE LOAF

6 ozs. flour.	4 ozs. castor sugar.
½ teasp. salt.	3 ozs. candied orange peel.
8 ozs. wheaten meal.	2 ozs. chopped walnuts.
3 ozs. butter or margarine.	1 egg.
2 teasps. baking powder.	¾ pint milk.

1. Sieve flour and salt into a bowl. Add the wheaten meal. Rub the butter into the flour. Add baking powder, sugar, chopped orange peel, and walnuts. Mix well together.

2. Mix to a stiff batter with beaten egg and milk. Pour into a greased loaf tin.

3. Bake in a very moderate oven. Time—about 1 hour. Cool on a wire tray.

NUT AND FRUIT LOAF

1 lb. wheaten meal.	3 ozs. chopped walnuts.
½ teasp. salt.	3 ozs. prepared currants,
3 ozs. butter or margarine.	sultanas or dates.
2 teasps. baking powder.	2 eggs.
3 ozs. castor sugar.	About ½ pint milk.
2 ozs. flour.	

1. Make as for Nut and Orange Loaf, substituting fruit for orange peel.

2. Bake in a very moderate oven. Time—about 1 hour.

CHELSEA BUNS

12 ozs. flour.	2 ozs. castor sugar.
½ teasp. salt.	½ oz. yeast.
2 ozs. butter or margarine.	1 egg.
About ¼ pint tepid milk.	

Cinnamon Mixture :

2 ozs. butter or margarine.	2 ozs. brown sugar.
1 large teasp. ground cinnamon.	4 ozs. sultanas.

1. Sieve flour and salt into a bowl. Rub in the butter, add the sugar.

2. Cream the yeast with ½ teaspoonful of sugar and 1 tablespoonful of tepid water. Make a well in the centre of the flour, pour in the creamed yeast, beaten egg and sufficient tepid milk to mix to a fairly loose dough. Knead until pliable.

3. Place in a floured bowl, cover with a damp cloth and leave in a warm place until it has doubled its size—about 1 hour.

4. Turn on to a floured board and knead lightly for a few minutes to redistribute the yeast throughout the dough. Roll out into an oblong shape about ¼ inch in thickness.

5. Cream butter and sugar, add cinnamon and mix well. Spread this mixture over the dough, keeping back a little to rub

over the sides and bottom of a deep Yorkshire tin. Sprinkle with the prepared sultanas and roll up.

6. Cut into pieces ½ inch in thickness, place on tin, cut side up and side by side. Cover with a cloth and leave in a warm place to prove for about 20 minutes. Bake in a fairly hot oven for 25 minutes.

7. Turn out, divide into buns and cool on a wire tray.

MADEIRA CAKE

4 ozs. castor sugar.	2 eggs.
4 ozs. butter or margarine.	¼ teasp. baking powder.
5 ozs. flour.	Flavouring.
1 slice of citron peel.	

1. Put the butter and sugar into a bowl and beat until white and creamy.

2. Beat the eggs and flavouring and add gradually to the creamed butter and sugar. Beat well. If preferred the eggs may be broken and beaten into the mixture one at a time. A little sieved flour may be stirred into the mixture between each addition of egg.

3. Fold in the remainder of the sieved flour and baking powder, using a metal spoon.

4. Put into a greased and lined 7-inch round or 8-inch loaf tin. Bake in a very moderate oven. Time—about 1 hour. When the mixture is just set, place the slice of citron peel on top.

5. Turn out and cool on a wire tray.

MARBLE CAKE

4 ozs. butter or margarine.	½ teaspoonful baking powder.
4 ozs. castor sugar.	1 oz. chocolate powder.
2 eggs.	1 tablespoonful milk.
5 ozs. flour.	Pink colouring.
Vanilla, lemon and almond essence.	

1. Make as for Madeira Cake and divide the mixture into three parts.

2. Mix the chocolate powder with the milk and add with vanilla essence to one portion, add pink colouring and almond essence to another, and lemon essence to the third.

3. Put the mixture into a prepared 7-inch tin in dessert-spoonfuls, using a different colour each time.

4. Bake in a very moderate oven. Time—about 1 hour. Cool on a wire tray.

CHOCOLATE CAKE

4 ozs. butter or margarine.	1 egg.
6 ozs. castor sugar.	1 gill of buttermilk.
2 ozs. chocolate powder.	8 ozs. flour.
1 tablesp. water.	¼ teasp. bread soda.

¼ teasp. vanilla essence.

Icing :

1½ ozs. butter.	½ lb. icing sugar.
1¼ tablesps. water.	1 oz. chocolate powder.

¼ teasp. vanilla essence.

1. Cream the butter and sugar.

2. Blend the chocolate powder in the water, when cooled add to the creamed mixture and mix well.

3. Add the beaten egg and buttermilk, and sieved flour alternately, beating well after each addition.

4. Dissolve bread soda in a little buttermilk, add to the cake mixture with the vanilla essence and mix thoroughly.

5. Divide the mixture between two greased sandwich tins, and bake in a moderate oven for about 35 minutes.

6. Put the butter and water into a saucepan and heat until the butter is melted, add to the sieved icing sugar and chocolate powder. Flavour with vanilla essence and beat well.

7. When the cakes are cold spread each one with the icing and sandwich together. Spread the top with icing, smooth over and decorate or pipe it on, using a bag and small rose pipe.

GINGER CAKE

4 ozs. butter.	2 eggs.
4 ozs. sugar.	8 ozs. flour.
1 dessertsp. golden syrup.	2 ozs. preserved ginger.
1 tablesp. treacle.	½ teasp. ground ginger.

½ teasp. baking powder.

1. Cream butter and sugar. Add syrup and treacle, mix well. Drop in the eggs one at a time, beat well. Add a little sieved flour after beating in each egg. Add the remainder of the flour, mix well.

2. Add ginger cut in cubes, ground ginger and lastly baking powder. Mix thoroughly. Put into a greased 7-inch tin.

3. Bake in a very moderate oven. Time—about 1¼ hours. Cool on a wire tray.

VICTORIA SANDWICH

4 ozs. butter or margarine.	2 eggs.
4 ozs. castor sugar.	¼ teasp. baking powder.
4 ozs. flour.	¼ teasp. vanilla essence.

2 tablesps. jam.

Glacé Icing :— 4 ozs. icing sugar. Boiling water.

To decorate : Cherries and angelica.

1. Grease two 7-inch sandwich tins, dust them out with a mixture of equal quantities of castor sugar and flour.

2. Cream the butter, beat in the sugar and continue to beat until white and creamy.

3. Add the eggs one at a time, beating until the mixture thickens again before adding the second egg.

4. Mix in the sieved flour lightly, adding the baking powder with the last addition of flour. Add flavouring.

5. Divide the mixture between the tins and spread evenly. Bake in a fairly moderate oven for about 20 minutes.

6. Cool on a wire tray, spread them with jam while still warm, and put together.

7. Make Glacé Icing to the consistency of thick cream with a little boiling water and beat well. Spread the top of the cake with the icing and decorate with cherries and angelica.

RASPBERRY LAYER CAKE

4 ozs. butter or margarine.	6 ozs. flour.
6 ozs. castor sugar.	4 eggs.
¼ teaspoonful baking powder.	

Icing :

½ lb. sugar.	1 white of egg.
4 tablesps. water.	2 tablesps. of raspberry jam.

1. Make and bake as for Madeira Cake and leave on a wire tray to cool.

2. Dissolve the sugar for the icing in the water and boil for 1 minute. Whisk the white of egg until stiff, add the syrup slowly, whisking all the time. Continue to whisk over boiling water until white and very thick. Add the sieved jam and mix well.

3. Split the cake in two places, spread a little of the icing on each piece and sandwich together. Coat the cake with the remainder of the icing.

CHOCOLATE LAYER CAKE

4 ozs. butter or margarine.	2 ozs. chocolate powder *or*
4 ozs. castor sugar.	1 oz. cocoa.
2 eggs.	3 tablesps. milk.
5 ozs. flour.	¼ teasp. vanilla essence.
½ teasp. baking powder.	

Butter Filling :

4 ozs. icing sugar.	2 ozs. butter.
A few drops vanilla essence.	

Chocolate Icing :

2 ozs. chocolate powder	¼ teasp. vanilla essence.
2 tablesps. cold water.	8 ozs. icing sugar.
½ oz. butter.	Hot water.

To decorate :—Crystallized Violets.

1. Put the butter and sugar into a bowl and beat until white and creamy.

2. Beat the eggs and vanilla essence and add gradually to the creamed butter and sugar. Beat well. Stir in a little of the sieved flour between each addition of egg.

3. Blend the chocolate powder with the milk, if using cocoa add ½ oz. sugar. Stir over a gentle heat until dissolved. Cool and add to the mixture.

4. Fold in the remainder of the sieved flour and baking powder, using a metal spoon.

5. Put into a greased and lined 7-inch cake tin. Bake in a very moderate oven. Time—about 1 hour.

6. Cool on a wire tray. Split in two places. Spread with Butter Filling (page 188). Sandwich together again. Coat with Chocolate Icing (page 190) and decorate.

CHOCOLATE SANDWICH

6 ozs. butter or margarine.	3 ozs. chocolate powder.
6 ozs. castor sugar.	¾ gill milk.
3 eggs (separated).	7 ozs. flour.
½ teasp. baking powder.	

Filling :—1½ ozs. Butter Filling.

To ice :—½ lb. Chocolate Icing.

To decorate :—A few walnuts.

1. Cream the butter and sugar. Add yolks of eggs and beat for five minutes.

2. Blend the chocolate powder in the milk, add to the mixture and stir well. Add sieved flour and baking powder and mix well.

3. Fold in the stiffly-beaten whites of eggs and divide between two greased sandwich tins.

4. Bake in a moderate oven. Time—about 30 minutes. Cool on a wire tray.

5. When cold spread with butter filling and sandwich together. Ice with chocolate icing and decorate with walnuts.

NOTE.—1 oz. cocoa may be used instead of chocolate powder. Blend with the milk, add ½ oz. sugar and heat until the sugar is dissolved. Cool and add to the mixture.

COFFEE SANDWICH

6 ozs. butter or margarine.	1 tablesp. coffee essence.
6 ozs. castor sugar.	7 ozs. flour.
3 eggs (separated).	½ teasp. baking powder.

Filling :—1½ ozs. Butter Filling.
To ice :—½ lb. Coffee Icing.
To decorate :—Crystallized violets.

1. Make as for Chocolate Sandwich, using coffee essence instead of dissolved chocolate powder.

2. When cold spread with Butter Filling flavoured with coffee essence.

3. Make Glacé Icing, flavour with coffee essence and ice sandwich with it. Decorate.

PINEAPPLE CAKE

4 ozs. butter or margarine.	½ teasp. baking powder.
4 ozs. castor sugar.	½ teasp. pineapple essence.
6 ozs. flour.	3 eggs.
American Fondant Icing :	
½ lb. coarse sugar.	¼ teasp. pineapple essence.
1 white of egg.	4 tablesps. water.

To finish :—2 ozs. preserved pineapple.   2 glacé cherries.

1. Make mixture and bake as for Madeira Cake. Make American Fondant Icing as on page 190.

2. When the cake is cold, split, spread a little of the icing on each piece, sprinkle with some of the chopped pineapple and sandwich together.

3. Coat with the icing. Decorate with preserved pineapple and cherries.

SIMNEL CAKE

8 ozs. butter or margarine.	¼ teasp. spice.
8 ozs. castor or brown sugar.	½ teasp. grated lemon rind.
5 eggs.	1½ lbs. prepared mixed fruit
12 ozs. flour.	(sultanas, raisins, currants).
¼ teasp. baking powder.	½ teasp. almond essence.
12 ozs. almond paste (page 188).	

1. Cream the butter and sugar, add the beaten eggs, beating well between each addition. Fold in the sieved flour and baking powder, fruit, spice, lemon rind and flavouring. Put half the mixture into a prepared 9″ tin.

2. Roll ⅓ of the almond paste into a round shape a little smaller than the cake tin, place on top of the mixture and put in the remainder of the cake mixture.

3. Bake in a slow oven. Time—about 4 hours. Allow to cool, turn on to a wire tray.

4. When cold cover the top with almond icing. Brush lightly with beaten egg. Make small balls of almond paste and place around the top of the cake. Place on a flat tin. Put into a cool oven until lightly browned.

SLAB FRUIT CAKE

1 lb. butter.	1 lb. raisins.
1 lb. castor sugar.	1 lb. currants.
1½ lbs. flour.	1 lb. sultanas.
8 eggs.	½ lb. cherries.
½ teaspoonful baking powder	½ lb. mixed peel.

1. Make as for Madeira Cake. Add the prepared fruit and mix well.

167

2. Line an oblong cake tin about 12″ × 9″. Put in the mixture and bake in a slow oven for about 3½ hours.

3. Allow to cool in the tin, then turn out, wrap in greaseproof paper and keep for about a week before cutting.

RICH PORTER CAKE

½ lb. butter.
¾ lb. brown sugar.
1 lb. flour.
4 eggs.
About ¼ pint porter.
¼ teasp. bread soda.
1 lb. currants.
1 lb. sultanas.
¼ lb. chopped citron peel.
¼ teasp. grated nutmeg.
¼ teasp. mixed spice.
Grated rind 1 lemon.

1. Cream the butter and sugar, add the beaten eggs gradually, beating well. Stir in a little of the sieved flour between each addition.

2. Heat the porter a little, pour on to the bread soda and add to the mixture with the remainder of the flour.

3. Mix the prepared fruit, citron, spice, nutmeg and lemon rind together and stir into the mixture.

4. Put into a greased and lined 9-inch cake tin and bake in a slow oven for about 3½ hours. Allow to cool in the tin before turning out on to a wire tray.

PORTER CAKE

½ lb. currants.
½ lb. raisins.
4 ozs. peel.
½ lb. butter.
½ lb. brown sugar.
1 lb. flour.
3 eggs.
About ¾ gill of porter.
½ teasp. salt.
1 teasp. spice.
Grated rind of one lemon.
¼ teasp. bread soda.

1. Prepare all the fruit. Chop peel.

2. Cream butter and sugar. Add sieved flour and beaten eggs alternately until all the egg has been added, add porter and mix in the remainder of the flour.

3. Add the salt, spice, lemon rind, fruit and soda and mix well. Put into a greased and lined 9-inch cake tin.

4. Bake in a very moderate oven. Time—about 2 hours. Allow to cool in the tin. Turn on to a wire tray.

RUSSIAN LAYER CAKE OR CHAPEL WINDOW CAKE

6 ozs. butter or margarine.
6 ozs. castor sugar.
8 ozs. flour.
4 eggs.
½ teasp. baking powder.
1 oz. chocolate powder.
1 tablespoonful milk.
Pink colouring.
Lemon, vanilla and almond essence.

Jam.
6 ozs. Almond Paste.

1. Make as for Madeira Cake and divide the mixture into three parts.

2. Flavour one part with lemon essence, add pink colouring and almond essence to another and blended chocolate powder and vanilla essence to the third (1 dessertspoonful of coffee essence may be used instead of chocolate).

3. Cook in three prepared oblong tins, $7\frac{1}{2}$ by $4\frac{1}{2}$ ins., in a moderate oven. Time—about 20 minutes. When cold trim the edges and cut each cake in four. Brush over the sides with jam.

4. Put together so that the adjacent colours in each line across and down are different. Press well together. Trim edges if necessary. Brush over with jam.

5. Roll almond paste into an oblong $\frac{1}{4}$-inch in thickness. Wrap around the cake. Press edges together. Smooth the paste with a knife.

6. Mark the top into squares with a knife, pinch the edge. Dredge castor sugar over.

GÂTEAU MÉLANGE

1 Genoese Slab (page 172).	1 Marble Cake (page 163).
2 tablesps. sugar.	Juice $\frac{1}{2}$ lemon.
2 tablesps. water.	$\frac{1}{2}$ glass rum.

Raspberry jam.

Glacé Icing :

6 ozs. icing sugar.	Boiling water.
$\frac{1}{2}$ oz. chocolate powder.	Pink colouring.

1. Put the sugar and water into a saucepan, heat until the sugar is melted. Boil for a few minutes. Cool a little, add the lemon juice, rum and about 1 tablespoonful of jam.

2. Break the Marble Cake into small pieces, moisten with the syrup mixture.

3. Prepare a square or oblong tin by lining it with greaseproof paper.

4. Cut a piece of sponge slab to fit the tin, split it in two. Spread with jam and put one piece in the bottom of the tin. Pack the soaked marble cake into the tin and press into place.

5. Put the second piece of sponge cake on top, cover with a piece of paper and place a light weight on top. Leave for several hours to press the cake together.

6. Turn out the cake, coat the top with white Glacé Icing. Pipe lines of chocolate and pink icing about 1-inch apart and draw the point of a knife through the lines to give a marbled pattern.

NOTE.—Pieces of stale cake are sometimes used up as a filling in this cake.

MADELEINES

2 ozs. butter or margarine.	2 ozs. castor sugar.
2½ ozs. flour.	1 egg.
¼ teasp. baking powder.	Flavouring.

Apricot jam.	¼ gill whipped, flavoured and
Cherries and angelica.	sweetened cream.

1. Make as for Madeira Cake. Cook in greased patty tins, in a fairly hot oven. Time—about 15 minutes.
2. When cold remove the centres with a pointed knife. Put ½ teaspoonful of jam in the hole made, fill up with cream. Cut " cap " in two, and place on the cream, butterfly fashion. Decorate with a piece of cherry and angelica.

CARAMEL CAKE

5 ozs. butter or margarine.	2 ozs. cornflour.
5 ozs. castor sugar.	3 eggs.
8 ozs. flour.	2-3 tablesps. caramel (page 222).
	1 teasp. baking powder.

Icing :

2 ozs. butter.	1 tablesp. caramel.
5 ozs. icing sugar.	1 tablesp. cream.

To decorate :—Chopped browned almonds.

1. Cream the butter and sugar.
2. Sieve flour and cornflour, beat eggs, add each alternately to the creamed mixture, beating well after each addition. Mix caramel thoroughly through the mixture. Lastly add baking powder, mix well.
3. Put into a greased and lined 8-inch cake tin and bake in a fairly moderate oven. Time—about ¾ hour. Turn out cake and cool on a wire tray.
4. Cream butter, add icing sugar, beat until smooth and creamy, mix in caramel and cream.
5. When cake is cold, split and spread some of the icing over, put together again. Spread the remainder of the icing on top, sprinkle chopped browned almonds over.

LITTLE ORANGE CAKES

3 ozs. butter or margarine.	4 ozs. flour.
3 ozs. castor sugar.	Grated rind of ½ an orange.
2 eggs.	1 teasp. orange juice.
	¼ teasp. baking powder.

To ice :—4 ozs. Orange Glacé Icing (page 189).
To decorate :—Orange rind and angelica.

1. Cream the butter and sugar. Add beaten eggs and sieved flour alternately, beating well after each addition. Add orange rind and juice and lastly the baking powder. Mix thoroughly. Put spoonfuls of the mixture into small, flat, well-greased patty tins.

2. Bake in a fairly hot oven. Time—about 15 minutes. Cool on a wire tray.

3. When cold coat the top of each cake with a little orange icing. Decorate with orange rind and angelica.

LUNCHEON CAKE

$\frac{3}{4}$ lb. flour.	2 ozs. candied peel.
Pinch of salt.	2 ozs. cherries.
$\frac{1}{4}$ lb. butter or margarine.	Grated rind of $\frac{1}{2}$ lemon.
$\frac{1}{4}$ lb. castor sugar.	$\frac{1}{2}$ teasp. baking powder.
$\frac{1}{4}$ lb. sultanas.	2–3 eggs.

A little milk.

1. Sieve flour and salt into a bowl. Rub in butter until like fine breadcrumbs.

2. Add sugar, cleaned sultanas, chopped candied peel, cherries cut into quarters, grated lemon rind and baking powder. Mix all well together.

3. Beat eggs until light and frothy, pour into the centre of the dry ingredients. Mix to a stiff batter, using a little milk.

4. Line a loaf tin about 8 inches in length. Put in the mixture and bake in a very moderate oven. Time—about $1\frac{1}{2}$ hrs.

FLORENTINES

1 oz. butter or margarine.	2 ozs. flour.
2 ozs. brown sugar.	$\frac{1}{2}$ teasp. ground ginger.
2 ozs. golden syrup.	1 oz. chopped cherries.

1 oz. chopped almonds.

Wafer paper.

1. Put wafer paper, smooth side uppermost, on a baking tin.

2. Weigh the sugar, spread it out on the scales and weigh the golden syrup on to sugar. Pour off into a saucepan, add the butter and heat until melted, add the sieved flour and ground ginger. Mix well.

3. Put on the prepared tin in teaspoonfuls and cook in a very moderate oven for about 5 minutes.

4. Sprinkle cherries and almonds on top and bake until nicely browned—about 10 minutes. Allow to cool, then remove from tin and trim wafer paper.

BOILED FRUIT CAKE

1 lb. sultanas or raisins	½ teasp. ground cloves.
½ lb. butter.	½ teasp. grated nutmeg.
7 ozs. sugar.	¼ teasp. bread soda.
1 gill water.	⅛ teasp. salt.
10 ozs. flour	2 eggs.
½ teasp. mixed spice.	

1. Boil prepared fruit, butter, sugar and water together for 10 minutes. Stir well while cooling. Stir in the flour, spice, ground cloves, nutmeg, bread soda, salt and beaten eggs. Turn into a greased 7-inch square tin.

3. Bake in a very moderate oven. Time—about 1½ hours. Turn out and cool on a wire tray.

GENOESE SPONGE

4 eggs.	4 ozs. flour.
4 ozs. castor sugar.	¼ teasp. baking powder (if liked).
1½ ozs. butter.	

1. Grease a 7-inch square or 8-inch round cake tin and dust over with a mixture of castor sugar and flour.

2. Whip eggs slightly, sprinkle in the castor sugar, whisking all the time. Place the bowl over a saucepan of hot water and whisk until the mixture is thick and creamy and until it holds the imprint of the beater.

3. Remove and whisk for a few minutes until cool. Fold in the sieved flour, baking powder and lastly the tepid melted butter.

4. Pour into the prepared tin and bake in a fairly moderate oven for about 40 minutes. Cool on a wire tray.

GENOESE SLAB

Make as above. Bake in a lined Swiss Roll tin. Time—20-25 minutes.

ICED ORANGE CAKE

4 eggs.	4 ozs. castor sugar.
4 ozs. flour.	1½ ozs. butter (melted)
Rind of ½ orange.	¼ teasp. baking powder

Butter Icing :—2 ozs. butter. 4 ozs. icing sugar.
Orange juice.

Orange Glacé Icing :—½ lb. icing sugar.   Orange juice.
Yellow colouring.

To decorate :—Orange peel cut into fancy shapes. Angelica.

1. Make a Genoese Sponge (page 172), adding the grated orange rind. Bake in prepared tin in a fairly moderate oven for about 40 minutes. Cool on a wire tray.

2. Prepare Butter Icing, flavour with orange juice, split cake in two and spread with this icing. Sandwich together. Coat top with Orange Glacé Icing (page 189). Decorate with orange peel cut into fancy shapes and angelica.

ICED COFFEE CAKE

Make exactly as for Orange Cake, substituting 1 dessertsp. coffee essence for the grated orange rind in the cake, and 1 tablesp. of coffee essence for the orange juice in the filling.

CHOCOLATE GÂTEAU

Make a Genoese Sponge (page 172) flavoured with vanilla essence. Split in three, spread with Chocolate Butter Cream (page 188) and sandwich together again. Coat with Chocolate Icing (page 190) and decorate with crystallized violets.

CHOCOLATE ROLL

3 eggs.	1 dessertsp. cocoa *or* 1 tablesp.
3 ozs. castor sugar.	chocolate powder.
2 tablesps. warm water.	$\frac{1}{2}$ teasp. vanilla essence.
3 ozs. flour.	$\frac{1}{4}$ teasp. baking powder.

Filling :—Whipped, sweetened and flavoured cream or Butter Icing.

1. Whisk eggs and sugar for a few minutes, place over a saucepan of hot water. Add the water and continue to beat until the mixture is thick. Bring back to the table and beat until cool.
2. Sieve flour and mix with the cocoa or chocolate powder.
3. Add vanilla essence, flour and cocoa or chocolate powder and sieved baking powder to the whisked egg and sugar mixture. Fold lightly and carefully through. Pour into prepared Swiss roll tin.
4. Bake in a moderate oven for about 10 minutes.
5. Turn on to a sheet of kitchen paper which has been lightly dredged over with castor sugar. Roll up quickly and leave in the paper on a wire tray until it cools a little.
6. Remove paper and leave on wire tray until cold.
7. Unroll and fill with cream or Butter Icing. Roll up again, dredge a little castor sugar over.

FRENCH CREAM CAKE

4 eggs.	Flavouring.
4 ozs. castor sugar.	1$\frac{1}{2}$ ozs. butter (melted).
4 ozs. flour.	$\frac{1}{4}$ teasp. baking powder.

1–2 tablesps. sherry.	Apricot jam.

$\frac{1}{4}$ pint whipped, sweetened and flavoured cream.

To decorate :—Cherries and angelica.

1. Make Genoese Sponge as on page 172.
2. Bake in a greased square 7-inch cake tin in a fairly moderate oven for about 40 minutes.

3. Cool on a wire tray. When cold split in two.
4. Cut the centre out of the upper half with a large round cutter.
5. Sprinkle sherry over the cake, spread each piece with jam, and the lower piece with a little cream. Sandwich together.
6. Fill in the centre space with cream put through a bag and pipe.
7. Lay the cap on, allowing the cream to show. Decorate with cherries, angelica and roses of cream.

SPONGE CAKE

5 ozs. sugar.	3 eggs.
½ gill water.	4½ ozs. flour.
Flavouring.	

1. Prepare a 7-inch cake tin by greasing and then dusting with equal parts of flour and castor sugar. Beat eggs.
2. Put sugar and water into a saucepan, dissolve the sugar slowly, bring to the boil and boil for 3 minutes. While hot, but not boiling, pour over the beaten eggs whisking all the time, continue to whisk until the mixture is thick and creamy and holds the imprint of the whisk.
3. Add flavouring and fold in the sieved flour. Pour into the prepared tin.
4. Bake in a fairly moderate oven for 40 minutes. Turn out and cool on a wire tray.

PETITS GÂTEAUX

1 Genoese slab about 1 inch in thickness.

Filling :—3 ozs. Vanilla Butter Icing or jam.
To ice :—4 ozs. Glacé Icing. Carmine.
To decorate :—Glacé cherries, crystallized violets or rose leaves.

1. Split sponge, spread with filling and sandwich together.
2. Divide in two, ice one half with white glacé icing and the other half with pink glacé icing. Cut into fancy shapes and decorate.

PETITS FLEURS

1 Genoese slab about 1 inch in thickness.

To coat sides :—Apricot jam.
¼ lb. chopped browned almonds.

To decorate :— Apricot jam.   2 ozs. almond paste.
Chopped pistachio nuts.

1. Cut sponge into rounds with 2-inch cutter. Brush the edges with apricot jam, roll in the chopped almonds. Brush over the top with jam.

2. Colour half the almond paste pink and half green. Roll out very thinly, cut into small rounds.

3. Arrange the rings of almond paste around the edge of the cakes alternating the colours and overlapping them. Fill in the centre with chopped pistachio nuts.

WALNUT SANDWICH

4 ozs. butter or margarine.	3 eggs.
4 ozs. castor sugar.	1 oz. chopped walnuts.
6 ozs. flour.	Vanilla essence.
¼ teasp baking powder.	

Butter Filling :— 3 ozs. butter.   6 ozs. icing sugar.
A few drops vanilla essence.
To decorate :—2 ozs. chopped walnuts.

1. Cream the butter and sugar.

2. Add sieved flour and beaten eggs alternately, beating well after each addition. Add chopped walnuts. Flavour with vanilla essence, lastly add baking powder.

3. Put into 2 greased sandwich tins. Bake in a moderate oven—about 30 minutes. Turn on to a wire tray and leave aside until cold.

Filling.

1. Cream the butter, add sugar gradually beating well all the time. Beat until soft and creamy. Flavour with vanilla essence.

2. Spread each piece with filling and sandwich them together.

3. Spread the remainder of the filling over the top and sides of the sandwich. Coat all over with chopped walnuts. If liked, American Fondant Icing (page 190) decorated with whole walnuts, may be used instead of Butter Icing and chopped walnuts.

YULE LOG

3 eggs.	3 ozs. flour.
3 ozs. castor sugar.	¼ teasp. baking powder.
¼ teasp. vanilla essence.	

8 ozs. Chocolate Butter Icing (page 189).

To decorate :—1 robin ornament.   ½ oz. chopped pistachio nuts.

1. Beat the eggs and sugar until thick and creamy. Add flavouring.

2. Fold in the sieved flour and baking powder. Bake in a lined Swiss Roll tin in a fairly moderate oven. Time—10–15 minutes.

3. Turn on to sugared paper, roll up. When cold unroll and spread with Chocolate Butter Icing, re-roll.

175

4. Pipe Chocolate Butter Icing all over the log in straight lines. If liked spread the icing with a knife and mark in straight lines with a fork.

5. Sprinkle pistachio nuts on top. Take a hard lump of icing sugar, and sieve a little on to the log to represent snow. Perch robin on log.

MINCE PIES

Rough Puff, Flaky or Puff Pastry.

Mincemeat :

¼ lb. mixed peel.	¼ lb. brown sugar.
2 ozs. almonds.	1 teasp. mixed spice.
¼ lb. suet.	½ teasp. ground nutmeg.
½ lb. raisins.	1 orange.
¼ lb. sultanas.	1 lemon.
¼ lb. currants.	2 cooking apples.

½ glass whiskey.

To Glaze :—White of egg.   Castor sugar.

To Make Mincemeat.

1. Chop the peel, blanched almonds and suet very finely.

2. Stone and chop the raisins. Wash the sultanas and currants.

3. Mix the suet, sugar, almonds and spices together. Add the grated lemon and orange rind.

4. Peel the apples, chop and add to other ingredients. Add the fruit and strained juice of orange and lemon. Mix all thoroughly and leave until the next day.

5. Add whiskey and mix again, then pack into dry jars and cover as for Jam.

6. Store in a cool place and keep for at least a month before using.

To Make Mincepies.

1. Roll out pastry thinly. Stamp out into rounds the same size as patty tins. Lay all trimmings one on top of the other and roll out again. Stamp out into slightly larger rounds, and use these as far as possible for the bottoms of the pies.

2. Place the larger rounds in the tins. Put a large teaspoonful of the mincemeat in the centre of each round of pastry. Damp around the edges.

3. Cover with the smaller round of pastry, press the edges well together. Flake and decorate. Make a hole in top of each pie with a skewer.

4. Bake in a very hot oven for the first 8-10 minutes, then reduce the heat until the mincepies are cooked—about 35 minutes.

5. Beat the white of egg, and brush over the tops of the pies with it. Dredge with castor sugar. Return to a cool oven for about 5 minutes.

MERINGUES

2 whites of eggs. 4 ozs. castor sugar.

Filling :—Whipped, sweetened and flavoured cream.

1. Prepare the tin by rubbing over lightly with butter.

2. Beat the whites, sprinkle in half of the sugar and beat until the mixture stands in points at the end of the beater.

3. Fold in the remainder of the sugar.

4. Put the mixture into a forcing bag fitted with a plain pipe or rose pipe, and pipe in rounds or ovals as desired, or shape with 2 dessertspoons. Dredge with castor sugar.

5. Place in a cool oven and leave until dried out. Time— about 3 hours according to size.

6. Remove from the tin. Leave aside until cold. Fill with cream, putting 2 cases together. Serve on a d'oyley on a silver or glass dish.

NOTE.—Meringue cases may be stored in an airtight tin and kept for some time if required.

CHOCOLATE CRISPIES

1½ ozs. butter. 1 oz. chocolate powder.
1½ tablesps. water. ¼ teasp. vanilla essence.
½ lb. icing sugar. ½ pkt. rice crispies.

1. Put the butter and water into a saucepan and heat until the butter is melted, add to the sieved icing sugar and chocolate powder. Flavour with vanilla essence and beat well.

2. Mix in the rice crispies and put in spoonfuls into paper cases. This amount makes about twenty-four crispies.

NOTE.—A slab of chocolate may be put in a warm place until soft and mixed with some rice crispies instead of making the above mixture.

WELSH CHEESE CAKES

3 ozs. Short or Rough Puff Pastry.

Raspberry jam.

Filling :—2 ozs. butter or margarine. 1 egg.
2 ozs. castor sugar. About 1 tablesp. milk.
3 ozs. flour. ¼ teasp. baking powder.
Flavouring.

1. Make pastry, roll it out to ¼-inch in thickness. Cut into rounds about 3 inches in diameter. Line 9 greased patty tins with the rounds of pastry. Put a half-teaspoonful of jam in each.

2. Cream the butter and sugar. Add the sieved flour and beaten egg alternately, beating well after each addition.

3. Add the milk and flavouring, lastly stir in the baking powder. Half-fill the lined patty tins with this mixture. Cross two match-like strips of pastry on each cake.

4. Bake in a moderate oven for about 20 minutes. Cool on a wire tray.

ALMOND CHEESE CAKES

3 ozs. Rough Puff Pastry.

Filling :—1½ ozs. ground almonds.   1 oz. rice flour.
    3 ozs. castor sugar.   2 or 3 drops of almond essence
    2 whites of eggs.

Raspberry jam.

1. Prepare pastry and line 9 patty tins with it as for Welsh Cheese Cakes (page 177). Put a half-teaspoonful of jam in each.

2. Mix almonds, rice flour, sugar and flavouring together, and fold through the stiffly-beaten white of egg.

3. Put a teaspoonful of the filling on top of the jam.

4. Bake in a moderate oven for about 25 minutes. A few minutes before they are cooked brush over with heated jam. Cool on a wire tray.

MELTING MOMENTS

8 ozs. butter or margarine.   1 egg.
4 ozs. castor sugar.   ¼ teasp. vanilla essence.
6 ozs. flour.   Cornflakes.

1. Cream the butter and sugar. Add the egg and beat well. Mix in the flour and flavouring.

2. Crush the cornflakes, drop a small teaspoonful of the mixture into the flakes and coat the ball with them.

3. Place on a greased baking tin, well apart, and bake in a moderate oven for about 15 minutes. Leave to cool on the tin.

CHERRY TARTLETS

4 ozs. Biscuit Pastry (page 155)

Filling :—¼ oz. gelatine.   ½ tin cherries.
    Syrup from cherries.
To decorate :—¼ pint whipped, sweetened and flavoured cream.

1. Soak leaf gelatine in a bowl of tepid water, leave until soft, squeeze out of the water when required. If using powdered gelatine mix with 2 tablespoonfuls of water, leave for a short time and use.

2. Roll the pastry out thinly, cut into rounds about 3 inches in diameter. Line some greased tartlet tins with the pastry. Prick the bottom of the pastry with a fork, cover with a small

round of greased paper (greased side on the pastry) and place a crust of bread on the paper to prevent the pastry from rising in the centre.

3. Bake in a moderate oven until a biscuit colour, remove crust and paper and leave in the oven for a further 5 minutes to dry out. Cool on a wire tray.

4. Heat the syrup, add the gelatine, stir until dissolved. Leave in a cool place until beginning to set.

5. Cut the cherries in two and remove the stones. Fill each pastry case with the cherries and pour a little of the jelly over. Leave until set.

6. Decorate with roses of whipped, flavoured and sweetened cream.

FRUIT TARTLETS

Make as for Cherry Tartlets, using any fresh fruit. Mask the fruit with Jam Glaze (page 224) instead of jelly.

ECCLES CAKES

½ lb. Rough Puff Pastry.

Filling :

4 ozs. prepared currants.	1½ ozs. finely-chopped peel.
1½ ozs. butter (melted).	2 ozs. sugar.
½ teasp. mixed spice.	

1. Roll pastry out to ¼-inch in thickness, stamp into rounds with a 4-inch round cutter. Moisten the edges with water.

2. Mix the ingredients for the filling together and put a dessertspoonful of it in the centre of each round of pastry.

3. Gather up the edges over the filling and flatten the cake with the hand. Turn over and roll out lightly until the currants begin to show through.

4. Score twice each way with a knife, bake in a fairly hot oven for about 20 minutes. Brush over with slightly-beaten white of egg, dredge with castor sugar and return to the oven for 5 minutes. Cool on a wire tray.

APPLE CHEESE CAKES

3 ozs. Short, Biscuit or Rough Puff Pastry.

Filling :

½ lb. apples.	Sugar to taste.
1 tablesp. water.	A nut of butter.
4 cloves.	1 yolk of egg.

Meringue :—1 white of egg   2 ozs. castor sugar.

1. Line some patty tins with the pastry.

2. Peel, core and slice the apples. Stew with the water and cloves until soft. Add sugar and butter, allow to dissolve. Sieve and add beaten yolk of egg. Leave until cold.

3. Put a teaspoonful of mixture into each pastry case.

4. Bake in a moderate oven for about 20 minutes.

5. Beat white of egg stiffly, fold in the castor sugar.

6. Just before the cakes are cooked put one teaspoonful of meringue on top of each, put back into a cool oven until set and lightly browned. Cool on a wire tray.

CHOCOLATE ÉCLAIRS

½ pint Choux Pastry (page 155).

Filling :—Whipped, sweetened and flavoured cream.

Chocolate Icing :

1 oz. chocolate powder.	A few drops vanilla essence.
1 tablesp. cold water.	4 ozs. icing sugar.
¼ oz. butter.	Hot water.

1. Put Choux Pastry into a bag with a plain pipe. Force it out on to a greased and floured tin in strips 4 inches in length.

2. Bake in a moderate oven for about 40 minutes. Slit and put back into the oven for 5 minutes to dry out. Cool on a wire tray.

3. When quite cold split along one side and fill with prepared cream. Make the Chocolate Icing as on page 190. Spread a little on top of each éclair. Leave aside in a cool place to set.

CREAM BUNS

½ pint Choux Pastry (page 155).

Filling :—Whipped, flavoured and sweetened cream.
A little finely-sieved icing sugar.

1. Put Choux Pastry into a bag with a rose pipe. Force on to a greased and floured tin in medium-sized roses.

2. Bake in a moderate oven for about 40 minutes. Make a slit in the side and put back into the oven for 5 minutes to dry out. Cool on a wire tray.

3. Split half-way round. If there is a soft centre scoop out with the handle of a teaspoon. When cold fill with prepared cream. Dust a little icing sugar over the top of each bun.

GINGER CRISPIES

2 ozs. butter or margarine.	Pinch of bread soda.
4 ozs. flour.	½ egg.
¼ teasp. ground ginger.	1 teasp. treacle.
2 ozs. sugar.	1 dessertsp. milk.
A few whole almonds.	

1. Rub butter into the flour with the tips of the fingers. Add all the other dry ingredients and mix well. Moisten to the consistency of a stiff dough with beaten egg, treacle and a little milk.

2. Knead on a floured board, shape into balls about the size of a marble, place on a greased tin, put a split almond on each.

3. Bake in a fairly moderate oven till set and crisp. Cool on a wire tray.

COCONUT CONES

2 whites of eggs.	6 ozs. dessicated coconut.
4 ozs. castor sugar.	1 drop vanilla essence.

Wafer paper.

To decorate :—Cherries.

1. Whisk whites of eggs to a stiff froth. Sprinkle in half the sugar gradually, whisking all the time. Whisk until stiff and until it stands in points.

2. Fold in the remainder of the sugar, coconut and essence.

3. Pile on wafer paper, forming into cones, put half a cherry on top of each.

4. Bake in a slow oven $1\frac{1}{4}$–$1\frac{1}{2}$ hours until pale fawn in colour. Cool on a wire tray.

CREAM HORNS

6 ozs. Rough Puff Pastry

To frost :—White of egg and castor sugar.
Filling :—Apricot or raspberry jam.
　　　　Whipped, sweetened and flavoured cream.
To decorate :—A few cherries and strips of angelica.

1. Roll pastry out until about $\frac{1}{8}$-inch in thickness. Cut into strips $\frac{3}{4}$-inch in width and almost the length of the pastry board.

2. Damp the right-hand edge of each strip of pastry, roll strips around the cornet tins, covering about one-third of the previous strip each time, and starting at the point of the tin. Do not allow the pastry to turn to the inside of the tin at the top.

3. Bake in a hot oven for 10 minutes, reduce the heat and cook for a further 20–30 minutes.

4. Remove tins from the horns 10 minutes before the pastry is cooked. Brush the horns over with slightly-beaten white of egg, dredge with castor sugar and return to the oven for a few seconds.

5. Lift out on to a wire tray, when cold put 1 teaspoonful of jam in each, fill up with whipped cream forced through a bag and rose pipe. Decorate with pieces of cherries and angelica.

VIENNA CHOCOLATE FINGERS

2 ozs. butter or margarine.	2 drops vanilla essence.
$1\frac{1}{2}$ ozs. castor sugar.	4 ozs. flour.
A little beaten egg.	1 oz. chocolate powder.

1 tablesp. water.

Filling :

2 ozs. butter.	2 drops vanilla essence.
4 ozs. icing sugar.	$\frac{1}{2}$ oz. grated chocolate.

1 dessertsp. water.

1. Cream butter and sugar. Beat egg, add vanilla essence. Sieve flour.

2. Dissolve chocolate in the warm water, cool, add to the creamed mixture.

3. Stir in the flour, add sufficient beaten egg to mix to a very stiff consistency. Put through a bag and plain pipe on to a greased tin in fingers about 3 inches in length.

4. Cook in a very moderate oven for about 20 minutes. Cool on a wire tray. When cold put chocolate filling between each pair.

To Make Filling.

1. Cream butter, add sugar, beat until white and creamy.

2. Add vanilla essence and dissolved chocolate. Mix well.

ALMOND FINGERS

6 ozs. flour.	$\frac{1}{4}$ teasp. baking powder.
3 ozs. butter or margarine.	1 yolk of egg.
2 ozs. castor sugar.	About $\frac{1}{4}$ gill milk.

Apricot jam.

3 ozs. icing or castor sugar.   3 ozs. chopped almonds.
1 white of egg.

1. Sieve flour into a bowl. Rub in butter, add sugar and baking powder, mix well. Mix to a stiff dough with beaten egg yolk and milk.

2. Turn on to a floured board, knead lightly, roll out to $\frac{1}{4}$-inch in thickness. Line a greased Yorkshire tin with the pastry. Spread jam over.

3. Beat the white of egg stiffly and fold the icing sugar through it. Spread over the jam, sprinkle chopped almonds over.

4. Bake in a fairly moderate oven for about 30 minutes. Cut into fingers and cool on a wire tray.

ALMOND MACAROONS

6 ozs. castor sugar.	$\frac{1}{4}$ teasp. lemon juice.
4 ozs. ground almonds.	2 egg whites.
1 oz. rice flour.	$\frac{1}{2}$ oz. whole almonds.

Wafer paper.

1. Mix the sugar, ground almonds, rice flour and lemon juice together.

2. Beat the whites of eggs. Add dry ingredients to them and mix well together. Put into a bag with a plain pipe. Pipe on to wafer paper on a flat tin. Each macaroon should be the size of a penny.

3. Place a split almond on the centre of each macaroon.

4. Bake in a fairly moderate oven, reducing the heat after the first ten minutes. Cook for about 30 minutes. Cool on a wire tray.

3. When firm, break away wafer paper even with the macaroons.

SHREWSBURY BISCUITS

2 ozs. butter or margarine.	Grated rind of ½ lemon, *or*
2 ozs. castor sugar.	½ teasp. vanilla essence.
A little beaten egg.	4 ozs. flour.

1. Cream butter and sugar. Beat egg and add flavouring. Add sieved flour and beaten egg alternately, beating well after each addition. Mix to a stiff paste.
2. Turn on to a floured board and roll out to ¼-inch thickness. Stamp into biscuits with a fluted cutter. Place on a greased tin.
3. Bake in a very moderate oven for about 15 minutes until a pale biscuit colour.

ESS BISCUITS

8 ozs. butter or margarine.	9 ozs. flour.
4 ozs. castor sugar.	Almond essence.
1 egg.	Cherries and angelica.
2 ozs. ground almonds, if liked.	

1. Cream the butter and sugar, add the beaten egg (keeping back a little) and essence and beat well. Mix in the ground almonds and lastly the sieved flour.
2. Put the mixture into a forcing bag with a large rose pipe. Pipe on to a greased baking tin in strips about 3 inches in length.
3. Brush over with beaten egg and decorate with pieces of cherries and angelica.
4. Bake in a fairly moderate oven for about 15 minutes.

SHORTBREAD BISCUITS

4 ozs. butter or margarine.	5½ ozs. flour.
3 ozs. castor sugar.	1¼ ozs. semolina.

1. Cream the butter and sugar, work in the flour and semolina and knead well.
2. Roll out on a floured board to ¼-inch in thickness. Cut into biscuits, lift on to a greased baking sheet and prick well.
3. Bake in a very moderate oven for about 15 mins. Leave to cool on the baking sheet.

ALMOND SLICES

3 ozs. ground almonds.	Juice of ½ a lemon.
3 ozs. castor sugar.	1 egg.
2 ozs. cake crumbs.	Jam.

To ice :—Water icing.

1. Mix almonds, sugar and cake crumbs together in a clean bowl. Add lemon juice and sufficient beaten egg to mix to a fairly stiff dough.

2. Turn on to a lightly-floured board and knead until free from cracks. Roll out into a strip about 5 inches in width. Cut into two equal pieces.

3. Spread one piece with jam and place the other piece on top. Cut into fingers 1 inch in width, lift on to a greased tin.

4. Bake in a very moderate oven for about 20 minutes. Cool on a wire tray.

5. When cold coat the top of each with a little Water Icing.

ALMOND CRESCENTS

4 ozs. flour.	1 oz. castor sugar.
2 ozs. butter or margarine.	2 yolks of eggs.
1 drop of almond essence.	

Almond mixture :

2 whites of eggs.	1 teasp. rice flour.
3 ozs. castor sugar.	2 ozs. ground almonds.

To decorate :—Chopped almonds.   Cherries.

1. Sieve flour into a bowl. Cut in butter and rub in with the tips of the fingers. Add sugar.

2. Beat yolks of eggs and add flavouring to them. Mix the dry ingredients to a stiff dough with the yolks.

3. Turn on to a lightly-floured board and roll out to $\frac{1}{4}$-inch in thickness. Stamp into crescents with a fluted cutter.

4. Beat the whites of eggs, mix in the dry ingredients for the almond mixture. Put a spoonful on top of each crescent, sprinkle with chopped almonds and decorate with half a cherry.

5. Place on a greased tin and bake in a very moderate oven for about 15 minutes. Cool on a wire tray.

BRANDY SNAPS

2 ozs. butter or margarine.	2 ozs. flour.
2 ozs. demerara sugar.	$\frac{1}{2}$ teasp. ground ginger.
2 ozs. golden syrup.	$\frac{1}{2}$ teasp. lemon juice.

Filling :—Whipped, sweetened and flavoured cream.

1. Weigh the sugar, spread it out on the scales and weigh the golden syrup on to sugar. Pour off into a saucepan, add the butter and heat until melted.

2. Add sieved flour, ginger and lemon juice, stirring well all the time. Beat well for a few minutes.

3. Put in small teaspoonfuls on a greased tin about 3 ins. apart.

4. Cook in a very moderate oven for about 10 minutes. Allow to cool slightly and roll round the handle of an oiled wooden spoon.

5. When cold, fill centres with whipped cream flavoured with brandy.

FANCY BREAD AND CAKES
GINGER NUTS

6 ozs. flour.	1 teasp. ground ginger.
Pinch of salt.	¼ teasp. ground cloves.
2 ozs. butter or margarine	1 tablesp. treacle.
2 ozs. castor sugar.	1 egg.

1. Sieve flour and salt into a bowl. Rub in the butter, add sugar, ground ginger and ground cloves and mix well.
2. Heat treacle and mix with the beaten egg. Add to the dry ingredients, mix thoroughly.
3. Form into small balls of a uniform size.
4. Place on a greased tin, bake in a very moderate oven for about 20 minutes.

SPONGE FINGER BISCUITS

2 eggs.	2 ozs. flour.	1¾ ozs. sugar.

1. Separate yolks from whites of eggs. Cream yolks thoroughly with the sugar, add flour, mix well and fold in the stiffly-whisked whites of eggs.
2. Put the mixture into a bag with a plain ½-inch pipe. Pipe in finger lengths on to a greased and floured tin, dredge with castor sugar and shake off what does not adhere to the biscuits.
3. Bake in a fairly moderate oven until golden brown and crisp.

BELFORDS

6 ozs. flour.	2 ozs. castor sugar.
3 ozs. butter or margarine.	½–1 egg.
	Flavouring.

Jam.

To ice :—¼ lb. Glacé Icing.
To decorate :—Violets or Cherries.

1. Sieve flour into a bowl. Rub in the butter, add sugar, mix well. Beat egg, add flavouring. Mix dry ingredients to a stiff dough with beaten egg.
2. Turn on to a floured board and roll out to ¼-inch in thickness.
3. Cut into biscuits with a fluted cutter and place on greased tin.
4. Bake in a very moderate oven, 15–20 minutes. Cool on a wire tray.
5. When cold put two together with jam. Coat with a little Glacé Icing. Decorate with a piece of cherry or a violet.

GERMAN SLICES

½ lb. flour.	3 ozs. castor sugar.
¼ lb. butter or margarine.	2 yolks of eggs.

Vanilla essence.

Filling:

2 whites of eggs.	4 ozs. castor sugar.
4 ozs. ground almonds.	Vanilla essence.

1. Sieve flour into a bowl. Rub in the butter, and add sugar.
2. Drop in yolks and vanilla essence and mix well together.
3. Turn on to a floured board and knead lightly until smooth. Divide in two, and roll out into strips about 3 inches by about 11 inches. Place on a greased tin.
4. Beat the whites of eggs stiffly and fold in the almonds, castor sugar and essence. Spread on the pastry. Bake in a fairly moderate oven for 30 minutes. Cool slightly on tin, slice and cool on a wire tray.

WEDDING CAKE

Lowest tier:

1¾ lbs. raisins.	½ teasp. ground nutmeg.
1¾ lbs. sultanas.	½ teasp. mixed spice.
1¾ lbs. currants.	Grated rind of 1 lemon.
¾ lb. mixed peel.	1¼ lbs. butter.
¾ lb. cherries.	1¼ lbs. brown or castor sugar
1 apple.	13 eggs.
4 ozs. chopped almonds.	1½ lbs. flour.
4 ozs. ground almonds.	3 glasses of whiskey or rum.

Almond Paste:	1½ lbs.	(page 188).
Water Icing:	1 lb.	(page 189).
Royal Icing:	3 lbs.	(page 190).

Middle tier:

12 ozs. raisins.	¼ teasp. nutmeg.
12 ozs. sultanas.	¼ teasp. mixed spice.
12 ozs. currants.	Grated rind of ½ lemon.
4 ozs. mixed peel.	8 ozs. butter.
4 ozs. cherries.	8 ozs. brown or castor sugar.
½ apple.	6 eggs.
2 ozs. chopped almonds.	10 ozs. flour.
2 ozs. ground almonds.	2 glasses of whiskey or rum.

Almond Paste:	1 lb.	(page 188).
Water Icing:	½ lb.	(page 189).
Royal Icing:	2 lbs.	(page 190).

Top tier :

6 ozs. raisins.
6 ozs. sultanas.
6 ozs. currants.
2 ozs. mixed peel.
2 ozs. cherries.
½ apple.
1 oz. chopped almonds.
1 oz. ground almonds.

¼ teasp. nutmeg.
¼ teasp. mixed spice.
Grated rind of ¼ lemon.
4 ozs. butter.
4 ozs. brown or castor sugar.
3 eggs.
5 ozs. flour.
1 glass of whiskey or rum.

Almond Paste : 6 ozs. (page 188).
Water Icing : 4 ozs. (page 189).
Royal Icing : 1 lb. (page 190).

1. Prepare fruit and mix it with the spice, nuts, lemon rind and half of the whiskey.

2. Cream the butter and sugar.

3. Break in an egg and beat until the mixture thickens, mix in a little sieved flour. Continue in this way until all the eggs have been added. Stir in the remainder of the flour.

4. Mix in the prepared fruit. Put the mixture into the prepared tin and bake in a slow oven.

5. Leave the cake in the tin until next day. Turn it out and remove the paper. Place the cake upside-down on a large sheet of greaseproof paper. Pour the remainder of the whiskey over the bottom of the cake and leave to soak. Fold this sheet of paper around the cake. Wrap in more paper. Store until required for icing.

SIZE OF TIN AND TIME FOR BAKING.

Lowest tier		*Middle tier*		*Top tier*	
Round	12″	Round	9″	Round	6″
Square	11″	Square	8″	Square	5″
About 6½ hours.		About 4 hours.		About 2½ hours.	

Fillings and Icings

ALMOND PASTE OR ICING

1 lb. ground almonds.	1 tablesp. whiskey.
1 lb. castor sugar.	1 tablesp. sherry.
¼ teasp. almond essence.	2 eggs.

¼ teasp. ratafia essence.

1. Crush all the lumps out of the almonds and sieve the castor sugar, mix both well together.

2. Beat the eggs (keeping back a little white of egg), add flavouring, sherry and whiskey to them. Pour into the almonds and sugar and mix to a stiff paste.

3. Turn on to a sugared board, knead well and roll out. Brush the cake with white of egg and put on the almond paste.

BUTTER FILLING OR ICING

4 ozs. icing sugar.	2 ozs. butter.

Flavouring.

Cream the butter, add sugar and beat well until soft and creamy. Add flavouring and mix well.

BUTTER CREAM

¼ pint water.	1 egg.
4 ozs. sugar.	4 ozs. butter.

Flavouring.

1. Put the sugar and water into a saucepan and stir over a slow heat until the sugar is melted. Boil, without stirring, until a little of the syrup forms a soft ball when dropped into cold water. Do not over boil. Cool a little.

2. Beat the egg and whisk on the syrup in a thin stream.

3. Soften the butter and whisk into the egg mixture.

4. Flavour as required, i.e., vanilla, chocolate and vanilla, lemon, orange, rum, etc.

FILLINGS AND ICINGS

CHOCOLATE BUTTER FILLING OR ICING

2 ozs. butter.	2 ozs. icing sugar.
2 ozs. chocolate powder.	¼ teasp. vanilla essence.

Make as for Butter Icing.

CHOCOLATE FILLING OR ICING

1½ ozs. butter.	½ lb. icing sugar.
1¼ tablesps. water.	1 oz. chocolate powder.
	¼ teaspoonful vanilla essence.

Put the butter and water into a saucepan and heat until the butter is melted, add to the sieved icing sugar and chocolate powder. Flavour with vanilla essence and beat well.

COFFEE OR MOCHA BUTTER FILLING OR ICING

4 ozs. icing sugar.	2 ozs. butter.
	1–2 dessertsps. coffee essence.

Make as for Butter Icing, flavour with Coffee Essence.

ORANGE BUTTER FILLING OR ICING

4 ozs. icing sugar.	Grated rind of 1 orange.
2 ozs. butter.	Yellow colouring.
	1 teasp. orange juice.

Make as for Butter Icing, flavour with orange juice and rind, colour with yellow colouring.

GLACÉ or WATER ICING

¼ lb. icing sugar.	Boiling water.
	Flavouring and colouring as desired.

Sieve the icing sugar and put into a bowl.
Add boiling water slowly until it is of the consistency of thick cream. Add flavouring and colouring and beat until smooth and glossy.

ORANGE or LEMON GLACÉ ICING

¼ lb. icing sugar.	Orange or lemon juice.
Yellow colouring.	Boiling water.

Make as above, adding orange or lemon juice first, and then sufficient water.

189

COFFEE GLACÉ ICING

¼ lb. icing sugar.   1 tablesp. coffee essence.
Boiling water.

Make as for Orange Glacé Icing.

ROYAL ICING

1 lb. icing sugar.   2 whites of eggs.
Juice of 1 lemon.   A few drops of laundry blue.

Roll out the sugar on a piece of kitchen paper. Put through a very fine sieve. Mix with the half-beaten white of egg and lemon juice. Beat for about 15 minutes.

NOTE :—Albumen powder may be used instead of whites of eggs. Follow the instructions supplied with it.

CHOCOLATE GLACÉ ICING

2 ozs. chocolate powder.   ¼ teasp. vanilla essence.
2 tablesps. cold water.   8 ozs. icing sugar.
½ oz. butter.   Hot water.

1. Put the chocolate powder into a saucepan with the cold water, add the butter and vanilla essence and stir over a gentle heat until the chocolate is dissolved.
2. Put the icing sugar into a bowl, add the dissolved chocolate and sufficient hot water to mix to a consistency when the icing will coat the back of a wooden spoon.
3. Beat until smooth and glossy.

AMERICAN FONDANT ICING

½ lb. granulated sugar.   1 white of egg.
4 tablesps. water.

Dissolve the sugar in the water and boil for 1 minute. Whisk the white of egg until stiff, add the syrup slowly, whisking all the time. Continue to whisk over boiling water until white and very thick. Spread quickly over the cake.

Preservation of Food in the Home

A good housewife takes a great pride in stocking her larder with a plentiful supply of home preserves. Her pride is justly founded because these preserves are the reward for meticulous care and careful preparation and cooking to obtain successful results. Food which is not properly preserved decomposes after a short time due to the growth of micro-organisms. Thorough sterilization of food and containers and the complete exclusion of air to eliminate the existence of these micro-organisms is necessary. Sugar, salt, vinegar, alcohol and spice are valuable in the preservation of different foods, as their presence is unfavourable to the growth of micro-organisms. Most gardens produce more fruit and vegetables than is necessary to meet the immediate need, the surplus can easily be preserved by carefully following the instructions in the recipes which follow.

JAM AND JELLY-MAKING

Home-made jams and jellies are a wholesome supplement to any meal. They cost less than bought jams and are far superior to them in flavour and in nutrient value. A good jam keeps well, has a clear bright colour, is well set but not too stiff, and has the flavour of the fruit from which it is made. A reliable recipe and a knowledge of the principles of jam-making are essential to make a really good quality jam. Even when using a reliable recipe it is possible to make a jam poor in quality if the condition of the fruit is not up to standard. For example, the fruit itself varies according to the season, whether it is wet or sunny, also in variety and ripeness. Jam made from over-ripe fruit lacks flavour and does not set satisfactorily. Again, the amount of water lost through evaporation varies according to the shape and size of the pan used and also to the amount of heat applied. Never try to make a large quantity of jam at one boiling. The preserving pan should be about half full to allow the jam to boil vigorously without boiling over, and also to avoid undue evaporation. If it is necessary to make a small quantity of jam, use a large saucepan instead of a preserving pan, remembering to have it just half-full.

Pectin.

The fact that fruit when boiled with sugar will set depends on a substance called pectin which is contained in the cell walls of the fruit. Therefore when making jam the first thing is to extract the pectin from the fruit. It has been found that this is more easily done when the fruit is slightly under-ripe. Some fruits are richer in pectin than others, e.g., plums, damsons, gooseberries, blackcurrants, redcurrants, and apples, while others contain little or no pectin. When using vegetable marrow the pectin must be supplied, as the marrow contains none. Strawberries contain little pectin, and it must therefore be supplemented by adding fruit juice or commercial pectin. Acid helps in the extraction of the pectin and is necessary to obtain a good set. If fruits themselves lack acid it should be added before the preliminary cooking of the fruit. Acid also improves the colour of the jam and helps to avoid crystallization of the sugar. It may be added in the form of lemon juice or other acid fruit juice, or citric or tartaric acid.

Test for Pectin.

After the preliminary boiling of the fruit, take 1 teaspoonful of the juice and place in a small bowl or cup, cool and add 3 teaspoonfuls of methylated spirits. Shake well together and then leave to stand for one minute. If the clot formed is firm and in one lump the amount of pectin present is good ; if the clot is not very firm, the amount of pectin is medium ; whereas if the clots are broken there is little pectin present.

Average Composition of Some Fruits.

FRUIT	Total Solids	Sugar	Acid	Pectin
Gooseberries	11·1%	3·5%	2·2%	·8%
Strawberries	11·1%	5·5%	·9%	·5%
Raspberries	14·1%	3·6%	1·7%	·5%
Red-currents	16·2%	4·8%	2·5%	·6%
Black-currants ...	19·9%	6·4%	3·5%	1·1%
Plums	13·7%	7·4%	1·6%	·8%
Apples	14·3%	7·6%	1·1%	·75%
Blackberries	18·7%	5·1%	·8%	·6%

PRESERVES

RULES FOR JAM-MAKING

1. The fruit should be freshly picked, dry, sound and slightly under-ripe if possible.
2. Pectin and acid should be present to make a good, well set jam.
3. Have the jam jars clean and hot and the covers, etc., to hand.
4. Never try to make a large quantity of jam at one boiling. The preserving pan should be about half full to allow the jam to boil vigorously without boiling over and also to avoid undue evaporation. It must always be remembered that the depth of the contents in the preserving pan and the rate at which they boil determine the length of time which the jam takes to cook.
5. Sugar is the preservative in jams, therefore the correct proportion should be used. Too little sugar may cause the jam to ferment, whereas too much may cause crystallization.
6. Skins of fruit must be softened by cooking before adding the sugar. If not, the skins become tough, because sugar has a hardening effect on fruits.
7. The sugar must be dissolved before allowing the jam to boil. It is recommended to heat the sugar because it will dissolve more quickly when heated than when cold. The jam should be stirred with a wooden spoon all the time while the sugar is being dissolved.
8. The fruit should be cooked slowly before adding the sugar, and after it is dissolved it should be boiled quickly.
9. Remove the thick grey scum which rises when the jam is nearly cooked. It is wasteful to skim continuously.
10. Test in good time to avoid overcooking because the setting point could be missed. Overboiling the jam darkens the colour and destroys the fresh fruit flavour. If a teaspoonful of jam wrinkles on a plate when it has been left in a cold place for a few minutes it is then ready to pot.
11. In the case of jam or marmalade where fruit is suspended, it is wise to allow the jam to cool in the preserving pan until a skin forms on the surface. The jam is then stirred before filling into the pots. This ensures that the fruit will remain suspended instead of rising to the top of the pot.
12. Fill the pots to the top to allow for shrinkage on cooling.
13. Press a round of waxed paper on to the surface of the jam immediately after filling. Turn the waxed side of the paper downwards.
14. Wipe the rim of the pot with a clean, damp cloth.
15. Cover, label and date.
16. Remember when storing jam that too much heat or damp may cause a growth of mould on top of the jam. It retains a better colour if stored in a dark place.

ALL IN THE COOKING

DAMSON JAM

6 lbs. damsons. 1½ pints water.
6 lbs. sugar.

1. Pick over the fruit carefully, wash and drain.
2. Put damsons into a greased preserving pan with the water. Stew until the skin breaks.
3. Add the heated sugar and stir over a gentle heat until the sugar is dissolved. Boil steadily.
4. Stir frequently and remove the stones as they rise to the top. Skim.
5. Test when it has boiled for 20 minutes, and pot.

DAMSON CHEESE

1. Wash the damsons, put into a large saucepan, adding about ¼-pint of water to each pound of fruit. Cover and cook until soft, stirring occasionally. Remove the lid and reduce a little if necessary to thicken the pulp.
2. Rub the pulp through a sieve, measure and return to a saucepan or preserving pan and add ¾–1 lb. sugar to each pint of pulp.
3. Stir over a gentle heat until the sugar is dissolved. Boil for about ½ hour. Test as for jam.
4. Pour into hot sterilized jars and cover immediately.

PLUM JAM

6 lbs. plums. 1½ pints water.
6 lbs. sugar.

1. Wash the plums, cut in halves and remove the stones.
2. Put the plums and water into a greased preserving pan and cook until the fruit begins to break.
3. Add the heated sugar and stir over a gentle heat until the sugar is dissolved. Boil briskly for about 20 minutes, skim, test and pot.

GREENGAGE JAM

Make as for Plum Jam.

RASPBERRY JAM

7 lbs. raspberries. 7 lbs. sugar.

1. Pick over the raspberries, put into the preserving pan and stew for about 10 minutes to extract the juice.
2. Add the heated sugar and stir over a gentle heat until dissolved.
3. Boil steadily for about 15 minutes, stirring frequently. Skim, test and pot.

PRESERVES

LOGANBERRY JAM I

Make, using the same recipe as for Raspberry Jam.

LOGANBERRY JAM II

5 lbs. loganberries.　　　　　　　**1 pint water.**
Sugar.

1. Pick over the loganberries and cook in the water for about 15 minutes. Put through a coarse sieve to remove the seeds.

2. Measure and add a pound of sugar for every pint of pulp.

3. Put into a preserving pan and heat slowly until the sugar is dissolved, then boil steadily for about 15 minutes. Skim, test and pot.

BLACKBERRY JAM

5 lbs. blackberries.　　　　　　　**5 lbs. sugar.**
½ oz. citric acid.

1. Pick over the fruit carefully and put into the preserving pan with the acid. Add about ¼-pint water if the fruit is hard and dry.

2. Crush the berries a little against the pan to extract the juice. Bring slowly to the boil, simmer until the fruit is soft and the moisture reduced.

3. Add the heated sugar and stir over a gentle heat until dissolved.

4. Boil steadily for about 15 minutes, stirring frequently. Skim, test and pot.

BLACKBERRY AND APPLE JAM

5 lbs. blackberries.　　　　　　　**2 lbs. apples.**
6 lbs. sugar.

1. Wash, peel, core and slice the apples, stew with about ½-pint water and beat to a pulp.

2. Pick over the blackberries, cook until soft, adding about ¼-pint water if the berries are dry. If liked, put through a coarse sieve, to remove seeds.

3. Put into a preserving pan with the apple pulp and the heated sugar and stir over a gentle heat until the sugar is dissolved.

4. Boil steadily for about 15 minutes, stirring frequently. Skim, test and pot.

195

BLACK CURRANT JAM I

4 lbs. black currants.   2½ pints water
6 lbs. sugar.

1. Remove the stalks from the black currants, put the fruit into a greased preserving pan, add the water and cook until the fruit begins to break.

2. Add the heated sugar and stir over a gentle heat until the sugar is dissolved.

3. Boil briskly for about 20 minutes, stirring frequently. Skim, test and pot.

BLACK CURRANT JAM II

4 lbs. black currants.   ¼ pint water.
4 lbs. sugar.

Make as for Black Currant Jam I.

GOOSEBERRY JAM

6 lbs. gooseberries.   2 pints water.
8 lbs. sugar.

1. Remove tops and tails from the gooseberries. Wash and drain the fruit, put it into a greased preserving pan, add the water and cook until the fruit is soft.

2. Add the heated sugar and dissolve it slowly.

3. Boil steadily for about 20 minutes. Skim, test and pot.

STRAWBERRY JAM I

6 lbs. strawberries.   9 lbs. sugar.   ½ teasp. citric acid.

1. Remove the stalks and hulls from the strawberries and wash if necessary.

2. Crush the fruit, put into a preserving pan and stew for 5 minutes.

3. Add the heated sugar, stir over a gentle heat until the sugar is dissolved, add citric acid. Boil steadily for 5 minutes. Skim, test and pot.

STRAWBERRY JAM II

4 lbs. strawberries.   4¼ lbs. sugar.
¼-pint red currant *or* gooseberry juice *or* juice of 2 lemons.

Prepare the fruit juice as on page 198, using about 1 lb. fruit to obtain ¼ pint of juice. Cook the crushed strawberries in the juice. Add the sugar, stir over a gentle heat until the sugar is dissolved. Boil for about 15 minutes. Skim, test and pot.

PRESERVES

RHUBARB JAM

7 lbs. rhubarb.   7 lbs. sugar.
1 teaspoonful of ground ginger.

1. Cut off the top and end from the rhubarb, wash the fruit and cut into 1-inch pieces.
2. Put into a large crock and cover with the sugar, allow it stand for 24 hours.
3. Turn the rhubarb into a greased preserving pan, add the ginger and heat slowly until the sugar is dissolved, stirring frequently.
4. Boil quickly for about half-an-hour. Skim, test and pot.

NOTE.—July, August and early September are the best months in which to make Rhubarb Jam.

VEGETABLE MARROW JAM

6 lbs. prepared marrow.   1 pint apple juice (page 198).
7 lbs. sugar.   1 oz. root ginger *or* 1½ teasps.
½ oz. citric acid.   of ground ginger.

1. Store the marrow for several weeks before using for jam-making.
2. Cut the marrow into ½-inch slices, peel, remove the pulp and seeds from the centre. Cut into ½-inch cubes and steam for about 15 minutes.
3. Place in an earthenware crock with the sugar and allow it to stand overnight.
4. Bruise the ginger and tie it in a piece of muslin.
5. Put the marrow, sugar, citric acid, ginger and apple juice into a greased preserving pan. Heat slowly until the sugar is dissolved.
6. Boil for about 20 minutes, skim, test and pot.

DRIED APRICOT JAM

2 lbs. dried apricots.   2 lemons.
6 pints tepid water.   8 lbs. sugar.
½ oz. almonds (blanched and chopped).

1. Wash the apricots and cut in four. Put into a crock with the water, grated lemon rind and lemon juice, and steep for 24 hours.
2. Turn into a greased preserving pan, add the sugar and almonds, stir over a gentle heat until the sugar is dissolved, then boil rapidly from ½–¾ hour. Skim, test and pot.

APRICOT PULP JAM

11 lbs. apricot pulp.	½ oz. citric acid.
8½ lbs. sugar.	¼ lb. chopped almonds.
1 teasp. salt.	1 teasp. almond essence.

1. Put the apricot pulp into a greased preserving pan and add the sugar, salt, citric acid and almonds. Stir over a gentle heat until the sugar is dissolved.

2. Boil for about an hour, stirring frequently. Skim and test. Add almond essence and pot.

GREEN TOMATO JAM

6 lbs. green tomatoes.   2 lemons.

5 lbs. sugar.

1. Wipe and chop the tomatoes. Put them into the preserving pan with the strained lemon juice, the grated lemon rind and the sugar.

2. Heat slowly until the sugar is dissolved. Boil steadily for about 20 minutes, skim, test and pot.

FRUIT JUICE (For Jelly or Jam)

1. Pick over the fruit carefully and wash well.

2. Put into a large saucepan with the water—apples, gooseberries and black currants about ¾ pint to each pound of fruit, red currants 1½ gills and blackberries about ¼ pint. Boil to a pulp—about 1 hour.

3. Tie a square of strong cheese cloth to the legs of an upturned chair. The seat of the chair should be resting firmly on a table. Allow the cloth to dip slightly in the middle to form a bag and place a bowl underneath.

4. Turn the cooked pulp into the cloth and allow to drip overnight until all the juice is extracted.

APPLE JELLY

6 lbs. apples.	4½ pints water.
2 lemons.	Sugar.

1. Wash the apples and cut into quarters. Peel and core must not be removed. Windfalls may be used if the bruised parts are cut off.

2. Put the prepared apples into a large saucepan with the water and thinly-pared rind of the lemons, cook until reduced to a pulp. Time 1–1½ hours.

3. Turn the pulp into a jelly bag and allow to drip until all the juice has been extracted.

PRESERVES

4. Measure the juice into a preserving pan, add the strained juice of the lemons and the heated sugar, allowing a pound of sugar to each pint of juice.

5. Stir over a gentle heat until the sugar is dissolved. Boil rapidly without stirring for about 10 minutes. Test, skim and pot.

NOTE.— If ginger or clove flavour is required, cook with the apples instead of the lemon.

CRAB-APPLE JELLY

Crab-apples are better after they have had a slight touch of frost. Make as for Apple Jelly.

RED CURRANT JELLY

4 lbs. red currants.   1 pint water.
Sugar.

1. Pick out any leaves but it is not necessary to remove the stalks. Wash the currants well.

2. Put into a large saucepan with the water and cook until the currants are reduced to a pulp.

3. Turn the pulp into a jelly bag and allow to drip until all the juice has been extracted.

4. Measure the juice into a preserving pan, add the heated sugar, allowing a pound of sugar to each pint of juice.

5. Stir over a gentle heat until the sugar is dissolved. Boil rapidly without stirring for about 10 minutes. Test, skim and pot.

NOTE.—A mixture of red and white currants may be used.

BLACKBERRY JELLY

5 lbs. blackberries.   ¼ oz. citric acid.
1 pint water.   Sugar.

Pick over the fruit carefully and put into a large saucepan with the water and citric acid. Cook until reduced to a pulp. Continue as for Red Currant Jelly.

MINT JELLY

3 lbs. apples.   3 pints water.
A large bunch of fresh mint.   Sugar.
¼ oz. citric acid or juice   A few drops of green colouring.
    of 2 lemons.

1. Wash the apples and cut into slices. Do not remove skin or core.

2. Put the apples into a saucepan with a sprig of mint and the citric acid or lemon juice, add the water and boil until soft and pulpy. Strain as for Fruit Juice (page 198).

3. Measure the juice and allow 1 lb. sugar to each pint of juice. Boil the juice for 10 minutes. Add the heated sugar and stir over a gentle heat until the sugar is dissolved.

4. Add a bunch of bruised mint tied in muslin and boil briskly for about 5 minutes to extract flavour from the mint. Lift out the mint and continue to boil until a little jellies on a cold plate in a few minutes.

5. Skim and add a few drops of green colouring. Pour into hot jars and cover.

LEMON CURD

2 lemons.	$\frac{1}{2}$ lb. castor sugar.
2 ozs. butter or margarine.	3 eggs.

1. Grate the rind from the lemons. Squeeze out the juice and strain.

2. Put the lemon rind and juice, butter and sugar into a saucepan. Stir over a gentle heat until the sugar is dissolved.

3. Add the well-beaten eggs and cook over a gentle heat until the mixture thickens. Pour into sterilised jars and cover as for jam.

PARSLEY HONEY

Parsley to fill a 6-pint saucepan. 3 dessertsps. brown vinegar.
Allow 1 lb. sugar to 1 pint of liquid.

1. Wash the parsley, put into a saucepan and cover with cold water.

2. Add the vinegar and boil until the parsley has lost its colour. Strain and measure liquid. Add the required amount of sugar and stir over a gentle heat until the sugar is dissolved. Boil until the syrup thickens. Pot and cover.

ORANGE MARMALADE I

3 lbs. Seville oranges (about 12). $\frac{1}{4}$ lb. sweet orange (about 1).
$\frac{1}{2}$ lb. lemons (about 2).
To each lb. of fruit allow 3 pints water (i.e., 11 pints).
To each pint of cooked pulp allow 1 lb. sugar (about 8 lbs.).

1. Wash the oranges and lemons. Cut them in two and squeeze out the juice on a lemon squeezer. Strain the juice into a large bowl containing the cold water.

2. Tie the pips and pulp in muslin and put into the bowl.

3. Slice the skin thinly either by hand or with a marmalade cutter. If liked, the rinds may be put through a mincer, but this does not give a good appearance. Add to the bowl and, if liked, leave to steep overnight.

4. Put into a preserving pan, bring to the boil and cook until the rinds are soft and the contents of the pan are reduced to half. This takes about 1½ hours.

5. Measure the pulp, return to the preserving pan and add the sugar, allowing 1 lb. to each pint of pulp.

6. Stir over a gentle heat until the sugar is dissolved, then boil rapidly for about 20-30 minutes. Test and skim. Cool a little, stir again and fill into the hot jars. Cover, label and date.

ORANGE MARMALADE II

3 lbs. Seville oranges.	½ lb. lemons.
4 pints water.	6 lbs. sugar.

1. Wash the oranges and lemons and put into a large saucepan with the cold water. Cover, bring to the boil and cook slowly until the fruit is soft—about 1½ hours. Lift out the oranges and lemons. The water should be reduced by one quarter. Make up to 3 pints by adding water if it has reduced too much.

2. Cut one end off the oranges and lemons, scoop out the pulp. Put the pulp and pips back into the water and boil for 15 minutes. Strain through a coarse strainer into a preserving pan.

3. Slice or mince the rinds and add to the juice. Add the heated sugar and stir over a slow heat until the sugar is dissolved. Boil rapidly for about 25 minutes. Skim, test and pot.

PRESSURE-COOKED MARMALADE

1 lemon, 1 sweet orange (combined weight ½ lb.)
2 pints water.   1¼ lbs. Seville oranges.   3 lbs. sugar.

1. Wash the oranges and lemons. Cut in two, and squeeze out the juice. Strain the juice. Tie the pips and pulp in muslin.

2. Cut the skins with a marmalade cutter or use a mincer.

3. Remove the trivet from the pressure-cooker and put in the water. Add the juice, rinds and pips. Very little, if any, evaporation takes place during cooking under pressure, and that is why so little water is needed. Be careful not to have the cooker more than half-full.

4. Put on the lid and put the cooker over the heat. When the steam comes in a steady stream from the steam escape, apply the pressure control (10 lbs.). Reduce the heat and cook under pressure for 10 minutes.

5. Remove pressure-cooker from the heat and allow to cool. Time to cool—about 10 minutes.

6. Lift off the pressure control, remove the lid and do not use it for the second stage (after the sugar has been added).

7. Add the sugar, stir over a gentle heat until the sugar is dissolved, then boil rapidly for about 15-20 minutes. Test and skim. Cool a little, stir again and fill into the hot jars. Cover, label and date.

LEMON MARMALADE

6 lemons   6 pints water.
To each pint of the cooked pulp allow 1¼ lbs. of sugar.

1. Wash and dry the lemons. Peel off the rind thinly and cut into thin shreds.
2. Remove the pith and cut finely.
3. Cut the lemons in four and slice thinly.
4. Tie the pith and pips loosely in a piece of muslin and steep in ½ pint of boiling water.
5. Steep the pulp and rinds in the water for 24 hours.
6. Put into a preserving pan with the pips and pith tied in the muslin bag and the water in which they have been steeped. Bring to the boil and boil until the rinds are soft, and the pulp is reduced to half.
7. Measure the pulp, return to the greased preserving pan and add the heated sugar.
8. Stir over a gentle heat until the sugar is dissolved, then boil rapidly for about 20 minutes, skim, test and pot.

GRAPEFRUIT MARMALADE

To each grapefruit allow 1 sweet orange and 1 lemon.
To each pound of fruit allow 3 pints of water.
To each pint of the cooked pulp allow 1¼ lbs. sugar.

1. Weigh, wash and dry the fruits.
2. Cut through the rinds only, making eight divisions, and peel off. Remove some of the pith and cut all the rinds into thin strips.
3. Cut up the fruits, removing the hard white centre from the grapefruit. Collect the pips and tie loosely in muslin.
4. Steep the pulp, rinds and pips in the water for 24 hours.
5. Put into a preserving pan, bring to the boil and boil gently until the rinds are soft and the contents of the pan are reduced to half. This takes about 1½ hours.
6. Measure the pulp, return to the greased preserving pan and add the heated sugar.
7. Heat slowly until the sugar is dissolved, then boil briskly for about 30 minutes. Skim, test and pot.

Bottling of Fruit

MOST foods are preserved commercially by methods such as canning, dehydration, deep-freezing and accelerated freeze-drying. A Deep-Freeze Cabinet may be purchased for use in the home. The housewife will find the following instructions useful for preserving surplus garden products. Bottling fruit by the water-bath method should give a sure seal and perfect appearance. The oven method and the quick method are suitable for preserving small quantities where appearance is not of first importance.

Stages.

Choice and preparation of bottles, covers, etc.
Making of syrup.
Preparation of fruit.
Packing into bottles.
Sterilization.

Bottles.

1. Special vacuum bottles are sold for bottling fruit. These can be obtained in various sizes ranging from $\frac{1}{2}$ lb.–4 lbs. Jam jars with special seals may be used as a substitute for the vacuum jar.

2. All bottles should be carefully examined before use to see that there are no chips off the rims, or round the necks of bottles.

3. The bottles should be sterilized before use. It is unnecessary to dry the inside of the bottle as the fruit slips more easily into position when the inside is wet.

SCREW-BAND BOTTLE.—This type of bottle has a lacquered metal cover and a screw-band to keep the lid in position. The cover must be renewed each time the bottle is used. The lid is placed on top and then the metal band is screwed on. During processing the band is loosened one half turn to allow air and steam to escape. It is screwed down as tightly as possible immediately after sterilization.

Seals to use on Jam Jars.—Various types of covers are available for use on jam jars. Special covers with synthetic skins are also on the market ; the manufacturers' instructions should be followed. This also applies when using synthetic skin covering.

To Test Seal.

Twenty-four hours after sterilization, remove the screw-band and test the seal, i.e., lift the bottle by the lid only, and if it adheres tightly to the bottle it shows that a vacuum has been formed. If the lid comes off it shows that there is a flaw somewhere in the bottle or lid. This should be remedied and the process of sterilization repeated. Dry the screw-bands and smear a little vaseline over before storing, to prevent rust.

Syrup.

Use $\frac{1}{4}$–$\frac{1}{2}$ lb. sugar to 1 pint of water. Put the sugar and water into a saucepan, stir over a gentle heat until the sugar is dissolved. Boil for 1 minute. Strain through muslin and leave until cold.

NOTE.—Water may also be used, but with syrup the fruit has a better flavour and colour. Syrup unfortunately may have the disadvantage of causing the fruit to rise in the bottle, which detracts from the appearance of the bottled fruit.

PREPARATION OF FRUIT.

Plums.

Remove stalks and wash well. Prick with a large needle to prevent bursting. Cut large plums in halves, remove stones and drop into a weak brine solution to prevent discolouration of the cut surface. Rinse in cold water before bottling.

Pears.

Wash and peel the pears, cut in halves and remove core. Drop immediately into a weak brine solution or subject to sulphur fumes as for Dried Apple Rings (page 207).

Gooseberries.

Top and tail the gooseberries. Prick the skin or cut a small piece from each end so that the syrup will penetrate the berry.

Raspberries.

Pick carefully into shallow baskets and bottle immediately.

Blackberries.

Remove stalks and leaves and handle as little as possible.

Apples.

Peel, core and cut into eighths. Drop immediately into a weak brine solution. Rinse in cold water and steam for 5 minutes before bottling.

Rhubarb.

Wash the stalks and cut into lengths.

Strawberries.

Remove the calyx and wash if necessary in cold water. Use syrup prepared from loganberries to improve the colour of the finished product (strawberries always lose colour during sterilization). Place the fruit in the syrup and bring to the boil. Leave overnight in the syrup, then pack into the bottles. Strain the syrup through muslin and pour over the fruit.

Loganberries.
Remove stalks and pick over carefully.
Black currants.
Remove stalks and leaves and wash.
Tomatoes.
1. Remove the eye from the tomato, dip in boiling water for 1 minute, then place in cold water. Peel off the skin.
2. Leave small tomatoes whole and cut large ones in halves or quarters.
3. Pack tightly into bottles, shaking a little salt and sugar between the layers—do not use any covering liquid. (½ oz. of salt and 2 teasps. of sugar to 4 lbs. tomatoes.)
4. If necessary use one bottle to fill up the others after sterilization, and re-sterilize at 190°F. for ½ hour.
NOTE.—If sterilization is carried out in the oven—the skins may be left on and the fruit covered with brine (½ oz. salt to 1 quart of water). *See* Oven Method, page 206.
Packing into Bottles.
1. Pack hard-skinned fruits tightly, press gently into place with the handle of a wooden spoon. Cover with the cold syrup, except for Oven Method.
2. When bottling soft fruits fill one-third of the jar with the fruit, add a little cold syrup and continue with the fruit and syrup alternately until the jar is full.

STERILIZATION OF FRUIT.

A.—In Water :
1. Have a pot deep enough to hold sufficient cold water to cover the bottles completely. If this is not possible the water should at least come to the shoulders of the bottles, in which case the pot should be fitted with a closely-fitting lid.
2. Prepare a false bottom to keep the bottles from resting on the end of the pot, *e.g.*,
  (*a*) Strips of wood nailed together in trellis fashion.
  (*b*) Straw.
  (*c*) A coarse piece of cloth.
  (*d*) Thick brown paper.
3. The water should be brought slowly to the temperature necessary for the proper sterilization of each fruit (see chart).
4. A floating dairy thermometer registering not less than 212°F. should be used.
5. When sterilization is complete :—
  (*a*) Remove some of the water.
  (*b*) Lift out the bottles with a dry cloth on to a wooden table.
  (*c*) Tighten the screw-band. Screw down occasionally until cold.

TIMES FOR BOTTLING FRUIT

Fruit	Temperature	Time Taken	Maintain Temperature
Plums	165°F.	1½ hours	20 minutes
Pears	190°F.	1½ hours	20 minutes
Gooseberries	165°F.	1½ hours	10 minutes
Raspberries	165°F.	1½ hours	10 minutes
Blackberries	165°F.	1½ hours	15 minutes
Apples	165°F.	1½ hours	10 minutes
Rhubarb	165°F.	1½ hours	10 minutes
Strawberries	165°F.	1½ hours	10 minutes
Loganberries	165°F.	1½ hours	10 minutes
Tomatoes	190°F.	1 hour	30 minutes

B.—In the Oven :

1. Pack the jars tightly with the fruit, without bruising. Fill almost to the top.

2. Place the jars in the centre of a very slow oven. Leave a space of about 2 inches between the jars.

3. Place a tin over the tops of the jars.

4. Leave until the fruit begins to shrink—about ¾ hour. Pears and tomatoes need 1½ hours.

5. If shrinkage is considerable use the contents of one jar to fill up the others, then replace in the oven for 10 minutes. The fruit should be up to the neck of the jar but not in it.

6. Have fast-boiling syrup or water ready, remove the jars one at a time, pour on sufficient liquid to cover the fruit. Place the cover and screw-band carefully in position, tighten immediately and leave for 24 hours. Test the seal as on page 204.

BOTTLING FRUIT (Quick Method)

Boil the syrup in a saucepan, add the prepared fruit, and cook until tender. Pack the cooked fruit quickly into the sterilized hot preserving jar. Reboil the syrup and pour over the fruit, put on the cover and screw-band, tighten the band immediately to seal. Complete one jar at a time.

Note.—Hard pears should be cooked first in water, as they may not soften (cook) in the syrup.

APPLE PURÉE

1. Wash the apples, cut them into pieces and put into a saucepan with a little cold water—about ¼ pint to each pound of apples. Stew until the apples are reduced to a pulp.

2. Press the pulp quickly through a sieve. Return to an open saucepan and boil until the purée thickens, stirring well. Add sugar, 2-4 ozs. to the pint.

3. Fill the purée into hot sterilized preserving jars—fill one at a time and seal immediately as for bottled fruit.

Drying of Fruit and Vegetables

1. Fruit should be perfectly fresh and ripe, vegetables young and tender.

2. Trays for drying may be made by nailing strips of wood together and covering them with wire gauze or cheesecloth. The cheesecloth should be washed before using to remove dressing.

3. Drying can be done in the retained heat of the oven after cooking ; in this way drying may continue intermittently, over a period of 2-3 days. The rack over a range can also be used, but in this case the fruit must be protected from dust.

4. The fruit should be heated slowly at first to prevent the outside hardening before the moisture has evaporated from the centre.

DRIED APPLE RINGS

1. Burn a sulphur candle inside a large inverted jar until the flame dies. Place a saucer over the mouth of the jar.

2. Wash the apples, peel, core and slice into rings ¼-inch in thickness.

3. Fill the jar with the apple rings and leave for 15 minutes, shaking occasionally.

4. Remove the rings and place them on trays in a cool oven (120°F.). If using an electric oven leave the door slightly open. After 2 hours raise the temperature slowly to 150° F. Time— about 4 hours.

5. Remove and leave in the heat of the kitchen for 1 day, when the texture of the fruit should resemble that of chamois leather.

6. Wrap in wax paper and store in a tin.

NOTE.—Cut apples discolour easily when exposed to the air due to oxidization caused by enzyme action. The apples are usually subjected to sulphur fumes (sulphur dioxide) to prevent this discoloration, while the same process bleaches and whitens the fruit.

DRIED PEARS

1. Peel and core the pears, cut into quarters or eighths according to size.

2. Place at once into cold salted water ($\frac{1}{2}$ oz. salt to 1 quart water) or expose to sulphur fumes as for Apple Rings.

3. Dry and store as for Apple Rings.

DRIED PLUMS

Wash the plums if necessary. Dry as for Apple Rings, taking care that the heat is kept low until the skins begin to shrivel.

DRIED BEANS AND PEAS

1. Prepare as for cooking and tie in a piece of muslin.

2. Have ready a pot of boiling water to which bicarbonate of soda has been added ($\frac{1}{2}$ teasp. bicarbonate of soda to 1 gallon of water). Dip the peas in for 2 minutes and the beans for 3 minutes.

3. Drain well, plunge into cold water, drain again and spread on trays to dry at a temperature of 120°F. Time—4–6 hours.

4. Cover and leave for 12 hours to cool.

5. Pack in bottles, cork tightly and cover with dark paper to protect them from the light.

Haricot Beans and Peas may also be naturally or air-dried as follows :

1. Allow the green pods to ripen fully on the plant.

2. Lift up the whole plants and tie in bundles. Hang up in an airy place to finish drying.

3. Remove the seeds from the pods and store in a dry place.

DRIED HERBS

All housewives should prepare their own mint, sage, thyme, parsley, etc., and store for the winter months. July is the best month to pick herbs for drying. Pick in the morning just after the dew has disappeared.

Thyme and all small-leaved herbs—tie in bundles and hang up to dry near a fire.

Parsley, Mint and Sage :

1. Pick the leaves off the stalks and tie them in a piece of muslin.

2. Dip in boiling water to which bicarbonate of soda has been added ($\frac{1}{4}$ teasp. bread soda to 1 pint of water).

3. Drain for a few minutes and spread on a drying tray.

4. Dry in a cool oven at a temperature of 120°F. for 1 hour, or near a fire, when they will take 3–4 hours.

5. When crisp and dry crush to a powder.

6. Wrap in grease-proof paper, place in a jar and cover with dark paper to protect them from the light and so preserve their colour.

PRESERVES

CANDIED LEMON OR ORANGE PEEL

8 lemons or oranges.
2 quarts of cold salted water (½ oz. salt to 1 quart water).

Syrup :—1½ lbs. sugar.   1 pint water.

1. Wash the fruit, cut in halves and remove the pulp carefully.

2. Put the skins into a bowl, pour the cold salted water over and leave them to soak for 2 days. Pour off the salted water and drain well.

3. Put into a saucepan with sufficient fresh cold water to cover the skins and cook slowly until tender—about 1 hour. Drain off the water.

4. Dissolve 1½ lbs. of sugar in 1 pint of water, bring to the boil, and boil for one minute. Pour the boiling syrup over the peel, cover and stand in a cool place for 3 days.

5. Drain off the syrup and bring it to the boil. Put in the skins and simmer until they are clear.

6. Lift the peel from the syrup, drain well, place on a cake tray in a cool oven (110°F.) or any warm place and leave for 12 hours.

7. Boil the syrup again until it is reduced and thick. Dip each skin in the syrup and pour a little into each round of peel. Leave until dry and store in a tin box or in a jar with a lid.

NOTE.—Any surplus syrup may be used for stewing fruit, or for fruit salad, etc.

TO PRESERVE EGGS

Buy eggs when they are at their cheapest in the summer months and store them for winter use. When preserving is properly carried out the eggs can be boiled, fried and poached as well as being used for other cooking purposes. It is absolutely essential to preserve them when they are new-laid. See that the eggs are clean ; slightly-soiled eggs may be wiped with a damp cloth. Washing should be avoided and rough-shelled eggs should be rejected.

There are many different methods of preserving eggs : e.g., Water-Glass and other commercial preparations. In all cases care should be taken to follow directions given by the manufacturers.

TO PRESERVE BUTTER FOR WINTER USE

1. Cut muslin in 12-inch squares.

2. Remove paper from the butter.

3. Place each pound of butter in a square of the muslin, roll up and tie at both ends, with fine white twine, leave a long piece of string free on one end.

4. Write date on a small label, tie to the free end of the twine.

5. Dissolve salt in water in the proportion of 1 lb. salt to 1 gallon of water. Bring to the boil and boil for 1 minute.

6. Pour into a large earthenware crock. When cold, lower the butter into the crock, keeping the label hanging over the rim of the crock.

7. Place a plate on top to keep butter submerged in brine.

8. Use the pounds of butter in rotation.

PICKLES

Pickled vegetables are a welcome addition to the supper table, when serving cold meats. Their food-value is also considerable. Vegetables for pickling should be perfectly dry and fresh.
Pickles may be divided into three main types :—
1. Pickled vegetables (sour pickle).
2. Pickled fruit (sweet pickle).
3. Piccalilli (mustard pickle).

To cover Pickles and Chutneys.

Tie a piece of grease-proof paper over the jar, and over this, place a circle of cotton material dipped in melted wax or fat.

SPICED VINEGAR (for pickles)

1 quart of vinegar.	$\frac{1}{4}$ oz. whole allspice.
3 blades of mace.	$\frac{1}{2}$ oz. bruised ginger.
6 cloves.	$\frac{1}{4}$ oz. cinnamon.

Tie the spices in a piece of muslin. Put into a saucepan with the vinegar. Bring slowly to the boil and boil for 10 minutes. Leave until cold before removing the spices.

PICKLED ONIONS

Small onions of uniform size.   Brine.
Spiced vinegar (page 210).

1. Peel the onions and put into a bowl.

2. Make brine by adding 2 tablesps. salt to 1 pint water. Bring to the boil. Pour over the onions and leave until cold.

3. Pour off the brine and bring it to the boil again. Pour over the onions and leave until cold again.

4. Remove the onions and pack into sterilized jars. Pour the cold spiced vinegar over. Cover and store.

PICKLED BEETROOT

Beetroot.   Spiced vinegar (page 210).

1. Choose medium-size beetroot. Cut off leaves 2 inches from beet, do not remove root, wash well.

2. Cook in boiling water for about 2–2½ hours until tender. Test by pressure with the fingers. Leave to cool in the water.

3. Peel and slice thinly. Pack into sterilized jars, pour boiling spiced vinegar over. Cover and store.

NOTE.—If a sweet pickle is required add 2 ozs. sugar to each quart of spiced vinegar.

PICKLED RED CABBAGE

Red cabbage.   Spiced vinegar (page 210).
          Salt.

1. Remove any discoloured outer leaves, cut the head in quarters, wash well and slice thinly.

2. Put in layers in a large basin and sprinkle each layer with salt. Leave for 24 hours.

3. Drain well, then pack into jars and cover with cold spiced vinegar. Cover, label and store for at least a week before using.

PICKLED WALNUTS

Green walnuts.   Brine (2 ozs. salt to
Hot spiced vinegar (page 210).   1 pint water).

1. Pick the walnuts before the shells have begun to form (beginning of July).

2. Prick well with a needle and do not use any that feel hard.

3. Put into a bowl, cover with brine and leave for a week. Change the brine and leave for another week.

4. Drain well, put on to a dish and leave exposed to the air until they turn black.

5. Pack into jars and cover with hot spiced vinegar.

6. When cold, cover and store for 4 or 5 weeks before using.

PICKLED MIXED VEGETABLES

1 lb. green tomatoes.   2 cucumbers.
½ lb. vegetable marrow (prepared).   1½ lbs. of small onions.
¼ head hard cabbage.   Salt.
1 small cauliflower.   1 quart of spiced vinegar
                          (page 210).

1. Prepare the vegetables.

2. Slice the tomatoes, cut the marrow into small cubes, shred the cabbage, separate the cauliflower head into flowerettes, cut the cucumber into small pieces and leave onions whole.

3. Make brine by adding 1 tablesp. salt to each pint of cold water.

4. Put the prepared vegetables into a crock and cover them with the cold brine, allow to stand for 24 hours.

5. Drain the vegetables and pack them into sterilized jars. Pour the spiced vinegar over. Cover and store for at least a month to mature before using.

PICKLED DAMSONS

6 lbs. damsons.   3 lbs. sugar.
1½ pints spiced vinegar (page 210).

1. Remove any stalks from the damsons and wash them.
2. Dissolve the sugar in the spiced vinegar. Add the fruit and cook until soft but unbroken.
3. Drain off the vinegar and boil until it has thickened slightly.
4. Pack the damsons into sterilized jars and cover with the vinegar.
5. When cold, cover and store.

PICKLED VEGETABLE MARROW

3 lbs. vegetable marrow.	½ oz. mustard.
4 ozs. salt.	½ oz. tumeric.
6 peppercorns.	¼ oz. curry powder.
½ oz. root ginger.	1 quart of vinegar.
4 chillies.	6 ozs. Demerara sugar.

1. Prepare the marrow and cut into ½-inch cubes. Put it into a crock, sprinkle the salt over it and leave for 24 hours.
2. Tie the peppercorns, ginger and chillies in a piece of muslin. Put into a saucepan with the mustard, tumeric and curry powder and add the vinegar. Boil for 5 minutes. Remove spices tied in muslin.
3. Drain the marrow and add with the sugar to the vinegar. Cook slowly until the marrow is transparent. Put into jars, cover and store.

PICCALILLI

1 lb. marrow (prepared).	¼ head cabbage.
1 large cucumber.	1 cauliflower.
1 lb. small onions.	2 lbs. green tomatoes.

4 ozs. salt.

Spiced Vinegar (for Picallili) :

1 oz. mustard.	½ oz. flour.
½ oz. ground ginger.	1 quart vinegar.
¼ oz. tumeric.	6 ozs. sugar.

1 teasp. peppercorns.

1. Cut the marrow into small cubes.
2. Cut the cucumber into pieces, remove the skin, cut into quarters lengthwise and then into slices ½-inch in thickness.
3. Peel the onions.
4. Remove outer leaves from the cabbage, wash it thoroughly and shred it finely.
5. Break the cauliflower into flowerettes and wash well.
6. Wash the tomatoes and cut them into quarters.
7. Place the vegetables and salt in alternate layers in a crock and leave for 24 hours, then drain well.

8. Mix the mustard, ginger, tumeric and flour together, blend with a little of the vinegar. Put into a saucepan with the remainder of the vinegar and the sugar. Add the peppercorns tied in a piece of muslin.

9. Heat slowly until the sugar is dissolved, stirring frequently, then boil for 10 minutes. Remove peppercorns.

10. Add the drained vegetables and simmer for about 15 minutes. Pack into sterilized jars. Cover and store for at least a month before using.

RED TOMATO CHUTNEY

4 lbs. red tomatoes.	½ oz. mustard seed.
2 onions.	6 ozs. sugar.
6 cloves.	2 teasps. salt.
½ teasp. whole allspice.	¾ pint white vinegar.

1. Skin the tomatoes and slice them. Prepare the onions and chop them.

2. Tie the cloves, allspice and mustard seed in muslin.

3. Put all the prepared ingredients into a saucepan with the sugar, salt and vinegar. Heat slowly until the sugar is dissolved.

4. Bring to the boil, simmer until thick and pulpy, stirring frequently. Time 1–1½ hours. Remove spices tied in muslin. Pour into sterilized jars and cover.

GREEN TOMATO CHUTNEY

½ lb. sugar.	4 red chillies.
3 pints vinegar.	4 lbs. green tomatoes.
1 oz. salt.	3 lbs. apples.
¼ oz. ginger (bruised).	½ lb. shallots.
½ teasp. white peppercorns.	1 lb. sultanas.

1. Put the sugar, vinegar and salt into a saucepan, add the ginger, peppercorns and chillies tied in muslin. Heat slowly until the sugar is dissolved, boil for about ¾ hour.

2. Add the chopped tomato, apple and shallots and the cleaned sultanas.

3. Simmer gently, stirring occasionally until the mixture is of a thick consistency. Remove spices tied in muslin. Pour into sterilized jars and cover.

APPLE CHUTNEY

4 lbs. apples.	1 lb. sultanas.
½ lb. onions.	1½ lbs. sugar.
1 teasp. white peppercorns.	1 oz. salt.
½ oz. mustard seed.	1 teasp. ground ginger.
1½ pints of wine vinegar.	

1. Peel, and chop the apples and onions.

2. Tie the peppercorns and mustard seed in muslin.

3. Put the prepared ingredients into a saucepan and add the vinegar, cleaned sultanas, sugar, salt and ginger. Heat slowly until the sugar is dissolved.

4. Bring to the boil and simmer until thick and pulpy, stirring frequently. Time—about 1 hour. Remove spices tied in muslin. Pour into sterilized pots and cover.

VEGETABLE MARROW CHUTNEY

4 lbs. prepared marrow.	1 pint of wine vinegar.
1 oz. salt.	$\frac{1}{2}$ lb. sugar.
4 chillies.	6 shallots.
3 peppercorns.	$\frac{1}{4}$ teasp. ground ginger.

Mustard.

1. Peel the marrow, remove seeds and cut it into small cubes. Sprinkle the salt over and leave to stand overnight.

2. Tie the chillies and peppercorns in a piece of muslin.

3. Put the vinegar, sugar, shallots, chillies and peppercorns into a saucepan. Stir over a slow heat until the sugar is dissolved, boil for 15 minutes.

4. Add the well-drained marrow. Bring to the boil, simmer until thick and pulpy, stirring frequently. Time—1 hour. Remove spices tied in muslin.

5. Add ground ginger and mustard to taste, mix well. Pour into sterilized pots and cover.

PLUM CHUTNEY

4 lbs. hard plums.	6 ozs. sultanas.
3 onions.	8 ozs. brown sugar.
1 oz. salt.	1 teasp. whole allspice (tied
$\frac{1}{4}$ teasp. ground ginger.	in muslin).
	1 pint of wine vinegar.

1. Wash and slit the plums, put into a saucepan with the chopped onion and other ingredients. Stir over a slow heat until sugar is dissolved.

2. Bring to the boil, simmer until thick and pulpy, stirring frequently. Time—1 hour. Remove stones and allspice. Pour into sterilized pots and cover.

GOOSEBERRY CHUTNEY

4 lbs. gooseberries.	1$\frac{1}{2}$ lbs. brown sugar.
4 onions.	$\frac{1}{2}$ lb. sultanas.
1 oz. salt.	$\frac{1}{4}$ oz. mustard seed (tied in muslin).
$\frac{1}{4}$ teasp. cayenne pepper.	1 pint of wine vinegar.

1. Top and tail the gooseberries, chop the onions and put into a saucepan with the other ingredients. Stir until the sugar is dissolved.

2. Bring to the boil, simmer until thick and pulpy, stirring frequently. Remove mustard seed, and pour into sterilized pots and cover.

PRESERVES

BEET RELISH

5 medium-sized beetroots.	1 medium-sized onion.
1 red pepper (seeded and chopped).	1 stick of horseradish
½ pint vinegar.	(grated).
5 ozs. sugar.	2 teasps. salt.

1. Prepare and cook the beetroot, cut into small pieces.

2. Put into a saucepan with the other ingredients, stir until the sugar is dissolved, and boil for about half an hour.

3. Pour into hot sterilized jars. Cover immediately and store.

TOMATO KETCHUP

2 lbs. red tomatoes.	1 teasp. salt.
¼ pint of spiced vinegar (page 210).	2 ozs. sugar.
Pinch of cayenne pepper.	

1. Wash and slice the tomatoes. Put into a saucepan with the vinegar and cook until soft.

2. Rub through a fine sieve, return to the saucepan, add the salt, pepper and sugar. Heat slowly until the sugar is dissolved, then boil until of a creamy consistency.

3. Pour into hot sterilized bottles. Secure well-fitting corks, sterilize, fit into the bottles, leave until cold, then brush over with melted paraffin wax.

MUSHROOM KETCHUP

7 lbs. freshly-picked mushrooms.
½ lb. salt.
1 dessertsp. peppercorns ⎤
½ oz. bruised ginger ⎬ To each quart of juice.
1 piece of mace ⎦

1. Remove the stalks from the mushrooms and pick over carefully. Do not peel, wash. Put into a crock and break into pieces with a wooden spoon. Add the salt, cover and leave for several days, stirring occasionally.

2. Put into a large saucepan and heat gently until all the juices are extracted.

3. Tie a piece of huckaback or strong cheesecloth to the legs of an upturned chair, letting it dip to form a bag. The seat of the chair should be resting firmly on a table. Put a bowl under the cloth.

4. Pour in the ketchup and allow to drip until all the juice has come through. Do not squeeze or press.

5. Turn into a pot, add the spices, tied in muslin, and simmer gently for about 1¼ hours. Remove spices.

6. Pour into hot sterilized bottles. Secure well-fitting corks, sterilize, fit into the bottles, leave until cold, then brush over with melted paraffin wax.

TO PRESERVE RUNNER OR FRENCH BEANS

3-4 lbs. young tender beans.
1 lb. salt.

1. Wash the beans, top, tail, string and slice them.
2. Place a layer of salt in the end of a glass jar. Add a layer of beans.
3. Repeat the layers until all the beans are used, finishing with a layer of salt and pressing well down.
4. Weigh down and leave for 48 hours, when enough brine should have formed to cover the beans—if not, add extra brine ($\frac{1}{4}$ lb. salt to 1 pint water) and cover.
5. When required, rinse in fresh water and steep in warm water for 2 hours before cooking.

HOME-MADE SWEETS

TOFFEE

1 lb. granulated sugar.	¼ lb. butter.
¼ pint water.	Pinch of cream of tartar.
½ gill of golden syrup.	1 teasp. lemon juice.

1. Put the sugar, water, syrup and half of the butter into a saucepan and stir over a gentle heat until the sugar is dissolved.

2. Bring to the boil, brush down the sides of the saucepan with warm water. Add the cream of tartar and boil to 260°F.

3. Add the remainder of the butter cut in small pieces and the lemon juice. Mix well.

4. Pour into a greased tin and mark into squares when half cold. When cold turn out and break into squares.

BUTTERSCOTCH

1 lb. sugar.	½ cup of water.
4 ozs. golden syrup.	2 ozs. butter.

1. Put the sugar, syrup and water into a saucepan and stir over a gentle heat until the sugar is dissolved.

2. Bring to the boil, put on the lid for 2 minutes, remove the lid and brush down the sides of the saucepan with a brush dipped in warm water.

3. When boiling steadily put in the thermometer and boil to 315°F. Take off the fire and when it ceases to boil stir in the butter and pour into a greased tin.

4. Mark into shape when lukewarm. When cold, break into pieces.

PULLED TOFFEE

1 lb. Demerara sugar.	2 ozs. butter.
¼ pint water.	¼ teasp. cream of tartar.
1½ tablesps. golden syrup.	A few drops of peppermint essence.

1. Put the sugar, water, golden syrup, butter and cream of tartar into a saucepan and stir over a gentle heat until the sugar is dissolved.

217

2. Brush down the sides of the saucepan, using a brush dipped in warm water, and boil to 290°F.

3. Grease a tin with olive oil and pour in the toffee.

4. Leave until beginning to set at the edge, sprinkle a few drops of peppermint essence over and keep turning the sides in to the centre until cool enough to handle, using a palette knife.

5. Pull into long lengths, fold in two, keep on pulling and folding until you feel toffee getting hard ; then draw out into a strip ½-inch in thickness.

6. Cut into 1-inch pieces with an oiled scissors, give a twist to each piece when cut.

FUDGE

A tin of unsweetened milk.	2 ozs. butter.
2 lbs. granulated sugar.	2 tablesps. golden syrup.
1 dessertsp. lemon juice.	

1. Put the milk and sugar into a saucepan and stir over a gentle heat until the sugar is dissolved.

2. Boil to 240°F. or until a little of the mixture forms a soft ball when dropped into cold water. Stir all the time.

3. Add the butter, golden syrup and lemon juice, mix until it thickens slightly.

4. Pour into a greased tin and mark into shape before it sets, when cold cut into pieces.

NOTE.—Chopped nuts or raisins may be added to this mixture.

CHOCOLATE FUDGE

1¼ lbs. sugar.	1½ gills milk.
2 tablesps. golden syrup.	Pinch salt.
1 oz. cocoa.	1½ ozs. butter.

1. Put the sugar, syrup, cocoa, milk, and salt into a heavy saucepan. Stir over a low heat until the sugar is dissolved.

2. Boil until it forms a soft ball when a little of it is dropped into cold water—240°F. Stir frequently.

3. Draw aside. Mix in the butter. Cool a little and beat until creamy. Put into a greased tin and mark into squares with the back of knife.

TURKISH DELIGHT

1 oz. leaf gelatine.	1 lemon or 1 orange (rind and juice).
½ pint water.	1 tablesp. sherry.
1 lb. granulated sugar.	A little carmine.

To coat :—1 tablesp. icing sugar.   1 tablesp. cornflour.

1. Soak leaf gelatine in a bowl of tepid water, leave until soft, squeeze out of the water when required.

2. Put the sugar, water and the lemon rind into a saucepan. Stir over a gentle heat until the sugar is dissolved. Add the gelatine and mix well. If using powdered gelatine only use ¼ pint of water to dissolve the sugar and put the gelatine to soak in the remainder until soft. Mix into the syrup.

3. Boil for 10 minutes. Add the strained fruit juice and sherry. Pour half the mixture into a wet tin, colour the remainder pink and pour into a second tin. Leave for 24 hours.

4. Sieve the icing sugar and mix with the cornflour.

5. Dip the tin quickly into boiling water and turn out the jelly. Cut into 1-inch squares with a knife dipped in boiling water. Coat each square with the mixture of sugar and cornflour.

NOTE.—The mixture may be coloured green and flavoured with a few drops of peppermint essence.

PEPPERMINT CREAMS

Fondant :—

1 lb. granulated sugar.	1 teasp. glucose.
¼ pint water.	Large pinch of cream of tartar.

*Flavour :—*A few drops of peppermint essence.

1. Dissolve the sugar in the water. Add the glucose and cream of tartar and bring to the boil. Brush down the sides of the saucepan with warm water. Boil to 240°F.

2. Turn into a bowl, allow to cool a little, mix with a wooden spoon until thick and white and then knead until smooth. Add the peppermint essence and work into the fondant.

3. Take small even-sized pieces, roll into balls, flatten out a little, leave until dry.

NOTE.—Different flavourings and colourings may be worked into the fondant to provide variety.

MARZIPAN

1 lb. granulated sugar.	2 egg whites.
¼ pint water.	12 ozs. ground almonds.

1. Put the sugar and water into a saucepan and stir over a gentle heat until the sugar is dissolved. Bring to the boil and brush down the sides of the saucepan with warm water. Boil to 240°F. or to a soft ball.

2. Remove from the fire, stir until thick and cloudy, mix in the ground almonds and then the slightly-beaten egg whites. Stir over the fire for a few minutes. Turn into a bowl and leave until cool.

3. Knead until smooth and work in any flavourings and colourings required.

NEAPOLITAN SQUARES

Marzipan as above.   Colourings and flavourings.

Divide the marzipan into three, use different colouring and flavouring in each portion. Roll out each portion into a square shape, place one on top of the other, press lightly with the rolling-pin and trim the edges with a sharp knife. Mark the top into lines with the back of the knife and cut into squares.

Marzipan Apples.—Colour the marzipan a pale apple green. Dust with icing sugar and form into small balls. Insert a clove in one end, leave to dry for 1 hour, then paint a rosy cheek on it with a brush dipped in red colouring.

Pears.—Tint the marzipan with yellow colouring. Form into balls, pull out one end into a pear shape. Insert a stalk of angelica into the narrow end and a clove into the other end.

Strawberries.—Form the marzipan into small balls, then pull out the paste at one end. Make little indentations all over them. Paint each one red and put in artificial stalks and leaves.

Note.—The fruits should be dusted with castor sugar and allowed to stand on waxed paper for a few hours to dry.

CARAMELLED WALNUTS

2 doz. half-walnuts.   ¼ lb. marzipan.

Caramel :
  ½ lb. sugar.   ¼ pint water.

1. Roll the marzipan into small balls. Put each ball of marzipan between two pieces of walnut and press well together.
2. Put the sugar and water into a saucepan and stir over a gentle heat until the sugar is dissolved. Boil until a light brown colour.
3. Dip each sweet into the caramel and drop on to waxed paper to set.

MISCELLANEOUS

ASPIC JELLY

2 ozs. gelatine.	1 qt. Bouillon or White Stock.
1 white of egg.	A little salt.
2 tablesps. wine.	1½ tablesps. wine vinegar.

1. Soak leaf gelatine in a bowl of tepid water, leave until soft and squeeze out of the water when required. If using powdered gelatine, mix with ¼ pint of water, leave for a short time and use.

2. Put the white and shell of the egg into a saucepan and work on the stock slowly, add soaked gelatine, salt, vinegar and wine, place over a low heat. Whisk until it comes slowly to the boil.

3. Put the lid on the saucepan and remove from the heat, leave to settle for about 20 minutes.

4. Ladle carefully through double muslin which has been wrung out of cold water. Do not tip the saucepan, because this tends to upset the scum. Use jelly as required.

NOTE.—(1) The gelatine should be increased to 4 ozs. if the aspic jelly is to be chopped.

(2) The stock used for aspic jelly must be good and strong, and may be beef, game, chicken or fish stock, according to the dish for which it is to be used. The wine should also vary : white wine for fish, sherry or white wine for chicken, red wine for beef or game. Vinegar must be used carefully as the aspic should be pleasantly sharp and not crude.

TO DISJOINT A CHICKEN

Having cleaned out the chicken :—

1. Cut off the wings at the first joint. Place the chicken with the tail turned away from you.

2. Hold the leg and cut the skin attaching the leg to the body. Pull back the leg to the joint and cut off.

3. Remove the skin from the thigh towards the knee joint. Trim off the end of the bone and the skin. Divide the leg at the joint. Trim off the bone at both ends of the thigh. Press the meat of the leg up towards the top part of the bone to form a drum-stick. Repeat on the other side.

4. Remove the skin from the tail-end towards the neck and cut off. With a sharp knife cut along the breast bone and separate at the natural division, raising the wing from the breast. Repeat on the other side.

5. Cut the breast bone from the carcase, on the length. Cut the breast bone across in two to give two breast pieces.

TO CUT CUCUMBER GARNISH

METHOD A.—Notch and cut into thin slices.

METHOD B.—Slice thinly, cut each slice in halves, crease in two and stand on the cut edge.

FORCEMEAT BALLS

3 ozs. breadcrumbs.	Grated rind of ¼ lemon.
1½ ozs. chopped suet.	¼ teasp. chopped onion.
1 dessertsp. finely-chopped parsley.	Chopped cooked liver of hare.
	Beaten egg.
¼ teasp. mixed herbs.	

1. Mix all the dry ingredients together and bind with the beaten egg.

2. Turn on to a floured board and make into small balls about the size of a pea.

3. Fry in hot fat or cook in a little hot fat on a tin in the oven.

TO BOIL SPAGHETTI

Lower gradually into plenty of boiling salted water and cook until tender. Time—about 15 minutes.

CARAMEL

6 ozs. sugar.	¼ pint water.

Put the sugar and water into a saucepan, stir over a gentle heat until the sugar is dissolved. Boil until a dark brown colour but not burnt. Stir in sufficient hot water to make a thick syrup and bottle.

CHESTNUT STUFFING

¾ lb. chestnuts.	¼ lb. butter or margarine.
Stock or milk.	Pepper and salt.
¼ lb. breadcrumbs.	1 egg.

1. Wash the chestnuts, split the skin of each on the rounded side and put down in cold water. Bring to the boil and boil 5 minutes. Remove the skins and stew chestnuts in milk or stock until tender.

2. Drain off the liquid and rub the chestnuts through a sieve. Add butter and breadcrumbs. Season and bind with beaten egg.

MISCELLANEOUS

MACÉDOINE OF VEGETABLES

This is a mixture of cooked diced vegetables.

To serve hot :—Mix with a little melted butter or Béchamel Sauce.

To serve cold :—Mix with a little mayonnaise.

RICH COATING BATTER

2 ozs. flour.	¼ gill tepid water
Pinch of salt.	1 white of egg.
1 dessertsp. oil.	

1. Sieve the flour and salt into a bowl. Make a well in the centre of the flour, add the oil and about 1 tablespoonful of the water.

2. Mix with a wooden spoon, allowing the flour to fall in gradually from the sides. Mix until very smooth. Add the remainder of the water gradually.

3. Beat for 5 minutes, cover, and leave the batter in a cold place for about 1 hour.

4. Stiffly beat the white of egg and fold lightly through the batter. Use immediately, as required.

JULIENNE STRIPS

Match-like strips of carrot and turnip cooked until tender in boiling salted water.

FRIED PARSLEY

Divide some fresh parsley into large sprigs. Wash and dry very well. Put into smoking hot fat and remove immediately the effervescence stops, otherwise the parsley will discolour. Drain well and use for garnishing.

BOUQUET GARNI

4 parsley stalks.	2 thyme stalks.
½ bay leaf.	

Wrap the parsley and thyme stalks in the bay leaf and tie with thread or fine twine.

MEAT GLAZE

Method I.—Put 1 pint of good quality brown stock into a small saucepan and reduce to ¼ pint, skimming occasionally. This glaze should set when cold if there has been sufficient beef bones in the original stock. Use for glazing tongues, etc.

Method II.—Dissolve ½ oz. gelatine in ½ pint brown stock. Add a little Worcester Sauce and a pinch of salt. Leave aside until beginning to set, and use.

SAVOURY BUTTER

1 oz. butter.	½ teasp. lemon juice.
Pepper.	

Cream the butter with the lemon juice and pepper. A few drops of green colouring may be added if liked.

CURLED CELERY

Cut celery into lengths as required. Shred to within 1 inch of the end and place in cold water for 15 minutes to curl.

TO LINE A MOULD WITH JELLY

1. Have the mould perfectly clean and free from any trace of grease. Pour a little liquid jelly into it and leave on ice or in a cold place to set.

2. Dip the underside of each piece of decoration into a little liquid jelly. Place in position, using a fine skewer. Secure by a very thin coating of cold liquid jelly. Leave to set.

To Line Sides of Mould.

Have some broken ice ready. Cool the mould by standing it in the broken ice until required. Pour a little cold liquid jelly into the mould, revolve the mould slowly on the ice, until the sides are evenly coated with the jelly or brush the sides with cold liquid jelly. If decorations are required on the sides, dip the underside of each piece of decoration into a little liquid jelly. Place in position, using a fine skewer. Secure by a very thin coating of cold liquid jelly. Leave to set. Revolve the mould and continue until the decoration is complete.

TO CHOP JELLY

Make the jelly of a rather stiff consistency. Turn it out on to a wet board and chop.

TO UNMOULD A COLD SWEET

1. Run the point of a knife around the edge of the mould to a depth of about ½ inch.

2. Hold the mould between the thumb and finger-tips. Dip into hot water, allowing the water to come to the finger-tips.

3. Lift out quickly and allow to stand for a few seconds.

4. Put a flat dish over the mould and invert. Give it a quick shake and then gently lift the mould up and off.

APRICOT GLAZE

2 tablesps. of apricot jam.   2 tablesps. of water.   2 ozs. sugar.

Heat the jam and water, strain, return to the rinsed saucepan. Add the sugar and stir until dissolved. Boil until it coats the back of the spoon. Cool a little and use.

SWEET STUFFING (for Turkey or Chicken)

6 ozs. sultanas.
1 lb breadcrumbs.
1 tablesp. sugar.
Pepper and salt.
6 ozs. butter or margarine.
1 egg.
A little hot milk

Wash the sultanas and mix with the breadcrumbs, sugar and seasoning. Add the melted butter, beaten egg and sufficient milk to bind.

MISCELLANEOUS

VEAL FORCEMEAT

¼ lb. breadcrumbs   1 oz. chopped onion
1 teasp. chopped parsley   2 ozs. butter or margarine.
Pepper and salt.

Melt the butter, add the onion, cover with a round of greased paper and a lid, and cook for about five minutes. Add the other ingredients and mix well.

TO BOIL RICE FOR CURRY

1. Have a pot of boiling water ready, add salt (1 dessertsp. salt to 1 quart water).

2. Put in the rice and boil rapidly until the grains of rice are soft. Time—17 minutes.

3. Place the saucepan under the cold tap and let the water run into the saucepan until the water is clear.

4. Drain on a sieve, spread on a lightly greased or oiled tin.

5. Put in a warm place until hot and toss occasionally with two forks.

MAÎTRE d'HÔTEL BUTTER

1 oz. butter.   1 teasp. lemon juice.
1 teasp. finely-chopped parsley.   Pepper and salt.

Cream the butter, add parsley, lemon juice and seasoning. Mix well. Set on ice or in a cold place until required. Form into pats and serve.

OVEN TEMPERATURES IN APPROXIMATE DEGREES OF HEAT

	Temperatures F—Fahrenheit C—Centigrade		Lettered Control	Numbered Control
VERY HOT	500°F.	260°C.	About H	About 9
HOT	450°F.	230°C.	,, G	,, 7
FAIRLY HOT ...	425°F.	215°C.	,, F	,, 6
MODERATE	400°F.	205°C.	,, E	,, 5
FAIRLY MODERATE ...	375°F.	190°C.	,, D	,, 4
VERY MODERATE ...	350°F.	175°C.	,, C	,, 3
SLOW	300°F.	150°C.	,, B	,, 2
VERY SLOW	250°F.	120°C.	,, A	,, 1
COOL	200°F.	95°C.		,, $\frac{1}{2}$-$\frac{1}{4}$

ALL IN THE COOKING

EXPLANATION OF COOKERY TERMS

À la:—according to the style of.

Au gratin:—applied to a dish which has been coated with bread-crumbs or grated cheese and then browned in the oven, and served in the dish in which it has been cooked.

Au naturel:—applied to food served uncooked, or very plainly and simply prepared and cooked.

Baba:—small yeast sponge cake soaked in syrup flavoured with rum or any other spirit.

Bain-Marie:—a large vessel containing hot water in which saucepans of food can be kept hot.

Bavarois:—a rich cream mixture usually half-custard and half-cream.

Beignet:—type of fritter.

Bisque:—soup made from shell-fish.

Blanch:—put into cold water and bring to boiling point, then pour off this water. This is done to whiten, to cleanse, to remove skin from nuts or to remove strong flavour.

Bouquet garni:—bunch of herbs with other flavourings tied together.

Canapés:—rounds or fancy shapes of bread, toast, etc., on which small savouries are served.

Cassolette:—a small case made of potato purée for holding mince, etc.

Croissants:—crescents or horse-shoe shapes of a rich yeast bread.

Croquette:—minced meat, game, sieved potatoes, etc., made into a cork-shape, coated with egg and breadcrumbs and then fried.

Croustade:—a case of fried bread used for holding various savoury fillings.

Croûte:—slice of fried or toasted bread.

Croûtons:—dice or fancy shapes of bread which are fried.

D'artois:—a sandwich of a very light pastry with sweet or savoury filling inside.

En:—served in.

Entrée:—a dish which is complete in itself and which is served after the fish course in a dinner.

Flan:—an open pastry case.

Foie-gras:—preparation of goose liver.

Fricassée:—a white stew of chicken or turkey to which cream is often added.

Galantine:—a cold roll of meat or poultry without bone, pressed, glazed and decorated.

Gâteau:—a light fancy cake, usually iced and elaborately decorated.

Hors d'oeuvre:—small tasty morsels of cold food served before the soup to stimulate the appetite.

Kromeski:—a mixture of meat or any other savoury wrapped in bacon, dipped in batter and then fried.

Liaison:—binding or thickening used for soups and sauces.

Macédoine:—mixture of vegetables or fruit cut in dice or in fancy shapes.

Marinade:—a mixture of wine, vinegar or lemon juice, oil, flavourings and seasonings in which fish or meat is soaked before cooking to give additional flavour.

Menu:—bill of fare.

Mirepoix:—a mixture of vegetables and seasonings used as foundation for braising.

Mousse:—a light spongy mixture.

Purée:—smooth paste of meat, fish, vegetables, or fruit, which has been reduced to a pulp and then sieved.

Quenelle:—a smooth mixture of fish, meat or poultry shaped with a spoon and poached.

Ragoût:—a rich type of stew.

Rechauffé:—re-heat of fish, meat, or vegetables.

Rissole:—mince of cooked fish or meat coated with egg and breadcrumbs and then fried.

Roux:—equal quantities of butter and flour cooked over the fire and not allowed to colour unless required for a brown mixture. It is used for thickening soups and sauces.

Sauté-pan:—a shallow stewpan.

Sauté:—tossed over the fire in a small quantity of fat until brown.

Savarin:—a light yeast pudding.

Soufflé:—a very light mixture which is generally obtained by the addition of stiffly-beaten whites of eggs.

INDEX, ALPHABETICAL

INDEX, ALPHABETICAL

CLASSIFIED INDEX

CLASSIFIED INDEX

CLASSIFIED INDEX

CLASSIFIED INDEX

NOTES